A Twist of Lyme

a Twist of Lyme

Battling a Disease That "Doesn't Exist"

ANDREA H. CAESAR

Foreword by Joseph G. Jemsek, MD, FACP

Edited by Nancy Grossman

ARCHWAY
PUBLISHING

Archway Publishing books may be ordered through booksellers or by contacting:

Archway Publishing
1663 Liberty Drive
Bloomington, IN 47403
www.archwaypublishing.com
1-(888)-242-5904

Because of the dynamic nature of the Internet, any web addresses or links contained in this book may have changed since publication and may no longer be valid. The views expressed in this work are solely those of the author and do not necessarily reflect the views of the publisher, and the publisher hereby disclaims any responsibility for them.

Any people depicted in stock imagery provided by Thinkstock are models, and such images are being used for illustrative purposes only.
Certain stock imagery © Thinkstock.

ISBN: 978-1-4808-0264-3 (sc)
ISBN: 978-1-4808-0266-7 (hc)
ISBN: 978-1-4808-0265-0 (e)

Library of Congress Control Number: 2013918126

Printed in the United States of America

Archway Publishing rev. date: 10/29/2013

Dedication

—————◦◉◦—————

I dedicate this book to my daughter, Anelya. You are the reason I get up in the morning. You are the reason I fight to be well. You are, quite simply, a spectacularly magical little creature and I am blessed to be your mommy.

Gratitude

⸻ ◈ ⸻

I have an endless list of people to thank for so many different reasons, but that would be a book in itself. I have to start by thanking my parents, Porter and Susan Caesar, for their endless support of every aspect of this journey. You have stepped in as temporary parents to my daughter whenever duty called and have been selfless and a crucial part of my survival of treatment. I have no words to thank you enough.

My life's journey would have been incomplete without the love of my grandparents Edward and Mary Lou O'Rourke, and Allison Caesar who learned to understand this baffling illness that has infested every part of my body. Thank you for being so open-minded and loving through it all. I am fortunate to thank the rest of my family for also being there for me, calling me, and sending me cards, as I fight for my life.

I thank Dr. Steve Clark, ND, for finally diagnosing me and sticking with me through the seven years of testing it took us to find out what was really happening to me. I also thank you for putting up with me as my boss for those seven trying years.

To my sidekick and the best assistant I could ever ask for, Michaeleen Sicard, who always lights up a room no matter what the situation and always knows how to cheer me up. For knowing where everything is at all times and taking on Mini at the drop of a hat, you have been a savior. Thank you for being a part of our family.

To all of my friends who have cooked for me, sent gift certificates for my juice cleanses, dropped everything to stay with me for a weekend, and so on, thank you. I could not ask for better friends. This includes all of the incredible messages of hope and encouragement

I have received from my friends around the world: Sweden, Russia, Cameroon, Colombia, Germany, Switzerland, Slovakia, Japan, and more. Thank you for the strength your words offered me.

I would like to thank my friend of twenty-five years, Leah Palmisciano, not only for being a loyal and devoted friend, but for introducing me to a career that would save my financial life when I needed it most and for introducing me to Omar Benavides, an unexpected light at the end of a very dark tunnel. Omar, I will forever be grateful to you for opening my eyes and heart to the option of allowing myself to be truly happy again.

I want to thank my dear friends, Ava, Kim, and Frohman Anderson. You have provided me the freedom to earn a substantial income from home while in treatment. Our relationship now stems far beyond business and I am proud to call you dear friends. Thank you for what you have done for my family. You have forever changed our lives.

Dr. Joseph G. Jemsek, MD, I believe with all of my heart that you not only saved my quality of life, but my life itself. As you said many times, had the wind blown in the wrong direction I could have found myself immobilized, unable to speak, or in many other debilitating conditions. I thank you for sparing me that hell. I believe that you are a crusader for the helpless, for those who cannot find help in a broken medical system. Your cutting-edge willingness to go against the system approach has spared the pain of many people. Thank you for your bravery and your heart of gold. And I thank you especially for supporting me in sharing my story, by writing the Foreword to this book.

Foreword

By Dr. Joseph G. Jemsek, MD, FACP

———=◈=———

The Lie Too Big to Confess
" The person attempting to travel two roads at once will get nowhere."
Xun Zi, Chinese philosopher in the Confucius era…

When life brings change we, the human species, adapt to that change if the change threatens our survival or, perhaps as a lesser challenge, threatens the quality or comfort of our lives. We adapt by modifying our behavior, we invent or evolve new coping skills, we make concessions and we often compromise and move on – we adjust, we adapt, and we cope. The human species is arguably the most adaptable species to ever have inhabited planet Earth, other than the cockroach.

Andrea Caesar writes about an abiding affliction she has endured and continues to endure. This affliction is Borreliosis Complex, or Lyme Borreliosis Complex, which represents a complex set of infections involving all of the body systems, but in particular the nervous system and its most primitive and basic functions. Andrea writes about her affliction in real-time in her blog format, adapted into this book, and so this is not a story of challenge and triumph, but a story of a disease which so distorts human experience that self may become unrecognizable to the patient afflicted, and certainly to those who love and support this person.

In the scope of chronic illness, this is very dangerous territory, indeed; and Andrea reflects such during her treatment, especially in the early portions that are marred by a severe disconnect from normal life. When we become unrecognizable to ourselves and others, what have we become? Who will believe we are suffering, when the suffering is oftentimes questioned by the medical community or family and friends? The conundrum is complicated by the prevailing opinion in the medical community that Andrea's disease does 'not exist.' This struggle with reality and the surrounding confusion and frustration are all on full display in Andrea's journalistic diary in her quest for wellness.

————— o —————

As an Infectious Disease physician and a proud veteran of care for the initial wave of those afflicted with and dying with HIV/AIDS, I have been privileged to have learned a great deal in this time, not only about medicine but, more importantly, about the character of the soul and the patients and families affected. I have seen the best in the human spirit and I have seen the worst in the human spirit. I know about desperate causes; I know about desperate measures when there are no answers and no hope for resuscitation and survival. I have wept with numerous youthful dying patients, many of whom were marginalized and scorned by society, including being scorned by their own families. In the first decade and a half of the HIV/AIDS pandemic, affliction with HIV/AIDS had the inevitable outcome of an end to suffering by virtue of sweet death.

Our patients with Borreliosis Complex want to die, but cannot die and so suffer without relief. These individuals suffer interminably without access to care in a medical system which trivializes their complaints when it is often startling clear that previously highly functioning individuals are unable to function. Yet the arrogant medical community has no explanation for the inexplicable and obvious fact that the patient is not a malingerer where the 'usual workup' reports fail to reveal a plausible diagnosis. Typically, at this juncture, many physicians, particularly at academic centers where those in authority have either lost or never had any clinical skills, or simply don't care, the patient becomes 'the problem' because these arrogant academicians cannot conceivably be 'the problem,' and so they blithely default blame to those least able to debate them or defend themselves, because they are very sick.

So, arrogant specialists unload their ignorance onto the sick and vulnerable, and wash their hands of the matter. So far, the innumerable discourtesies afforded the suffering have not resulted in charges or recompense for such arrogant and anti-patient behavior, but the day will come when this will change. In the meantime, the patient is typecast as a psychiatric refugee who now needs to go into that black hole for treatment. In the course of all of this, our patients become not only desperate and hopeless, but also confused, disenfranchised, depersonalized, and often become scorned and cast aside to wallow in the netherworld Hell which is advanced Borreliosis, advanced infection of the brain with multiple organisms in a complex pathophysiology that the human species has never experienced and for which it has no innate defense, an infection complex of neural and other tissues to which our species cannot 'adapt.' Conservatively, given that there is no 'selection process' in our society, it will take millennia for the human species to take immunologic control of spirochetal-dominated complex infections.

With no chance for recovery of the life they once had, a life wrested away from them, a life they just would now be satisfied to only partially participate in once again, most patients lose hope and resign themselves to lives of 'nothing.' At our clinic in Washington, DC, and for many years prior to this in our locations in North Carolina and South Carolina, we see those patients who, either with their last remaining grasp of their innate being, or with the loving support of their family, who do not give up hope, who want to explore any avenues of hope that they feel may remain. And so it was with Andrea Caesar and her family.

As one of the very few physicians who has been heavily involved with both of the major epidemics of our time, I have to say that the suffering with Borreliosis Complex in its advanced state is simply worse than HIV/AIDS in the modern era. Many would argue that this is heresy, but then the critics don't have a thimble's worth of experience in Borreliosis Complex. They would argue that the carnage between 1980-1995 with HIV/AIDS was unprecedented and I would never disagree. But in the modern era, HIV/AIDS is a chronic and largely – in most parts of the world – manageable illness, albeit at tremendous expense to society; and in no way would I ever diminish the impact and suffering of this disease in which I was devotedly involved for over two decades. But there are virtually no other physicians who have witnessed both pandemics on full display and, for many of the reasons stated, Borreliosis Complex is worse, more insidious and ultimately more debilitating.

This disease, which is sweeping our nation and our world in breathtaking leaps, is unparalleled in its ability to invade the core brain and thereby rob its victims of their very souls. Our patients don't die immediately, but they do die from physical and mental exhaustion. They die without a soul, having been robbed of essential functions of life by this illness, whether physical or as a neuropsychiatric deterioration. They are often robbed of an innate awareness of their self, as Andrea Caesar portrays in her book. Our patients are depersonalized, robbed of their basic physical and emotional functions, terrorized by their own body in revolt, and cannot 'cope or adjust.' They are marooned forever with this illness, often without hope of significant intervention.

The knowledge and skills needed for intervention in this illness are complicated and tortuous, but therapy can be done with success, as we have at the Jemsek Specialty Clinic. However, formal protocols and research are held hostage by the editors of medical journals, under the influence of medical groups like the Infectious Diseases Society of America, the IDSA, where the vernacular of a modern discussion of Borreliosis Complex is not allowed. The end result, in large measure due to the oppressive force of those in power at the

IDSA: any opposition to the notion of a complex stealth pathogen set of infections involving basic neurologic function has been muted. Clearly, the IDSA and others of their ilk have their own agenda, which too often conflicts with the well being of patients and hampers their road to recovery. I fear they have forgotten to take the pill of humility; they could have avoided much acrimony by simply agreeing to open their discussion groups, but this has not been the case and now *the lie is too big to confess.*

Per Albert Schweitzer: 'Success in not the key to happiness. Happiness is the key to success.' The IDSA is now in the uncomfortable posture of defending an enormous lie, one abetted by numerous contradictions. Several of the 'Lyme cabal' at the IDSA have patents for diagnosis, immunization and Rx of 'chronic Lyme disease,' *202 patents in all*, which purport to promote diagnostics and vaccines for a chronic disease which they continue to deny, a disease which they continually quote as 'hard to get and easy to treat.' Nothing could be further from the truth. So Xun Zi, in a modern time, would certainly take the IDSA and their ilk of other scoundrels to task for 'walking two roads' – with one road being the lie and the other the profiteering to be done on behalf of those whose arrogant ambition is to feather their own nest in this lifetime.

I believe the biggest fools of all are those who don't understand their limitations on their limited time on Earth. In the case of the IDSA and the Lyme cabal, the damage these few have done to public health issues around the world and for generations to come is perhaps unparalleled and the largest public health scandal of the millennia. We let this happen due to our permissiveness, but this is the way of history in that humans in authority continue to regard their tenure on Earth as infinite and their power uncontestable. So the lesson appears to be that we trust those in power and continue to suffer the consequences.

The 'information age' has rapidly become the 'misinformation age.' As far as the Lyme cabal, the massive damage they have done will continue to have adverse effects for generations; the road to sanity and integrity, if it happens at all, will not likely begin until the scoundrels all die. Their day of reckoning will come soon enough; a new generation of physicians can do no worse.

I have spoken of 'happiness' on Earth, a vital subject, one to which we are all tethered. An article I enjoy, by Ryan and Deci, published in the *American Psychologist* in 2000, breaks down this core issue. It speaks of self-actualization, 'to be the best you can be,' and it speaks about what makes us fulfilled in our lives. It talks about three critical attributes for happiness which must be present in some combination: 1) autonomy, i.e. the extent to which we have the ability to control our own lives; 2) maintaining connectedness with others, i.e. love of family, a willingness to meet others and build on an interaction, and our continuing benefit from existing relationships; and 3) exercising competence using our gifts to continue to learn and experience. As one should plainly understand by now, Andrea Caesar has had none of these faculties in her power during her illness; they all evaporated into the mist of her mysterious malady. And the frightening truth is that this is happening to millions in our country and around the world, and getting worse. And the great thing is that Andrea has had sufficient neural connections to write about it and, in so doing, help millions with her book – and that she will recover during her long journey back to wellness. God Bless Andrea and all afflicted.

—Joseph G. Jemsek, MD, FACP

About the Author of the Foreword

Dr. Jemsek is a board-certified physician in infectious disease and internal medicine. He diagnosed the first documented case of AIDS in North Carolina in early 1983, and has been recognized with North

Carolina's Certificate of Appreciation, for his groundbreaking work in the field of HIV/AIDS treatment and research, as well as with the World AIDS Day Volunteer Service Award in 2004. In 2000, he founded a specialty infectious disease practice to serve patients with HIV/AIDS. His practice rapidly evolved to include a large influx of patients with Lyme Borreliosis Complex (LBC), commonly referred to as Lyme disease. In 2005, Dr. Jemsek focused his practice exclusively on LBC, and has treated thousands of afflicted patients from every state in the US as well as from multiple other countries. In January 2010, he opened the Jemsek Specialty Clinic in Washington, DC, where he continues to serve patients from around the world.

Preface

I originally wrote this book as a blog with the intention that it first and foremost be my outlet and release, perhaps to explain things to my friends and family who have a hard time understanding what it is like to live with and treat Lyme disease and the multiple infections that accompany the disease. It also served as an incredible outlet to help myself work through things that only I can understand. This book was written while in treatment. It was not written in retrospect, rather as a current account of what I was going through on the day I wrote each entry.

Throughout the book you will find some very good writing and some very poor writing. I have chosen to keep it as such to respect the authenticity of how I was functioning neurologically, feeling, and expressing myself at that moment. There is some foul language, most of it written when in a Lyme Rage or in a terrible mental, physical, and/or emotional state.

The purpose of sharing this material is to educate, support and validate all that comes with Lyme and the people who suffer from it without the support of a medical system to even recognize its existence. That said, please keep in mind as a disclaimer, that I am a patient, not a medical professional and the information presented is about my treatment and journey, and mine alone. It is not a suggestion of what anyone else may be going through, although I assume there will be many people suffering from Lyme out there who will relate to parts of the book. I do not claim, by any means, to be a Lyme expert. I am a "me" expert.

This book should be read by any family member or loved one who knows someone with Lyme, whether being treated properly or not. My hope is not only that Lyme patients will relate to pieces of my own fight against Lyme, but that they might also gain more emotional and logistical support from my experience and from those around them.

For the loved ones of Lyme patients, I hope this will open your eyes and provide *you* with some answers and prospective to what certainly must be a frustrating position to be in. I know those around me struggled for twenty-six years before my diagnosis to understand my behaviors and my physical, mental and emotional symptoms.

You may not like or agree with what you see or read in this book, but believe me, in that case, chances are I didn't enjoy writing about, feeling, or acknowledging it, either. Having been at a loss for verbal expression that might gain a listening ear after all of these years without a diagnosis, I desperately needed an avenue to release my thoughts and this was my chosen path. Perhaps this book will inspire some, even educate some, who may not be familiar with Lyme. But in the end, this is my story, my truth, and my journey.

With this book I ask for your support. I ask that you make some noise about chronic Lyme disease and associated co-infections to your state representatives. Thank you for joining me in my pursuit of wellness, to a desired state of long-term remission. Please spread the word. If you are unfamiliar with the severity of these tick-born diseases, please know that the experiences I share in this book could belong to you or someone you love. I wish to spread awareness, because I would never wish this upon my worst enemy.

When I Was Eleven

———— ◆ ————

I grew up in Pennsylvania until I entered the fifth grade. I was an active, happy, vivacious kid who loved to play kickball and play on the monkey bars. I had lots of energy and took gymnastics, ballet, and tap. I was on a soccer team and a good student.

We moved to Barrington, Rhode Island, a lovely town, when I was ten, and all was well with the world. There were some normal adjustments to be made, as would happen with any move, but in all it was good. And then when I was eleven, in the sixth grade as I recall, I found myself having a hard time running. All of a sudden I would lose my breath. And it burned to breathe. I was always getting notes to be excused from gym, mostly using illness as a reason.

All of a sudden I started to get migraines – the kind that require absolute darkness and silence to survive. I would throw up uncontrollably, which would help a bit and then I would go back into the darkness and silence of my parents' room, the darkest room in the house. I remember this like it was yesterday.

I was the kid who was *always* missing school. My friends from Rhode Island will definitely remember me as "that kid." My grades were good, though I didn't apply myself as much as I should have, because I didn't have the energy. I was always feeling fluish, my muscles hurt, and I had headaches all the time.

I got psoriasis on my elbows and knees. My bones started cracking a lot. I had just gotten my period, so the doctors blamed it all on hormones. They were wrong. We now know that this is when I changed as a person. This is when I contracted *Borrelia burgdorferi* (Lyme disease) and probably some of the other co-infections I am infected with today, such as *Bartonella*, *Babesiosis* (also known as *Babesia*) and *Ehrlichiosis* (also known as *Ehrlichia*).

Back then, in 1986, Lyme disease was not really on the radar beyond the breakout in Lyme, CT. I never had a bulls-eye or any signs of a tick-bite that I can recall, although I do remember getting what we thought were spider bites, which would leave similar traces. It never occurred to any of us to discuss that with the doctor. However, had we done so, he probably would not have said a word about Lyme anyway.

———◦———

By the age of twelve, I was certainly the only twelve-year-old I knew who had a weekly appointment with a massage therapist for muscle tension, constant migraines, and general body aches. By this time, I started needing daily naps to function. And when I say nap, I mean two to three hours. I didn't do one-hour naps or power naps. I mean full-on, pass-out, almost in a coma naps. I do that to this day. I needed those naps then, as I do now.

At fourteen I remember being on an eight-week summer trip to England, Scotland, and Wales with a summer camp group. I remember sitting outside Windsor Castle with the most unbelievable shin splints I have ever experienced. And from that day on, I have had no feeling in my shins. And I mean *no feeling at all in my shins*. Given my complete inability to play sports, I threw myself into the performing arts. If there is anything I am confident in doing, it's singing. And I love to sing. In fact, singing has gotten me through most of my life.

I was always smart and witty, always armed with a quick comeback. Throughout high school, I had a hard time with reading comprehension, concentrating, being motivated in general. There was never any discussion of ADD, because it clearly was not the issue, although it was all the rage those days. In fact, there was no real reason to account for any illness besides lethargy, pain, and migraines.

I have always been cold. I have craved the beach and the warm sun all my life. I would do anything to live in a warm climate. I have struggled with low body temperature since my teens. I have, for over twenty years, taken scorching hot baths every night before bed, just to be warm enough to fall asleep.

At seventeen, as this all continued, I started seeing a chiropractor for neck and back pain, as well as migraines. I spent my senior year of high school in Sweden as an exchange student. I was often sick, but mostly overlooked it all. I sang in a pop band, went to clubs, went mushroom picking in the woods, and was wooed by Swedish boys. That was not a bummer. I loved Sweden.

Boston

During the summer of 1998, I moved to Boston to work for a Swedish company doing what I had always wanted to do. It was a dream job – a dream company really. Everyone was my age. Everyone was hot. Everyone spoke multiple languages and was well travelled. Everyone was doing good work to help other young people see the world. I was used to partying being a serious full-time job from college. This was a company with the motto "Work Hard, Play Hard." And boy did we. The thing is, and perhaps I should have noticed this change then, but I was completely not interested in the weekend activities with my new friends. We all worked together and partied after work, sometimes *at* work, sometimes *as* work. But each weekend, I found myself back in my car, driving north to my parents' home in a sleepy New Hampshire town.

I've always wondered why I *hated* living in Boston so much when it really is such a great city, but I think in writing this I have realized why. I never really felt well in Boston. I lived there during the height of The Big Dig, when virtually the entire city was in upheaval recreating a roadway system that would make Boston a more pleasant place to be, with less traffic. This meant there was dirt in the air. *Everywhere.* Having moved from DC, a clean and well-kept city in most parts, I was not used to this filth – and now that I know more about Lyme, I know that being there was not good for my health. I was working long hours and not breathing good air. I felt awful. When I went to my parents' house, after a day or so, I'd feel better. Then I would leave at 6:00 a.m. on Monday mornings to return to Boston. I *loved* my job and the company, but *hated* living there.

During the weekends at my parents' house, I could have spent some time creating a social life, especially in the summer. Instead, I got in my pajamas the second I arrived and wore them until I left on Monday morning. I had migraines constantly and I would like to thank my Swedish friend Victoria for introducing me at that time to Excedrin Migraine. From the first time I tried it, I never left my home without it again, for almost fifteen years.

It was at this time my hip and knee issues began. My knee would hyper-extend, usually while going down the stairs, and man did that hurt. What a pain in the… knee. And the weird thing with my hip started. I'd stand up and then stumble, because one of my hips (usually my left hip) was not really up to cooperating. I would limp for a few minutes, my hip would readjust, and I'd be back to normal again. So why worry, right? *Sigh…*

The job I had in Boston, however, motivated me because it showed me that I had a mind that functioned on a very high level and a heart that beats for all people. When you are in the business of enriching people's lives, you begin to learn who you are. I will always be thankful to this company for the fun, the skills, the knowledge, and the drive it provided and helped me discover within myself.

Without that company, I am not sure I would have ever known these traits existed in me; and at this very moment, I use all of those attributes on a daily basis in my current job, which I am able to do from home with a constantly increasing income doing something I wholeheartedly believe in. This has become a crucial part of my life, because chronic Lyme disease treatment is not covered by insurance, as its existence is not recognized.

Sweden, the First Years

In 1999, I was afforded the opportunity by the company I was working for in Boston to move to Sweden to work on their end of what I had been doing for the past year and a half. Having been an exchange student, I already spoke fluent Swedish, albeit like a teenager, but through the years I would learn to speak as a native adult, at a level of fluency in which it would be hard to detect a foreign background.

It was so exciting and I often felt that I was living in a movie. But it was a very lonely time for me too. Swedes can be quite reserved and while I was living in the heart of Stockholm, which boasts an incredible array of all things cultural, social, and gastronomical, I really didn't know anyone. I had moved from an office, which was the center of my social life, to a new office across the ocean where the employees left right at five o'clock. It was so strange to me and I was surprised that I had not been prepared for how different the culture of that office was.

And so for the first time in all my life, I was alone. And I mean *really* alone. Yes, I had my host family from years before when I was an exchange student, but they were in another city, and the loneliness, the quiet, would set in during the evening and nighttime hours. I quickly became an expert on Swedish pop culture. Thank goodness the internet had become the norm in people's homes (wow, I just dated myself) because I could actually chat with people at home and even get to know new people in Sweden online.

Amidst the quiet, I began to notice just how much my body hurt. My muscles were like rocks. Migraines were almost daily. I was so tired, but I couldn't sleep. And I was sad. For the first time in my life, I was very sad. And it was because I was lonely.

I am well-versed in the stages of culture shock and expatriation and knew that I would have to force myself to go out and start inviting people to do things and asking them if I could go along with them. That was a bit of a blow to my pride, as I had never had to *ask* for a social life, but with time, I got one.

One of my best friends in Sweden was its scenery. It's something I miss to this day. Stockholm is like no other place I have been. I have been to thirty-four countries to date. Its clean and peaceful beauty, sharp professional atmosphere, gorgeous people, its proximity to water in every direction, its urban feel with a dose of old world European charm and sleek modern Scandinavian style – yet always so close to nature – took my breath away. I miss Stockholm.

———◦———

That first year in the Swedish office was honestly hell for me. I did my job, but I was also spending time trying to replace my lack of social support with other ventures. I always have big ideas. So I would present them to this person and that, and keep myself busy. The wonderful people in the Boston office knew how unhappy I was, but unfortunately I had a new manager who was also new to our division and who was not based in Stockholm, with whom I had zero connection. She did not know me at all and made no attempt to get to know me. She and I just did not like each other. She thought I was a wreck and I thought she was a bitch.

Now with more experience under my belt, I can see how I might have been any manager's nightmare, but as a manager, she could have made an effort to lead with less of an iron fist and find out what might help me feel more content in the Swedish office. She made no effort whatsoever and it only made the situation worse.

I would cry at the drop of a hat, I was looking for a way out at any turn I could find one, and I was just generally miserable. My job was less challenging than my previous job, although it was considered a promotion because of the overseas move. But less of a challenge meant I was *bored* and sad. But now with a decade more experience in high levels of leadership positions, I can see that really, she was not nice to me at all which just made the situation worse. Honestly, I think she just wanted me out.

The company tried as hard as they might to work with me. Remember, I hated Boston, I now know, because I felt so sick there, but at the time I just plain hated it and most of the available jobs I could return to were there. So I was sent to Miami for a few days to see if I might like a job they had available there. When the company sends you on these trips, they assume you will take the job. And I was sure I would when I went. But again, there was no effort to share with me any type of social possibilities and I wasn't really fond of the job itself and, to be frank, with a few years in the company and an offer for my second transatlantic move, I was not moving for the low salary I was offered for such a move.

It was in the hotel room during those evenings when they should have been showing me a good time that I realized I had not completed what I had set out to do in Sweden. It was a shock to me. Yes, I was miserable, but had I really done everything I could do to make sure that my years spent in Sweden were not a waste of time? I knew it would be an ugly announcement when I would tell the company I was going to leave because they had no other attractive positions for me and that I did not know what would be next for me. But I knew it was the right decision.

I now know this constant state of indecision and emotion were neurological symptoms of Lyme. I burned bridges by leaving that company I actually loved. Bridges that I may never repair, but I did what was right for me. I did it because I realized that Sweden feeds my soul.

Sweden, the Later Years

Writing this chapter means revisiting a part of my past that I often try to avoid, although in some capacity, it always lingers.

As I mentioned, it dawned on me while interviewing for a job in Miami that I had not yet accomplished all I wished to accomplish during my time in Sweden. I had a vision in my mind that had not yet come to be. I wanted to make close friends, be wildly successful at what I did, and maybe fall in love. By this time, I was forming some good friendships and loved my new job.

Once I secured my new job and knew I'd be settling in for a while, I decided to sell the apartment I had for another in the most desirable part of the city. With tree-lined streets, swanky stores and restaurants, and some of the loveliest parks you can imagine, I found myself at a showing of an apartment in a part of Stockholm called Östermalm. There was a bidding war for this apartment, as was the norm at the time for all apartments in Stockholm. I had the highest bid on an apartment I had set my heart on; my new home.

On the day of the closing, I went to the realtor's office to sign the paperwork. It turned out the apartment owners were away on vacation and so they had given Power of Attorney to a neighbor and member of the condo board. Gustaf.

When I walked in, I saw this perfectly Swedish – you know, 6′4″, broad build, blue eyes, and a smile that knocked me over – man. And at that moment, I knew. I just knew. We waited for the realtor and during that time discussed what I did and what he did, etc. It turned out he was in a relationship with a woman from New Hampshire (go figure) who was divorcing, and he was in the process of moving there within a couple of months. My heart sank a bit, but not too much, because I knew.

We signed the papers and the apartment was mine, but who cared? All I saw was Gustaf. He asked me if I would like to walk with him to the subway. *Obviously,* but I played it cool. "Oh, how nice of you." So we walked the couple of blocks to the subway and I found myself feeling a bit of a twinge in my heart because I didn't want it to end. But I had to go off to work, so I reached out my hand to shake his and looked up in his eyes and, with that look, my knees buckled and I found myself in his friendly embrace.

The weeks flew by and finally I moved in and there was a knock at the door. Who could that be? I peeked through the peephole and there was Gustaf, on my first night in my new apartment, with an exquisite bottle of wine and two wine glasses, rightly assuming mine were probably still packed. We had the best time. We talked about everything. It was so fun and I was so sad to think that he would soon be leaving, within the next week actually, to go to live with his girlfriend in New Hampshire.

But life went on and I unpacked and settled in. Right away I built a balcony off of the kitchen towards the open courtyard that looked to all of the other buildings like mine that were built in the 1880s. I was truly happy there. It was a small apartment, but perfect for me. I walked to work in the morning through the streets of Östermalm and into Gamla Stan (Old Town) where the Royal Palace is and where my office was. I walked along the water and stopped and look at the architecture on Strandvägen and then crossed the bridge. On my way home one day, I remember stopping dead in my tracks, looking across the water that I was about to cross, thinking to myself, "I live here!" It was such an emotional, breathtaking feeling to know that I lived in a postcard.

It was at this point the minor paranoia began, a typical trait of those with neurological issues from Lyme. I had no idea. I woke up at all times of the night and ran to the door to look through the peep hole and make sure no one was there. Sometimes I slept with my phone ready to call 112 (their version of 911) in case someone got in. I knew this was not normal, but for me it quickly became the norm.

After a month or so, there was another buzz at my door. Gustaf was back. His relationship hadn't worked out. And again, wine bottle in hand, he joined me for a perfect evening. We talked a lot and watched the movie *Spy Game*. I will never forget. My heart was pumping and at that moment I knew we would be together. The next night he invited me to join him with his friends on the roof deck for dinner. I didn't know he was a French trained chef.

We all got pretty hammered and it was such good fun. But I set my sights on him and of course I offered to help clean up after the others left. After all, I just lived one floor up. So we cleaned up and then, as I was leaving at about 3:00 a.m. and went to give him a hug, he leaned down from his 6'4" to my 5'4" and kissed me. At that moment I knew that Gustaf would forever change my life.

We fell in love. We moved in together. We were happiest at the summer homes on both of Sweden's coasts. I felt safe when he was with me. No paranoid trips to the peephole to see who was coming to kill me.

I grew very close to his mother and father, who were divorced and had a troubled relationship, which troubled Gustaf even more. And it didn't make things easy on us. Of course, a trained diplomat, I somehow always ended up in the middle of things and while I really felt like a member of the family, I wanted nothing to do with the drama. It was hard for me, but I loved him. God, I loved him.

At times we would fight. I was about twenty-eight, and this is when the rage started. The smallest things would set me off. We would get in fights because I was *sure* I had told him something and he would fight back saying I hadn't. Of course my take was that he was not listening to me, when in fact, knowing what I know now, I had very likely not told him what I thought I had. I would scream. I would tell him to go away. I would sleep on the couch. I would do things that the person who I am at my core, within my heart and soul, would never do to someone that I loved. It was never physical, but it was *loud*.

——◦——

One night in Stockholm, Gustaf attended one of his exclusive "Men's Club" evenings. Once a month he would dress in white tie tuxedo and go to an old school men's club, Timmermans Orden, which had existed for hundreds of years and had boasted royalty as members. He loved this. I have no idea what they did at these meetings because it was top secret. I had no worries that they were doing anything naughty, but I don't like secrets, unless they are mine. *Giggle...*

Once a year, spouses and significant others were invited to attend a Christmas dinner. The building was immense and elegant. It was like visiting a royal summer home or small palace. It was an honor to be invited to be a member and an even bigger honor to climb the ranks of the Order. That's all I knew. It wasn't far from our home, perhaps a ten-minute walk. We walked everywhere. That's what you do there. But Stockholm is a big city and while it is safer than other big cities, there was still crime.

I had always begged Gustaf to take a cab home after these events. After all, the shortcut home was through Humlegården, a huge park that was very dark at night. But Gustaf had grown up in these very city blocks and liked to walk home. He was a big man, confident, and opinionated. It drove me crazy that he would walk home at that hour of the night.

He usually came home around midnight or shortly thereafter. One night, I woke up around midnight and he wasn't home. That was okay. Then it was 1:00 a.m. and I was a little worried, so I called his phone.

It was off. Okay, I knew he turned his phone off at the meetings. That was obviously appropriate. Then it was 2:00 a.m. *No way* was that event still going on. And my heart started pounding when I called his phone once again only to find it was still turned off. I called my parents in the U.S. It was 8:00 p.m. there. And I just started *wailing*. Where *was* he? Should I get a cab and go look for him? I was *panicked*. I was so scared that he'd been mugged or stabbed or beaten. I was so sick with worry it was all I could do not to vomit.

At 3:00 a.m., he came home to a completely hysterical life partner. I was inconsolable. He had gone out with some friends after the event and had simply forgotten to turn his phone back on. He was so sorry to have worried me. But I just couldn't stop crying. He couldn't help me. And all he ever really wanted to do was be the man in the relationship. He wanted to take care of me. But again, he couldn't "fix it." I imagine it was one of the events that made me impossible to live with. I now know I can thank Lyme for the paranoia.

Looking back, I realize these strange instances of inexplicable issues of fear, memory loss, and uncontrollable emotions were more frequent than I had ever realized and they would only progress.

At Gustaf's urging, I realized it was time to see a doctor about what was wrong with me. I went to my primary care doctor and I remember feeling deeply, deeply depressed about this change in my emotional well being. I had really wanted Gustaf to be there but he couldn't because of work. So there I sat in the waiting room, in tears, wondering what would become of me, wondering what was wrong with me. And after sitting for about fifteen minutes, I looked up and there he was. My Gustaf had come to sit with me in that meeting and find out what was wrong. I loved him so.

And so we sat with Dr. Lucia and she told me I was depressed and should go on antidepressants. She also told me that I was selfish and too wrapped up in myself and that we should just have a baby – that would cure the selfishness. That's when Gustaf slammed his hands on the desk, stood up, grabbed my hand and we walked out. Have a baby? We had talked about it. We had certainly talked about marriage. I wanted nothing more than to have this man's baby, but surely now was not the right time. I knew something was severely wrong.

That appointment was a train wreck. I started seeing a Shiatsu therapist for pain and a reflexologist that Gustaf's mother had suggested. Nothing helped. I tried so hard to hide the physical and emotional pain I was going through. I started seeing a sound therapist who also did an alternative energy treatment with something called a QXCI/SCIO machine, which really seemed to help. I realized in these sessions that I was holding in a lot of pain. She would make a sound with the symbol, and then I would try to find the sound, the tone within me that best represented my anger or sorrow or fear or desperation for that day, whatever it was. And when I found that sound, I would let it out as loud as I could, tears streaming down my face, my hands shaking, every ounce of energy drained from my being. But afterward, it was a feeling of pure euphoria. Gustaf thought it was a crazy cult and he did not recognize who I was becoming.

For his thirtieth birthday, I took him to Mexico for two weeks. We had a nice time, but I was so sick the entire time. All I wanted to do was sleep, just as I had wanted to do all summer, at the family summer home. People worked outside, enjoying the boat, taking walks – and I took four-hour naps. I was not all right.

One of the scariest moments of my life happened midday on a weekday in a busy but quiet part of Östermalm, just about a block from the bridge that leads to the walking trails, parks, and museums of Djurgården. I was on my way home, as I recall, and everything was so busy around

me, so loud, so fast. And there I was, in the middle of an intersection at a complete halt, watching it all spin around me. I couldn't move. I'm sure many people noticed the crazy girl standing in the middle of the intersection with a look of panic on her face, but some kind soul, not much older than I, realized that he could help get me across the street. And so, in very quiet Swedish, he said, "Let's get you across the street to the corner. It will be okay."

Once we were there, he said, "Who can we call?" I stared at him wide-eyed for a moment. Blinking a few times, my heart beating out of my chest and unable to take a breath, I said, "Gustaf," and handed him my phone. He dialed Gustaf and I wept into the phone and could only manage, "I don't know what's happening. I need you to come get me." And he did. I was not far from his work. He came running, and we took a taxi home. He had no idea what was going on. On some level, I think he had already checked out from all of my craziness, but I also think that he thought I was seeking attention.

Unfortunately, as I now look back, since I have had Lyme in various stages since I was eleven, he had only known me since my infection, as most people have, and so he had never gotten to know the real heart and soul that lies within me. In fact, I think I may be the only person who actually knows myself on that deepest of levels. Some people have seen a glimpse of my heart and maybe my soul every now and then, but then it is so often overshadowed by a Lyme episode which alters perception of who I am. It's not who I am at all. It's these squatters in my body.

———— ⋄ ————

One night, late at night in March 2004, just about a month after our return from Mexico, my world came crashing down when Gustaf started crying and told me that he "was having doubts about us." The conversation developed and he said that he would be moving out to his mother's apartment (since mine had been subleased) until we figured things out. "You need to figure out what's wrong with you, Andrea."

And within a week, the life I had built for myself overseas, in a country that I planned to spend the rest of my life in, was gone in a flash. I thought during all those years that he was the love of my life. I was already in so much physical and emotional pain and then this – it just broke me. So, a week later, my apartment was for sale, I left my job, from which I had been on disability, and I lost the love of my life and his family and left all of my friends, my entire social network, behind.

Gustaf drove me to the airport in silence, his hand holding mine on my leg. I stared straight ahead the whole time. "You are so quiet," he said. "There's nothing more to say," I replied. "Not for now, I guess," he responded. I checked in, barely able to speak, and we stood at the security check-in for what seemed to be an eternity. And he held me and kissed my closed eyes the way only he could do. I said once more, "You don't have to do this." To which he replied, "You need to get help. I cannot do it." And with that, I walked away, weeping my way through security. I could see him through the one-way wall. He could not see me, but I could see him. And he stood there, still, lifeless, for what seemed an eternity, and then he walked out the door.

That was the last time I ever saw Gustaf.

Twenty-nine Years Old and Back with Mom and Dad

Now don't get me wrong, I realize how lucky I am to have such a supportive family. But I am nothing short of independent, so going from living a completely independent life for twelve years, then in a life-partner relationship, to living in the spare room in my parents' house in a lakeside community which lies forty-five minutes from *anywhere* was an adjustment, to say the least.

I just didn't know what to do. I hadn't lived at home since I was seventeen and I had never lived in this town. The emotional impact of losing virtually everything I had created for my own adult life was too much to bear. I spent *hours* in the fetal position, wailing, creating sounds I had never heard a human make. Sometimes it was a very high-pitched cry, almost a scream that would go on and on. Other times it sounded like a dying cow. All I know is that I have never known such deeply rooted sorrow.

I was taken to a doctor in town, who has thankfully since relocated. She looked me over, drew some blood work and told me it was all in my head. I explained to her that I felt *grey* on my antidepressant, that I couldn't be happy, but I could definitely be sad. I am a happy person. I knew this was not the right solution to my problem. In the end, she basically told me I needed to suck it up and get on with my life. To treat my "obvious depression issues" she declared that she would double my dose of Zoloft. At this point, I walked out of yet another doctor's office.

In March 2004, I looked at my mother and said to her, "If we do not find out what is wrong with me, I am going to die. I can feel this." She suggested I see a naturopathic doctor around the corner. Since the twelve doctors I had already seen on two continents couldn't seem to help me, beyond offering that I was depressed, should get pregnant so I wouldn't be so selfish, and that it was all in my head, I happily obliged. I was also intrigued by what he would have in store for me since I'd had such success with the QXCI/SCIO machine in Sweden.

And so I went to see a naturopath for the first time and I told my story in amazement because he just sat there and let *me speak* for myself. Uninterrupted. I spoke for thirty minutes with my parents in the room, sharing all of the gory details of my emotional breakdown, my body pain, my debilitating fatigue, and how my life was ruined. He typed furiously every word that I said and that he said. And when I was finished, it was as if someone clicked the "on" switch and all of a sudden this human ency-clopedia started talking to me and asking me questions no one had previ-ously asked. It was clear that this guy knew his stuff. All of a sudden, I felt like I had someone. Someone got it. Someone might just figure this out.

As most Lyme patients will be able to relate to, I was tested for lupus, rheumatoid arthritis, thyroid disease, HIV/AIDS, autoimmune disease, and the list went on and on. While most of these were okay, my ANA (autoimmune indicators) demonstrated a connective tissue disorder which, at the time, didn't mean much to us, but most impor-tantly, my adrenal glands showed to be completely kaput.

Your adrenal, or suprarenal, glands are located on the top of each kidney. These glands produce hormones that you can't live without, including sex hormones and cortisol, which helps you respond to stress. They have many other functions. Mine were virtually dead, which ex-plained *a lot*. And so we set off on an adrenal treatment, which worked at first. We were still not sure *why* I had this problem and it would take years to investigate the cause.

In the meantime, we were also treating multiple gut infections that I had likely acquired in my travels to thirty-plus countries in my time.

I've stayed at the Ritz and I've stayed in stucco huts with tin roofs and no running water. I have seen a lot in my time, and so has my intestinal tract. When I travel, I like to interact with the locals, eat with the locals, and experience a piece of life in another place. And my poor doctor – every time we would fix one parasite or infection, I'd bring home another.

I was also diagnosed with multiple food intolerances, some that were causing issues in my intestinal tract, but also some that were causing inflammation. This continues to be a part of my process and I get my intolerances checked regularly, as they do change with elimination of foods and change of diet.

And so at least we had *something* to work with. It really was *something*. And the treatments were lightening me up a bit again. I was awake more. I wasn't wailing all the time.

My rage issues continued and were unbearable for all of us. When they happened, I always had the sensation that I was outside my own body, watching some screaming monster. It wasn't me and I couldn't control the anger. It was scary for my parents and completely unacceptable to my dad and his old-school upbringing. He could not begin to fathom that I would speak to my parents the way I did. For me it was torture; the anger I expressed was real, but I was ashamed of my actions, which I could not control.

We all figured it must have been because I was living with my parents again and was in an unwanted situation that was, for the first time in my life, out of my control. So, I sought a job in the Boston area once again. I was forcing myself to start over. I applied for a few jobs at independent schools, received offers from them all, and settled on living in an apartment in Lexington, a town in which I was very happy.

Lexington

I secured a job in the Boston. Given my previous unhappiness living in the city, I decided on an apartment in Lexington, a suburb. I loved the apartment, which had greenery everywhere and was newly renovated and bright and clean. I was happy to be in my own space again. There were only a few apartments in each of the three-floor Adirondack-style buildings, and people had to be buzzed in to get in. I lived on the top floor, the only apartment on that floor.

I worked from 8:00 a.m. to 4:00 p.m. at a private boarding school about fifteen minutes away. I liked the people I worked with. They were all so *funny*, and I needed that. I struggled to get up in the morning and struggled through midday to get through my adrenal crashes, but I had been open about my condition, so they were nice enough to bear with me. They were really quite lovely about everything, even though I am sure it was annoying for them.

Living in Lexington marked the first time I had lived alone for years. I missed Gustaf and everything about Sweden. I missed my friends. I missed Stockholm. I missed the vibe. I missed the life I had built for myself. But I forged on, knowing I just had to force myself to move on.

The paranoia set in again. I was scared to be alone. I bought those little sticky things you can put on the door where, if it is set and the door opens, a loud shrieking alarm siren erupted. It wasn't a security system. (I would have had one if I could have, but I was not allowed to install one in the apartment.) I woke up in the middle of the night and went to the window to see who was in the parking lot. What were they doing? Were they coming for me? I watched until I saw their cars pull away or saw them go into other buildings.

I needed to sleep and while I could have slept *all day*, I could never sleep at night. This is typical of Lyme patients, that their clocks get turned upside down. This is now 2005 and the upside down clock would continue to be an issue for me, an increasingly major issue, into 2012. I became, what I would fairly say, addicted to over-the-counter sleep drugs.

By now, I had a new primary care physician in New Hampshire and was still seeing my naturopath. He was so patient with me and my wacky emails. He wanted so much for me to get better, but it was clear my adrenal issues were *not* getting better as they should have with treatment and so, yes, there must be an underlying cause.

—————◦————

Since I have promised to share all of the nitty-gritty in hopes of helping someone else out there who may be undiagnosed or looking back and trying to pick up the pieces of their own shattered lives, I'm going to talk poop. I had been constipated my whole life, which was something I was addressing with my naturopath. Magnesium citrate sometimes helped. Treating the infections always helped. Obviously, I was on copious amounts of probiotics. But sometimes I was just plain constipated.

It was a time of year in my new job that I would need to travel; I had two back-to-back trips to California scheduled. On my first trip, I made it to Los Angeles and got through the event. I would say it was moderately successful, given the mess the job had been when I came in to clean it up. I returned to Boston and a couple of weeks later it was time to go back to California. Next up was San Francisco, and I was scheduled to leave the following day. I was incredibly constipated and uncomfortable, so I emailed my naturopath to see what I could do besides magnesium citrate to try and remedy this before my trip. He had suggested Triphala, which I could buy at the Whole Foods up the street.

The next morning, as I woke up, my hand brushed my thigh and felt something strange. I lifted the covers to see my legs were covered in hives; and not just a few hives, A *lot* of hives. I had never had hives before and had no idea what it was, but then remembered I had tried the new supplement the previous night. I figured it wouldn't be a big deal to travel to the event across the country since it was just on my legs. And then I looked in the bathroom mirror and saw it peeking up through my pajama top. I immediately stripped down to find that my entire body was not only covered in hives, but that they were all connecting as I watched. I was becoming one *big* hive.

My flight was to be that evening, so I drove straight to the Newton-Wellesley Hospital ER, having trouble breathing as I pulled in. They brought me in right away and shot me with all kinds of stuff. It was clear I was going nowhere that day. I felt so guilty that once again someone was going to have to pick up the slack for one of my dumb illnesses, but it was what it was. It was also the day I decided I would not renew my contract. I had hoped to be able to hold down a job and start my life anew, but that was not what the universe had intended for me.

Vermont

It was clear that I could not continue to work. My body was not going to allow it. I was terrified of losing my independence again, so I was desperate for an alternative. For many years I had considered grad school and when I realized this was the way I was going to go, I knew where I wanted to go. The School for International Training (SIT), in Brattleboro, VT, a part of the NGO (non-governmental organization) World Learning, was right up my alley.

Despite all I have been through, I have lived an extraordinary life. I have been all around the world, I have loved, and I have experienced great wealth and great poverty around me. I have seen a lot and I have been fortunate. After losing Gustaf, nothing made sense to me. It would be years before I would understand the roles that various life experiences have played in the story of my life and how it would affect the next stage.

I believe my time in Lexington had one purpose, which was for me to meet Brad and Kerry.

Brad and Kerry worked at the school where I had been that year and owned a log home in a tiny town on a river in Vermont. Everyone loved them. While they are some of the funniest and most fun people I know, they also have huge hearts that they share readily and openly with their friends. These are very good people.

It just so happened that they also owned a small red cottage located on a dirt road about twenty minutes from SIT, longer in the winter. And so, upon my acceptance to SIT and realizing that, in my condition, dorm life would not be an option – and really, country living might do me some real good – I asked if I could rent the cottage for that year starting toward the end of August.

I spent the summer in New Hampshire and all of my symptoms remained, but the proximity to my naturopath helped me focus more on my health. At this point, I knew things were rapidly declining and while I was hopeful that grad school would be a nice distraction, I was desperate for both help and my independence. I don't think anyone thought I would pull off grad school. As usual, I didn't care what anyone else thought.

I immersed myself in my health. It was my full-time job that summer. I saw a massage therapist every week and resumed my intense emotional therapy that I had started when I first found myself back in the United States. My therapist specialized in grief therapy and couldn't have been better-suited to guide and support me through the emotional trauma I was still reeling from after losing my life and love in Stockholm so suddenly. We took the approach of treating my loss as a death and I went through each of the stages of grief. Some days we would laugh, some days we would go to "the ugly." Other days I came to realizations which helped me move forward, one step at a time.

There was no question that the lingering emotional trauma was getting in the way of all aspects of my health – physical, mental, spiritual, and emotional. That summer, I realized that my life had forever changed, that I would never be the same again. My heart was raw from devastation and I trusted no one.

I wanted no one near me, including my parents. For the first time in my life, I didn't want hugs. I definitely didn't want sympathy, and I sure as hell didn't want anyone telling me they knew what I was going through. I feel this is an important part of being a friend to someone who is grieving or going through treatment or recovery of any kind: No matter *what* you have experienced in your life, you do not know what it's like. You *don't* understand. Feeling empathy is not the same thing.

We are all like snowflakes, our own intricate design of life experiences, histories, heritage, race, upbringing, trauma, memories, struggles, etc. And while many of us just want to reach out with support by saying "I understand," the truth is that saying that takes away from how personal the experience is for that person. None of us share all of the common denominators and so, none of us can truly understand what another is going through, feeling or thinking at any time.

For the first time in my life, I withdrew from the outside world to look within. And you know, "within" can be a pretty scary place. For me it was/still is like a maze. We make choices based on wants, needs, hopes, intuition, beliefs, and we never really know which one will lead us the right way. But through months and now years of introspection, I have learned that the answers that have never led me astray are those that come from the heart but are confirmed by my gut. The few times I have chosen to ignore what my gut has said, I have been burned.

During the summer of 2005, my naturopath thought we should test for Lyme. Not unlike most Lyme patients, the test came back "IND." Not negative, but not positive. Part of the problem with the diagnosis of Lyme in 2005 was that the testing was very flawed, only 30% accurate. The blood test tested for antibodies to fight Lyme disease, but these spirochetes are tricky little suckers and in many cases, such as mine, are able to avoid an immune response all together, therefore causing a negative test result.

And so we went on treating my adrenal issues and my continued gut issues, since I kept traveling. We assumed my PTSD from "losing Sweden," as I started to call it, was continuing to upset me and therefore upset my adrenal glands. It made sense. I spent the summer reading, watching movies, being disagreeable, and sleeping – mostly during the day. I hated my life at that point and honestly, I wonder if I would have survived that summer had I not had my calendar packed with appointments from my support team.

I moved to Vermont in August 2005 and pursued my MA in Teaching English to Speakers of Other Languages (TESOL). After all, how could I possibly have a future ahead of me if it did not include foreign cultures, languages, experiences, and peoples. I had to be very open with the administration and my professors about my condition and thankfully, though uncomfortably, I was considered a "special needs student" for the first time in my life.

I moved into my perfect little Swedish-like cottage and set up shop. The first night, I realized how isolated the cottage was. It was pitch black when you looked outside. This was a town of a thousand people. My Lyme paranoia set in. This was not a home in which I could just install a magnetic siren on one door. I needed a plan. I befriended my neighbor across the street, Scott. He made beautiful, high-quality furniture. His woodworking was immaculate. He had a ponytail all the way down his back, multiple tattoos, and was always chain smoking.

He lived there alone and was quite an angry divorced man. But he was really lovely to me and I told him that I was scared at night. You see, Scott did his best work in his workshop at night. I knew he was always awake when we should both be asleep. And so, we came up with a plan: if I got scared or if someone broke in, I would set off my car alarm and he would come right over with his gun(s). That was enough for me to sleep well in Vermont. Scott never went *anywhere*, so if anyone ever tried to get in my house I would just sound the alarm and he would shoot them. Super. As I write this, I howl with laughter realizing just how crazy the whole thing was. As you can see, I was losing my mind.

The first semester was not at all what I expected. We spent that time looking within, and I was so sick of myself at this point, that it qualified as moderate torture. After all the therapy and introspection, the last thing I wanted to do was look at my own train wreck of a life, now from an academic point of view. We were asked to share with our classmates things about ourselves that symbolized who we were and where we came from. But for me, to do this in front of people who I did not yet know at all and who did not know me, was profoundly disturbing to my emotional well-being. I thought of myself as more Swedish at that point. I knew I was American, but I still thought in Swedish, dreamed in Swedish, and had not yet allowed myself to feel 'at home' in the U.S. again.

I did it, but it was ugly. I wailed my way through the presentation. I later spoke with the administration about how strange I found it that this type of exercise would occur so early in the semester when none of us yet knew each other. In fact, many of my classmates came from countries of extreme situations. Many of them came from cultures where sharing is really not something that is done in such a public forum. They should have known this! Why had we not eased into this?

My saving grace in grad school was my advisor. Just typing her name brings tears to my eyes. I don't know where our instant connection came from, but she is a healer, a teacher, a mentor, like another mother. Her door was *always* open to me and probably to everyone. But she made us all feel special, and that was what I needed at the time. I trusted her. I didn't trust much of anyone at that point. It was nice to have someone who I considered a part of my health support team right there at school.

Much like in Lexington, I didn't have much of a social life at SIT, but I did choose a couple of select friends who could somehow deal with and see through my issues. I bonded specifically with my friend Katherine, who was going through her own emotional transition after returning from the Peace Corps in Cameroon, where she left her love as well. We would sit on the floor of my cottage and study, listen to music, often Swedish music, and sometimes we would cry. It was good to have a friend like Kath.

Other than that, my social life mostly consisted of the weekends when Brad and Kerry would come up from Boston. They were so wonderful to me. They knew how sick I was and we really did have a great time together. Kerry cooked, honestly the first proper thing I had eaten all week. We drank copious amounts of red wine and I just loved them. We went to breakfast at "The Dam Diner." They were like family.

Between semesters, we were to conduct a teaching internship of several weeks. I had planned on doing mine in South Africa. But during the fall semester, it was clear that I was very, very sick. *Why* was I not getting better? I cried myself to sleep in my Unisom-induced, drugged state and say out loud, "I am *doing* the emotional, mental, spiritual and physical work. *Why* am I not getting better?" It just seemed I was getting worse.

———————

And so while my friends traveled to my dreams, to South Africa and to Thailand on the Burmese border, to Chiapas, to Guatemala, or any place more interesting than my parents' house, I found myself back at my parents' house. And this is when the discussions began. It had been two years since I watched Gustaf walk out those automatic doors at the airport. I was getting worse and now I realized I might not get better. None of us wanted me living with my parents. To be fair, it sucked for them as much as it sucked for me.

By the time the school had given me special permission to do my internship out of the scheduled allotment time, we agreed I needed to live in their town and that they would buy a house for me to live in, not far from them. I didn't need much. I didn't think I would be here for more than a couple of years. I needed a home with two bedrooms and an office. That was all; a starter house. But I wanted it to be in a nice neighborhood and a house that wouldn't suck even more of the life out of me. Within weeks we closed on the smallest home in a nice development of families surrounded by apple orchards and beautiful trees, about seven miles from my parents' home.

While the first floor of the house was livable, the upstairs had not yet been touched. And so, when I returned to Vermont for the second and final semester, construction began on the two bedrooms and bath upstairs. It was to be completed by the time I got out of school. I spent my days attending one or two classes, came home and took a nap, then completed three to four hours of work each day. Lucky for me, most of our work was related to writing, and clearly I enjoy writing. So, I managed to get through the academic part of the program, with the constant support of my wonderful advisor. Honestly, looking back, I do not know how I did it.

By some miracle I completed the second semester, but for the first time in my life, I got horrible spring allergies. My body pain continued. I had migraines every day and I could not control my body temperature; I was always freezing. I had to take several scorching showers a day to warm up. My thyroid tests continuously came back fine, so this was an issue we just didn't know how to deal with other than to "get hot."

The very hardest part of leaving Vermont was leaving Brad and Kerry who had by this time made a permanent move to Vermont. I had grown so comfortable with them. These were people I could just relax with. I had very few others in my life I could do that with. I knew that we would be friends forever, and of course we always will be. But with time, I have lost contact with them, though we sometimes give one another a shout on Facebook. I hope they read this book at some point and know just how much I appreciate and love them for all they did for me.

Internship

—◦—

Once I had finished both academic semesters at SIT, I had two major components left to complete my MA in TESOL. I needed to complete the teaching internship, from which I had taken a leave in the winter, and then I needed to write my two-hundred-page Masters final project.

My therapist and I had a series of conversations about how I had a history of not really completing things I had begun. We realized that I had a profound fear of loss; perhaps if I cut things off before they fully developed or manifested, that left me in control so I would not have to deal with unexpected loss. It was this conversation that made me realize that I had to complete this degree. There was no option. I became determined to defy my inner fears and win the battle.

I was back, living close to my health team, and promptly resumed my previous appointment schedule with my naturopath, a new MD, massage therapist, and counselor. I did an internship at a local summer boarding school where I worked during the mornings six days a week as a teacher of students from around the world who were learning English. Many teachers sought out social opportunities with one another. I showed up for class, met my obligations, and went home and slept for the rest of the day.

At this time, I still had all of my symptoms, but the days were a brilliant distraction and, in retrospect, I have found that it's the distractions that very well may have gotten me through this so far.

Masters Degree Miracle

———◦◈◦———

After my internship was complete, my house was finally ready for me to move into. I had never lived in this town and I knew no one. At the time, this was just fine with me. I found myself suffering from social phobias I had never previously struggled with. I didn't want to meet anyone. I hated when my mom dragged me out to things, although she did the right thing. I had no idea social phobias were a typical neurological symptom of Lyme.

I had the perfect excuse to isolate myself in my misery. My final project for my Masters was a phenomenal distraction from my life.

I completed my Master's thesis in two weeks. Not because I am some master of the universe, but because I literally sat down and started to write and didn't stop until it was done. I had a lot to say and all of a sudden, the five-month complete mental shutdown I had experienced lifted and I began to pour out my work into words. I had words. It felt so good to finally speak.

I am not known for being at a loss for words. But for years I have felt that I have never really expressed myself. It had been so *long* since I actually *felt* something other than being numb, that the writing process figuratively dragged me out of my self-imposed silence with every word I put on paper. It was a deeply moving experience for me.

Against the odds, I completed my Master of Arts in Teaching English to Speakers of Other Languages on time in May of 2007. It was a big moment for me. I had completed something in its entirety.

Now What???

———◦◉◦———

I had thrown all of my being into my Master's thesis and once it was sent to the committee on its way to review, I felt not a sense of relief, but of dread. What would I do now? How could I *possibly* survive in this tiny town in my house all alone? Of course, my nighttime paranoia and insomnia continued. I had an alarm system put in and not only locks on my bedroom door knob, but a deadbolt as well, so real was my paranoia.

It was in this house that I was finally forced to fight my own demons: my fear of being alone, truly alone; my deeply rooted insecurities about body image no matter how skinny or chubby I was; my absolute inability to make a decision of any kind; and my still raw heart, screaming for relief. I found myself often thinking of women who are able to just move on from major relationships with little effort. I just could not get to that place.

There was really nothing I could do about it. I was hurting. I was dating here and there since the beginning, but really no one caught my attention in any way that could even compare. And so rather than heal, my heart began to harden, slowly but surely. And I became tough; really tough. I started saying exactly what I thought, sometimes without a filter. And I retreated, working hard on sculpting a cast iron shield around my heart.

While my parents will tell you that "no one has ever been able to control what she does," I would actually disagree with them by saying that while I have always been resourceful and independent since childhood, it was at this point that I began not caring what anyone thought about anything. I became aware that my distractions had come to an end and I needed to start really looking within to gain some direction, make some decisions, and pick up whatever pieces were left of me.

I had no idea where to begin, so I went to bed. And I slept and slept and slept. Then I would be "with it" for a few weeks, and then sleep and sleep and sleep again. The pain was excruciating; the migraines daily; the insomnia/sleep drug addiction ongoing; the mood swings a given; and the desperate need for an escape from my body a constant.

One day, during an appointment with my naturopath, I realized that it was, in fact, his fault that I lived here now, because I moved here to be close to treatment. And I told him so, only what I said, surprised him: "You know, Steve, it's your fault I live here, so you need to give me a job." He laughed at my audacity.

I started work the following Tuesday.

The Road Not Paid For

——⚫——

The agreement was that I would work Tuesdays and Thursdays from 2:30 to 6:00 p.m., just seven hours a week. I was working for *peanuts* and, clearly, working as an office coordinator (really just a glorified receptionist) was, ahem, not what I had just dropped $50K on a Masters for, in addition to four years in a private college. But I liked Dr. Steve. His approach to health and medicine had my attention – and it took a lot to catch my attention.

I pulled medical charts, made appointments, took payment, and after a while, I started working in the medicinary – a natural pharmacy of thousands of supplements and tinctures. It was fun and it was new. And it craved very little brainpower. Most of all, it got me out of the house, and Dr. Steve started to treat me for free which was a relief. My parents had been footing the bills for my visits with him, but honestly, that was getting old and I wanted not only my life back, but my financial independence as well.

I enjoyed Steve's quirkiness and understood his moodiness. We both thought that I might work there for a year or so, and that I might decide to start a company when I felt better, or perhaps decide to teach and put my new degree to use. By the following summer, we were in a groove and his wife, who worked all the hours I didn't work, had a baby. None of us were sure if I would be able to handle a full-time schedule, but neither of us wanted a third party to come in and ruin the good vibe we had going. Steve and I just got each other. I was constantly blown away by his intelligence, which really I have not personally experienced with another soul on Earth. I think one could certainly put him up there with minds like Steve Jobs, Bill Gates, etc.

We laughed a lot. I liked to shock him with my banter and instant comebacks. I was finally in a place where I really could say anything. We had some growing pains in the beginning, as is common in developing any kind of new working relationship, but in all, we were a good professional match. My job became a living classroom for me and I started to learn things about the body, and my own body, that had never previously interested me. I watched new patients come in suffering, and months later, walk out of the office feeling wonderful and not requiring a follow up.

Steve's strengths were my weaknesses and vice versa. I was a PC person. He was a MAC devotee. He eventually won that battle, much to his delight. His bedside manner needed some work and I was made to schmooze and make people feel happy about their experience in the office. I knew nothing about anything health-wise in the beginning, and he was like a walking medical journal. At the time, he was clueless about business and sales, and that was my specialty. We made a great yin and yang and eventually, after a few temper tantrums on my end, he gave up his need to micromanage me and we became trusting partners in moving his practice forward. We became friends, good friends, and in many respects I think I became a member of their family.

What we thought would be a temporary arrangement became a seven-year working situation and a forever friendship. Through the years, he began bouncing questions off me and I answered honestly. He would always take my opinions into regard. He taught me to work the medicinary entirely on my own. The practice grew at least six-fold during the time I was there. I learned a lot and while I no longer work at the practice as of just a few weeks ago. I don't think we will ever be rid of each other.

Steve was the first man I had learned to truly trust in years. I am not sure he has any idea of the depth of the effect he has had on my life beyond my medical situation. I have everything to thank him for, including his flexibility in my process of adopting a baby girl.

Bright

———◦———

Mini's real name means "bright." I cannot think of a better-suited name for my daughter. She lights up every room she walks into. She is remarkably smart. She is quite simply the bright light of my life. I had never heard her name before I first received her referral, but without even a thought, I knew I would keep her birth name. I still think it is one of the most beautiful names I have ever heard. Knowing its meaning makes it that much more beautiful to me.

Life as a mom, a truly single mom who has no one to share custody with, has been wonderful *and* challenging. In some ways, I think it's easier to be a truly single mom, because I make all of the decisions without having to compromise, argue, discuss, whatever. I just do what I think is right. But I never get a break without having to pay for it with a check or guilt. There is no such thing as a "sleep in" morning for me. *Ever.* And then of course, I am the sole breadwinner in this house. So within my freedom lies a lot of pressure.

I have been blessed with a child who sleeps better than any other child on Earth. This kid has slept twelve hours a night and taken two-hour naps since I brought her home. And I know the universe intended this for me. My exhaustion has been unbearable for several years now and when it is nap time, when most moms get productive, I dive into bed and sleep as much as I can, unless of course I am reading a wonderful book or catching up with friends, or working at hours when no one should be working, but I do nap with the best of them.

The whole being-a-mom thing has worked out pretty perfectly. We were made for each other and once again, I understand how the timing of various things in my life, even emotional trauma, has resulted in this path I am meant to follow. I still don't know why I am to follow this painful path when I have worked so hard to do so much good in the world, but it's clearly the path that is meant for me and when I am sure of what I am meant to do with my knowledge and experience, I will comply.

The first year Mini was home, I did quite well. My coping mechanism, for her sake and my own, was to come up with a rock-solid structure and never deviate from it for a year. I got a lot of flak from people for this, but as usual, I didn't care. I did what I knew was right for us. Mini had spent her first nine months in a place with a strict schedule and she was used to routine. I needed routine to maintain a manageable lifestyle and level of pain/fatigue.

No one knows the half of what I went through. My parents have always been very helpful with Mini and really everything else, but telling them every single weekend that my pain was unmanageable and that my eyes were burning from fatigue just didn't seem fair. So many times, I forged forward in silence, hoping that someday, something might make things easier for me to go through the daily motions that most people can do without a thought.

A Shot at Professional Freedom

Mini had been home for a few months and I was feeling guilty about picking her up at 5:15 p.m. after my workday. She was only in daycare three days a week in the beginning, but it was those evenings during the drive home that I would shudder at the thought that I would only have an hour with her before she would be asleep.

I remember exactly where we were one evening on the ride home when I clenched the steering wheel with all of my might. I said out loud, "I need a new professional situation. I look forward to finding a job that will keep me in this town, that I will believe in, that I will enjoy, and that will earn me well over six figures." I said it several times and never gave it another thought.

I had been looking for a couple of years for a line of personal care and home products that was *truly* safe to use with no harmful chemicals. Some companies had some good products, but no one boasted an entire line of safe (in my eyes) products. I knew that what I put *on* me went straight into my bloodstream and was as dangerously toxic to my system as what I put *in* me.

One day, I got a text message from my friend Leah who knew I was looking for something like this as well. She suggested that I take a look at a new company that had launched in Rhode Island just a couple of weeks prior. With one look at the ingredients, which were miraculously all listed (not always the case), and completely acceptable and safe, I ordered the starter kit immediately and became an Ava Anderson Non-Toxic consultant.

Little did I know that two years later, I would find myself in a battle for my life, but still able to sustain my financial security with this business alone. I would become a top Ava consultant nationally for forty consecutive months, and continue to remain there to this day. This company has not only changed the products we use in our family, but has become a financial rock for me during my roughest of times. I am grateful for the opportunity and passionate about sharing Ava Anderson's non-toxic message.

Detoxing plays a crucial role in treating Lyme, and what we put *on* us is as important as what we put *in* us. I am passionate about sharing the company's message and hope that many of you who suffer from Lyme will consider an external detox as important as an internal one.

What's Going On?

As Mini and I settled into our life together and regular life set in, I was never quite right. I was always seeing Dr. Steve for something. We always assumed it was the usual adrenal and gut stuff.

Because chronic Lyme is not only unrecognized, but actually claimed as nonexistent by the Infectious Diseases Society of America (IDSA), Lyme Literate Doctors (LLDs) around the country who have been recognizing, diagnosing, and treating the disease using the International Lyme and Associated Diseases Society (ILADS) protocol have mostly been doing so under the radar. This is because doctors who choose to treat Lyme disease and co-infections like Bartonella, Babesia, Ehrlichia, etc. are being brought before medical boards across the country, and having their licenses suspended and sometimes revoked.

What does this mean? It means that our government needs to take action regarding corruption that lies within the medical community on this issue (and likely other issues as well). Why haven't they? *Money*. You can learn more about this by watching the movie *Under Our Skin* – and if you have read this far without watching it yet, I'm going to spank you.

In 2011, the New Hampshire State Legislature passed a law saying that New Hampshire doctors who treat Lyme with long-term, high-dose antibiotics cannot lose their licenses, except for gross negligence. This was a *major* win for the Lyme community, especially in New Hampshire, where we have more Lyme per capita than anywhere else in the country.

At our clinic, we started using a relatively new test by IGeneX Labs. This test, rather than a blood test for Lyme antibodies, is a urinalysis taken over six days *while* the patient is on antibiotics for treatment of Lyme. Three urine samples are taken during this time period and the samples are tested for the actual die off of the bacteria in the urine.

We started retesting people who were not getting better with their treatments, more than a hundred who had already been tested using the ELISA and/or Western Blot tests, which had come back negative. Fax after fax began coming back positive with Lyme bacteria in the urine. Almost overnight we became a Lyme clinic, treating a majority of our patients with Lyme. With the change in legislation, Dr. Steve came out of the Lyme closet and started treating people who were desperate for help. It was astonishing how quickly our practice changed.

The entire tone of the practice changed. Lyme patients are in pain of every kind. Excruciating physical pain, unimaginable emotional pain, often after being told for years that they are crazy, that "the blood tests are fine," that "it's all in your head," to "get a psychologist," etc. People with Lyme are typically and understandably grumpy and can be *very* rude and *very* mean. So, we needed to create new boundaries as a place of healing, in order to prevent the unpleasant aspects of Lyme and to protect our goal of helping people.

I knew the Lyme protocol like the back of my hand. I knew the Chinese herb protocol as if I had written it myself. I could help people with the inevitable gut issues that come with Lyme treatment. And I could offer the emotional support that they needed when they just needed to talk to someone. In short, I got an intense crash course in Lyme. I knew what I was working with when it came to Lyme patients.

Lyme Gets Personal

I was watching patient after patient get diagnosed with Lyme. Many of them had been to some of the most highly regarded hospitals in the world – Dartmouth Hitchcock, Mass General, Cedar Sinai, you name it. Patients came in with diagnosis of Lou Gehrig's Disease (ALS), rheumatoid arthritis, MS, Parkinson's Disease, etc. I repeatedly watched these patients get properly diagnosed with Lyme, and start treatment using the ILADS protocol, along with herbal treatments, and watched their symptoms get dramatically better. They had been misdiagnosed. Now with a proper Lyme diagnosis, I was watching them improve, one after the other, as they returned for their appointments.

In the fall of 2010, the soles of my feet started to hurt. Of everything that had ever bothered me, my feet had not been one of them. And when I say they hurt, I mean burning, excruciating pain. It was like walking on shattered glass with every step I took. I immediately bought some Dansko clogs thinking maybe I needed more sole support. It continued. My toes started to hurt. They were scorching. The best way I can explain it is that if I looked down at my feet and could see their skeletons within, every single bone would be bright red.

One day I was making a tincture for a patient. I picked up a 32-ounce bottle of Holy Basil tincture and it went crashing onto the floor. My right elbow had given out. It hurt now too. This was the first time I ever experienced joint pain beyond the spine. And my spine, oh my spine. Dr. Steve adjusted me often and I got regular massages, but nothing helped. Migraines continued and my life was a living hell.

I looked at Dr. Steve one day and before I said it, he knew, "Yeah, we need to do the new Lyme test on you." So I went on the antibiotics, took the test, and fought my daily migraines. And we waited. It takes about three weeks to get the test back. I stalked the fax machine. And then one morning a fax came in while Dr. Steve was in with a patient. It was my test results.

"My labs came back positive," I sent him in a chat message. I heard his door open and his big feet walking toward reception. He turned the corner, tears in his eyes, and said, "I am so sorry. I am so very sorry." And suddenly it all made sense. Suddenly, my personal hell climbed to a whole new level.

The Start of Treatment

It's fair to say that very few people know about Lyme disease, much less about the treatment and its effect on patients. With most diseases, you get diagnosed, take some medicine and then start to feel better or at least some level of relief. This is not the case with Lyme.

Lyme treatments are known to cause Herxheimer reactions, which occur when your body is trying to get rid of toxins at a faster rate than the body is capable of eliminating them. It is often thought that the more severe the reaction, which can manifest itself in *any* form (pain, migraines, seizures, loss of mobility, hallucinations, emotional issues, tingling of the extremities or back, you name it), the more severe the infection. In short, when a Lyme patient is in treatment and is experiencing Herx reactions, they may feel even worse than they did prior to treatment.

These reactions can occur when you begin treatment, a few days into treatment or well into treatment. Dr. Steve wisely called my parents into my first Lyme appointment (with my permission). It's important for people treating Lyme to have the support of friends and family. Because it is such an unknown illness, it's crucial that the people close to the patient are aware of what can, and probably will, happen.

I knew what he was going to say because I had heard the speech dozens of times, but when I heard it and he was talking to and about me, it was as if I was hearing it for the first time. I was scared and so were my parents.

I did pretty well during my first three months of treatment. I felt relatively clear-headed, my stomach did not seem to be bothered by the meds, and I was able to work my normal schedule, although in anticipation of treatment we had hired a part-time administrative assistant.

My foot pain continued despite treatment. From my experience at the clinic, I knew this was very likely Bartonella. We were not yet treating that, so I suggested we do the full IGeneX panel for co-infections, which came back positive for Bartonella and Ehrlichia. While my Babesia test came back negative, we both agreed that I had enough symptoms and that the tests are unreliable enough to assume I had that too.

All fall I had started to complain of a weird feeling in my left side, just below my lowest rib. I saw both Steve and my primary MD about it, wondering if it could be related to a 2005 case of endometriosis which landed me in laparoscopic surgery. I explained that it felt "like a ball is in there or something." My primary did an ultrasound and x-ray of my abdomen and of my entire spine and while nothing was found on my abdominal x-rays, it was at this time that I was diagnosed with degenerative disc disease (osteoarthritis) in my upper cervical spine. Super. Thanks, Lyme.

Dr. Steve did frequent visceral manipulation to try to relieve my abdominal symptoms. Visceral manipulation is a gentle hands-on therapy that works through the body's visceral system (the heart, liver, intestines and other internal organs) to locate and alleviate these abnormal points of tension throughout the body in an effort to release connective tissue and adhesions, which are stuck and causing physical issues. The practitioner uses gentle hand movements to slowly disconnect tissues that have grown together in places they should not have. While it's a gentle procedure, it can be extremely painful, as it was for me, as my severe case of Lyme disease and associated co-infections had resulted in an equally severe case of connective tissue disorder. He would start by digging around with his hands until he found an adhesion. When he did, he would slowly tear the adhesions from each other and from my organs. I sweated, I cried, I screamed, I always told him to stop when I couldn't take anymore. Our agreement was that we'd then count to five and he would stop.

It helped for a while, as did the Vicodin my MD had prescribed. I had always been against pain meds, even after my surgeries, until I experienced this level of pain.

<hr />

Treatment continued, month after month. During each session I was in a constant state of Herx reaction, which were getting worse and worse. I was not sleeping at all at night, but I could sleep all day. When I did sleep, I would hear sounds similar to a cap gun going off in my head. I was never scared when it happened – I knew it was in my head, not an outside threat. It always took a while for me to come out of that kind of sleep.

When I slept during the day, it was the hardest sleep I could imagine. And when I awoke, I could not open my eyes. I knew I was awake – I was talking to myself inside my head trying to tell myself, "Okay, get up now. You have to get Mini. Pick your head up off the pillow." Because I could not open my eyes, I was never sure how long it took to get me out of that kind of sleep, but it usually felt like about fifteen minutes or so. I later found out that both of these sleep situations were actually seizures.

I later had a lengthy blood panel drawn and about four months into treatment, my liver levels presented as questionable. Because of all of my pain, we decided to stop treatment immediately. This was very frustrating. I had seen very few patients do this. Here I was again. Back at step one.

You Put the Lyme in the Coconut

—◦◉◦—

By February 2012, I had been off antibiotics for three months. Dr. Steve was worried about putting me back on them. He kept saying, "There's something we're missing." We agreed that I needed to see one of the best specialists in the world for Lyme, because clearly I was not tolerating the regular ILADS protocol. We went through several names. I decided I was most comfortable seeing Dr. Joseph Jemsek at the Jemsek Specialty Clinic in Washington, DC.

I had seen Dr. Jemsek in the movie Under Our Skin and admired that he was still in practice despite past legal troubles. I greatly appreciated his determination to help those of us who have no voice. And what I loved most, was that he opened his new practice right in Washington, D.C., just blocks from The White House. The more I learned about him, the more obvious it became that he was "my guy."

The pain in my side continued until it became unbearable. Under my lowest left rib I got shocking pains that were just too much to bear. If I did not have Mini loving on me every single day, I think this might have been the end of me.

I had tried acupuncture, visceral work, and took Vicodin, which really seemed to be the only thing that helped. This may be too much information, but I have vowed to tell the whole story so here goes. I have used a Mirena IUD for the past couple of years. Because of it, I rarely get a period. *Amen.* On February 3, 2012, I got my first period in months and simultaneously noticed that the Vicodin was no longer working for me. The pain had me in the fetal position, crying, screaming, unable to get remotely comfortable.

Even if you don't personally know me, you have probably gathered by now that I'm the type that gets things done. I made the connection of the worsened pain and my period, called my OB-GYN and said I needed to come in right away. Honestly, I was just fed up with my MD who kept referring to it as a muscle spasm. I have to say, my gynecologist is a great guy. He speaks so quietly and is just always very pleasant. I'll admit, sometimes I say things to get him to talk louder or catch him by surprise, but he is very steady and it never works. Oh well, project for another day.

I was in so much pain that I brought my mother with me. The conversation went something like this:

Me: "So, I have this raging pain right here and I'm going to need a pelvic and an abdominal ultrasound. I have all day. I can wait until we can make that happen."

He did the appropriate exams that we all dread and agreed to the ultrasounds because, really, what choice did he have? He didn't think it had anything to do with my pelvic region because the pain was so high, but clearly I was going nowhere. Alas, in this case what they found was a 9cm endometrioma on my left ovary. Oh yeah, I had a coconut-sized cyst and, yeah, the pain now made sense. I needed surgery, right away.

The surgery was to be laparoscopic, through the belly button, probably outpatient. But that's not how it happened. At all. One hour into surgery, he had to bring in a second surgeon. The gigantic cyst was so heavily adhered to two-thirds of my pelvis, uterine wall and urethra because of my Lyme-related connective tissue disorder that the surgery became a laparotomy. Basically, I had a three-hour C-section. I had a flipping C-section. I flew five thousand miles four times to "give birth" to my daughter, but still had a c-section. That's just rude.

Outpatient surgery turned into two nights in the hospital followed by one week of bed rest. It was hard on Mini. My parents took turns sleeping over and taking care of her. I was surprisingly pretty self-sufficient. And slept and slept and slept. Hallelujah. *Sleep at last.*

One major thing was hanging over me, making me *determined* to speed up the healing process. Nine days after surgery, my company's biggest conference of the year was to occur in Palm Beach, Florida. I had been the top-ranked consultant in the company, Ava Anderson Non-Toxic, since 2010. I could not wrap my mind around not going. The President of the company, my dear friend, Kim Anderson, managed to find a way to Skype me in so I could still do my presentations. I armed myself with fake palm trees and all kinds of tackiness to add a little light to the fact that I could not be there.

But I couldn't wrap my mind around it. I harassed my surgeon pretty much every other day. He kept saying "*no way* can you go this soon." The answer "*no*" has never really registered with me. On Monday, I marched into his office, showed him I was *fine* and got the go-ahead to go to the conference on Wednesday.

Dr. Jemsek _ Visit #1
March 2012

All that was happening was surreal. Dr. Steve, my rock, had agreed that I should go to see Dr. Jemsek of the Jemsek Specialty Clinic in Washington, DC. Unfortunately, I was clearly beyond the scope of his expertise. Hopefully this well-known specialist – known worldwide as one of the big names in Lyme – could help me.

It was a very emotional trip to DC. I had my father with me. We would be in DC for only one night. We made our way through the city where I had been happy so many years before, and found Dr. Jemsek's office on the second floor of a large office building. The walk down the corridor was not a long one, but getting there felt like it was happening in slow motion.

And then we came to the sign by the door. My dad stopped in his tracks, put a hand on my shoulder, and we both got very teary. *Could this be it?* Was this the man who could save my life? Apparently, walking into the Jemsek Clinic a complete wreck is not unusual, as about five feet into the reception area there was a four-foot-tall table with a teddy bear and some tissues.

I pulled it together, checked in, and then found myself taking pictures of the office. Who takes pictures in a doctor's office? I guess the answer to that is someone who has been suffering on various levels for twenty-six years and is perhaps losing the battle. We were first called in to see his really smart and lovely Physician's Assistant, Kim, who went through my vitals, etc. We went through *all* of the details of my life and how things had unfolded.

One thing I had done, that I suggest anyone dealing with chronic illness does, is to walk in armed with an entire life health history written out, as well as a complete list of medications and dosages. Doing this allowed me to take control of my own health and showed them (and other doctors since) that I am in control of my information and am ready to be approached as a serious patient.

They conducted several tests, which measured reactions from my nervous and neurological systems – some of which I did okay on, others that I failed miserably.

———

There was a knock on the door and there he was: Dr. Jemsek. My dad seemed kind of star-struck and honestly, so was I. Here was this expert we had seen in *Under Our Skin* and whom I had seen speak on several videos from the ILADS conference.

Dr. Jemsek is a warrior. He is a doctor who is in it to *save lives*. His demeanor is very even-keeled. He is rather quiet in his speech (likely because many of us, myself included, are sound-sensitive), and he is straightforward. He is also *very* focused on the individual, where you were, where you are, and finally, where you are going.

Well, the where you are going part was pretty overwhelming. When I walked into this world-renowned Lyme clinic, I figured he sees the worst of the worst. People get wheeled in here. Some can't talk. Some have daily seizures. Well, after this meeting it became clear that I was among the most serious cases too. And that was scary.

I was told that my system was so fragile at that moment that basically the wind could blow the wrong way and I could lose mobility, my speech, my eyesight, you name it. I would not be on antibiotic treatment at all for a while. The first priority would be to get my immune system to cooperate so it too could take part in fighting this disease. Second, he believed, and would send me away with tests to confirm, that I have some brain damage from the Lyme and as such, I would be treated with neurological meds. Dr. Jemsek also believed all of my pain was neurological and nerve-based. This does not mean it was in my head; it meant that the chaos in my brain was causing my body pain.

I was sent to have a blood draw at home, *thirty-two* vials of blood. I was also ordered to get a brain SPECT scan, a cardiologist evaluation, an ultrasound and a HIDA scan because, after poking around, he said, "Your gall bladder is probably going to have to come out."

"Oh well," I thought to myself, "what's another organ?"

GPS

During the winter of 2011-2012, after I went off the antibiotics, I started having the sleep seizures that I mentioned (the popping in my head that I had no idea were seizures), and new neurological issues began to appear.

Each morning I take Mini to her school, which is about twenty minutes away. I love that drive. We listen to her favorite music and she sings along at the top of her lungs with her little three-year old voice. Sometimes she negotiates stopping for chocolate milk and on the days I require a gallon of coffee to survive, I comply. Usually she has some very important things to say, like "Mommy, da tapir is scared of da puma," or "who is habbin da next birfday?" Mornings are hard for me, but she is good entertainment.

One day I was driving her to school, which takes literally two main roads to get there. About ten minutes into the drive, I suddenly felt completely disoriented and had no idea where we were going. I pulled over. Wait a minute. Where are we going? "Mommy, why you stop da car?" Mini asked, and I had to admit to my then two-year-old, "Well, baby, I can't remember where we are going." "You so silly, Mama. We goin to my school!" And panic set in. I didn't know how to get to school. I couldn't remember the name of her school to look it up on my iPhone map. "Let's go, Mommy."

"I don't know where to go. Mommy feels a little confused right now." Then my sweet two, almost three-year-old said, "Oh, it's just up there, up the road. I can tell you!" So I started driving again, trusting my girl and my instincts, and sure enough, she clapped her little hands when we got there and said, "Here we are! We did it! Good job, Mommy!"

I took her in to her classroom and went through our usual change of shoes, kisses, hugs, and high fives. And then I walked back to the car and sat there and cried. I knew where I was now and I knew how to get home, but what had just happened? What was happening to my mind?

It would be the first of several instances of disorientation, although thankfully now it happens more when others are driving. My mom often hears, "Wait, where are we going again?"

One thing that has tortured me since my twenties is not being able to find things. My whole life it would put me into a rage I could not control. I would get *so angry*. My keys. I hate my keys. I still avoid them at all costs because I can never find them, even though I put them in the same place every time. Yesterday for Mother's Day, it took me thirty minutes to find our matching Lilly Pulitzer outfits that I had bought for the occasion. I had just seen them the day before. I knew where they were, but I could not find them.

I have had to call my mom and ask her where things were. She has always been very nice about trying to help me keep my home picked up. I can leave quite a mess, especially with clothes. And when she'd tell me she didn't know, I would flip out and usually hang up, even though I know it's probably not her fault. And I always feel bad about it, but I can't articulate it. I just *hate* not being able to find things. It's one of my Lyme triggers.

If you speak to other people with Lyme, you will likely find that, while it may not their keys, they likely have their own triggers. Please know that these are real and that their reactions are uncontrollable, as strange as it sounds. If that is something you cannot accept, I suggest you walk away quietly during the Lyme rage or find out at a later time (*not* in the middle of a Lyme rage) what you can do to be supportive. The experience of these rages is highly emotional because they are real, though often unreasonable. Many times, the patient knows this, especially after the fact.

Since the summer of 2011, I'd had to reduce my hours at work. I started working nine to one, and to be honest, I didn't get much done. I was confused. I was tired. I was upset. Dr. Steve was so patient with me and I think the fact that he saw me every day in that state was just torture for him. We had built that business together, are very good friends and yet, I was the one patient whose body had rejected ILADS treatment.

One day, I was sitting at my desk in the back office with a nice view of the woods behind the building. We had hired a full-time receptionist to deal with the patients because I just couldn't deal with the social aspect of the job anymore, which used to be my greatest gift. Our solution was a good one. I could sit quietly in the back and pay bills, call in prescriptions, and talk to patients as a doctor's assistant. It was a good arrangement, but not on this day. A man, dressed in camouflage, was running through the woods. He was scary. I knew right away, I'd had my first hallucination. I was terrified – not of the imaginary man in the woods, but of my mind, which I knew I was losing. The years and years of paranoia since my twenties was one thing, but this was just too much. Now I was seeing what I had feared for so long.

To lose your mind and be fully aware of it is complete horror.

Jemsek Visit #1
The Aftermath

———— ⋅◍⋅ ————

After the first visit with Dr. Jemsek in March 2012, I realized, or perhaps accepted, that my life was about to change big time and that working for Dr. Steve would no longer be an option. I told him the week I came home. Actually, I told his wife because I couldn't face him to tell him I'd be leaving. We had already hired a new full-time person who we had wanted for a couple of years (the last one was moving on) and I'd thought I would be able to stay and train her through April. That didn't happen. In fact, that week seemed to be the last week I would show up for work at all. My body, my fatigue, my brain were all done. I had nothing left to offer the practice. I needed to put all of what little energy I had into the new treatment.

I previously shared that when seeing Dr. Jemsek for the first time, I had to be taken off all antibiotics and was put on a whole list of medications and supplements to help support my neurological function, try to get my immune system to help out a little more, and work on adjusting my "sleep architecture" so that my clock was not turned on its head. I took supplements for oxidation and, most importantly, detoxing. I was also told, as I had been by Dr. Steve many times, that keeping inflammation in the body low is key to treating Lyme, so I was immediately instructed to go gluten-free and avoid any foods that cause inflammation in my body specifically.

Upon my return home, I went straight to Dr. Steve and requested the following two tests: The ALCAT test (ALCAT.com) and the IgG

Food Allergy Assay from US Biotech. As a result, I have eliminated the following foods from my diet.: gluten, all dairy (including the milk protein casein), eggs, soy, peanuts, tapioca (which is in *all* prepared gluten-free products – *boooo*), codfish, mackerel, okra, shrimp, spelt, tuna and black-eyed peas. Many of these foods had already been removed as a result of prior testing by Dr. Steve, but food allergies in this regard do change.

I began my new treatment. My day now consisted of four handfuls of medications – upon waking, at noon, 4 p.m. and at bedtime. We are talking twenty pills, four times a day. At first it felt completely overwhelming, but now it's really not a big deal. Meds come with the package and they have helped. One of the things I was told during my first visit to DC was that virtually none of Dr. Jemsek's patients use traditional pain killers. This surprised me, but I was happy to hear it, as I am generally opposed to using prescription pain killers unless totally necessary. I would be using neurotrophic and nerve medications to control my pain. So, out with the Vicodin and be gone with the Percocet; we were trying something new.

Just to be clear, neurotrophic meds are used to regulate any part of the brain – I use them for mood stabilizing, sleep, pain (including itching and sunburn without sunburn...a lot more about that later), anxiety, and basically everything else that is wrong, brain-wise. What they do *not* do is kill infection.

———— ◦ ————

I had ups and downs in my first month. I couldn't claim to have been emotionally stable. I had real issues with patience and had to give myself a time out several times to prevent snapping at Mini. But sadly, I did snap at her a few times. Try as I might, I am only human. I cried, I mean *really* cried, for the first time in a long while and it seemed that once the floodgates opened, that was it. I found that very little made me happy. I found that for the first time in my life, I had very little interest in watching TV, a typical diversion for me, a sort of bubblegum for my broken mind.

I think I was probably disinterested because I was more photo-sensitive than ever before. My computer does not seem to bother me though, so I live for Facebook, which keeps me connected to the world and prevents me from becoming the next hermit/Unabomber in the woods. *Just kidding, FBI.* That's a positive thing, I suppose, although I would make a much hotter Unabomber than the last one.

One thing I noticed right away was that with the meds I was given for bedtime came sleep. And not just your run of the mill "night-night" experience. No, this stuff is full-on, pass-out, knock you almost in a coma, see you next Thursday kind of medicine. And I couldn't have been happier about it. Mini knew Mommy slept harder now and she knew she could come in to get me. I also started using the baby monitor again and heard her every time she called me, so no worries there. But I was sleeping, which I had not done without meds in twenty years. In fact, when there were days I could not fit a nap in, I seemed to actually survive quite well.

Most incredibly though, was that most of my pain was gone. As I said before, I had never left my house in over fifteen years without Excedrin Migraine. But now I hadn't had a migraine since March. I left my house without one *every day.* There've been some real downers though, including the aforementioned emotional instability.

I discovered this in a special ninety-minute Lyme massage that I attend twice a week. My massage therapist was working on my legs. I have always had problems in my legs. On this day, she was using hot stones. My body sucked in the heat. Lyme hates heat, which is why I loved it so much. When I was warm, I felt better. As she dug in my legs with the stones, she got to my shins. And I said, "Gayle, oh my God. I can feel it." I'm not sure she realized the significance of this. She replied, "What do you mean?" I got teary and said, "I can feel you working on my shins." For the first time in twenty-three years, I had sensation in a part of my body that had been dead to me since that moment outside Windsor Castle in 1989. I knew at that very moment the loss of sensation had been neurological and the new meds had brought that part of my body back to life.

⸻

While working one day in April of 2012, giving a presentation, I felt a headache begin like none I had ever experienced. It was in a new place. And it was different. It was as if it was in my head, but then also extended into a bubble outside my head. That's the only way I can explain it. I got a little panicky after I was done with my presentation, but I tried to tough it out, thinking it was a migraine of some kind.

Finally, my presentation ended and I got in my car. The drive home was about twenty minutes. A few minutes into the drive, when I was able to release myself from my job, I started sobbing and went into a full panic attack. I called my dad right away. My mom answered, but I asked to talk to him. "Are you okay?" "No, I need to talk to Dad." Once he got to the phone, I realized that my eyes were twitching a little back and forth and I had more saliva than I was used to. Then I realized I couldn't swallow. I held my tongue as I spoke with my father, because I realized I was having my first seizure while awake.

My father asked me where I was several times:

Me: "I don't know. I don't know."

Dad: "Pull over the car."

By this time he was calling me on his cell and was getting into the car to come find me. I knew I needed to pull over, but I couldn't reason with myself. My only focus was to get home. I kept sobbing. I was so scared.

Me: "No, I want to go home."

Dad with a shaky voice: "I'm sure you do. I think you should stop at the ER."

Me: "No, Dad, no way am I having a Lyme fight with that fucking hospital. I just want to go *hoooome!*"

My lip was quivering and by that time I was able to tell Dad where I was as I made my way closer to town. I would like to add that I was driving perfectly fine. It was so weird.

Dad had parked on Main Street right where he knew I'd be turning. He waited for me and when he saw my car, he pulled in front of me, probably to control my speed and keep an eye on me, because he knew by then I was not going to stop the car. We got home safely and I parked the car in the garage. I stumbled out of the car and had trouble walking, bumping into things as I walked upstairs. Thankfully, Mini was already asleep and Maxi, my assistant who was babysitting, was in the kitchen, unaware of what was happening. I remember going for the checkbook to pay her, with no balance at all (physical, not monetary, I hasten to add.). We decided I would pay her the next day.

I called Dr. Jemsek's office immediately to speak with the triage nurse on call. I went to bed, settled into the fetal position and lay there still for what seemed an eternity. The phone rang; it was triage. We went through the whole thing. I was surprisingly lucid and able to explain what had happened. I think it was then that I was able to let go of the trauma and snap out of the terror of what had just happened. She suggested when this happens to take an Ativan ASAP and settle into a safe place. The following day the same thing happened at home and this strategy worked. I was able to ward off the seizure with Ativan once I felt it approaching.

Dad saw that I had come out of it, went home to get some clothes and stayed at my house that night. I think we were sufficiently freaked out, thank you very much. We had originally thought he wouldn't need to join me on my next trip to Dr. Jemsek in DC, but the game had just changed and the following day he made his airplane and hotel reservations.

My memory continued to serve me poorly and my vision became blurred from that moment on. That seizure was a signal to me of what was to come. And what was to come, I mean, we had no idea…

Testing, Testing 1, 2, 3 — 4, 5, 6?

"Who is your team?" they had asked me at my first visit with Dr. Jemsek. I had no idea what they were talking about. I was thinking, "*You* are my team. That's why I flew down here, duh." They noticed my blank stare and continued, "You know, your cardiologist, neurologist, general surgeon." Oh, yeah. I had none of those.

I was sent home with scripts to get *a lot* of stuff done before Visit #2. I needed to get a HIDA scan for imagery and ultrasound, both to see if my gall bladder was okay. They explained that most Lyme patients' gall bladders cause major issues, because when they are not working properly, they act as a toxic magnet. Remember now, one of the biggest components of proper Lyme treatment is to detox. Okay, so the assignment was to get a HIDA scan, whatever that was, and an ultrasound. Gotcha. Had a thousand of those.

Also, get a brain SPECT scan. Huh? Note to self – brain = need neurologist. I had no idea what this meant other than it was imagery of my brain. More pictures of my insides.

"Oh, and don't forget you need to get a full cardiac evaluation." Okie dokie. I was on it. And so I came home, exhausted at the thought of all this homework. I suppose someone could have helped me get through all of this, but I have more medical knowledge than anyone in my family and I am a stubborn pain in the ass, so I did it all myself. I decided to do the ultrasound and HIDA scan locally at our little hospital in town, mostly because I could. Then I settled on making the trek to Dartmouth Hitchcock for neurology and The New England

Heart Institute for cardiology. The name sounds about right, wouldn't you agree?

———— ✦ ————

So, first up was my ridiculous blood panel of thirty-two vials. I showed up at the hospital and told them, "I realize this is a challenging script and I am prepared to wait as long as I have to for you to get these tubes and labels organized. Please let anyone who comes in go before me." The two ladies at the window looked at the script wide-eyed. One of them went out back, and suddenly there were four nurses gathered around the computer.

"Apparently this will be a big one," I thought. Meanwhile, I was busy drinking 64 ounces of water, knowing it would help with drainage of my blood supply.

It was really pretty funny. I could hear them saying, "I have no idea what that is. Look it up." Again and again. And I thought the thought I have a hundred times a day: "Lyme, you are so obnoxious." After an hour and a half, I went in for the blood draw. Finally, they called me, looking bewildered.

"Look," I said, "I am totally fine if you need to draw from multiple sites." The stone-faced scary manager wanted to use a big needle – you know, the harpoon. I said, "No way. Use the butterfly needle." And so they did.

Anyway, seventy-eight people in the room (okay, it was actually four). They all had a job: one drew the blood, the next grabbed the vial and handed the new one to the one doing the draw. Then the grabber passed the drawn vial off to the labeler, who made sure the right label went on the right color tube. Then the fourth one, "the rocker," took the labeled tube to my very own special rack that would be sent off later that day. It was kind of like a relay. I was quite amused by their bewilderment and all the commotion.

Obviously, the needle gave out at about twenty-four vials. They had to stick my other arm for the remaining eight vials. They told me the thirty-two was a record at the hospital. Overachiever. *Grin...* I estimated that blood work to be worth about $12,000, no kidding, but for once, it was covered by insurance; I probably hit my deductible on vial four. Good stuff.

Okay, so, ridiculous blood draw – *check!*

Next came the ultrasound. It was with Katie. She always does my ultrasounds. She went to college with one of my best friends, who is a college friend of Mini's godfather. So Katie did the ultrasound and it came back with no gall stones. *Hooray!* Something I *didn't* have!

Ultrasound of gall bladder et al. – *check!*

And then I went for the HIDA scan. *Ay ay ay*, the HIDA scan. Basically, you get in an open coffin from the year 2087, get an injection to fill your gall bladder, and lay there as still as a rock for thirty minutes while a creepy camera takes pictures all around you. Then, good times: *Injection! Of radioactive material.* Super!

"Um, okay, I am going to puke on myself now," I said to myself, "No, I really mean it. I am going to puke! No, no, WAIT! Okay, the pukey feeling is gone. Why does it feel like an electric snake is moving through my colon? This can't be good," I said, again talking to myself in silence.

HIDA scan – *fail.*

Yay! Time to make an appointment with a general surgeon for gall bladder removal. No problem. What's another organ? They just took

an ovary in February. Let's have a night cap. Appointment done. Gall
bladder comes out May 25, 2012.

———◦———

So, I made my way to Dartmouth Hitchcock to see the neurologist. I
arrived for this appointment armed with my extensive health history,
a very organized list of my personal pharmacy (my daily medications
list) and my blue medical file of virtually every doctor's note and test
done on me since 2001, because I am just that demanding. My file is
organized just as we did at Dr. Steve's, with my tests and meds info
clipped to the left and the appointment notes on the right. I was fully
prepared for the Lyme fight. You just have to be.

I gave the nurse the information I wanted the neurologist to see
before she came in. And when she came in, with her resident in tow,
she was absolutely lovely. She appreciated my copious notes and par-
ticipation in my own healthcare. She knew I knew my stuff. We had
some banter. I admit, I showed off a little, but I wanted to get the scans
done that Dr. Jemsek had ordered and I wanted it scheduled as soon as
possible. I also wanted the dud of a resident to lighten up a little.

After about ten minutes of a consultation, she said, "Well, what I
think is happening here is that Dr. Jemsek needs some tests done and
you need to get them done locally. I think I can learn a lot from your
case, and I am willing to be that person on your team who gets you what
you need in the neurology department."

I'm sorry, did she just really say that? Did she actually not give me
any shit for "claiming" chronic Lyme? I got teary (seriously, can we lose
the tears now?) and thanked her. "You know," I said, "New Hampshire
has more Lyme per capita than anywhere else in the country. It causes
neurological damage. If you pay attention to it and really take a look
at this, you could change lives and your entire field of medicine." She
heard me. And she ordered the SPECT scan of my brain.

Then, on the way out, since I was feeling triumphant, I thought I would enlighten the downer of a resident. "It might serve you well to crack a smile with your patients. Maybe participate with those patients who have some level of social skills and humor, because if you are going into neurology, you are probably not going to have many of those." As we walked out, without him, I heard the doctor say under her breath, "Amen." *Giggle...*

Brain SPECT ordered – *check!*

Resident *schooled* – *check!*

Maxi was unavailable the day of the SPECT scan, and my dad was working on something out of town. Mom was no longer allowed to take me to medical appointments because we stress each other out in these situations, so she had pleasantly been dismissed from this duty. So, my sister offered. This was kind of a big deal to me and I was grateful. Since the seizure, I have not driven out of town.

So, my sister took me to get the SPECT scan. This was awesome. Enter a room with a blood draw chair, get injection of radioactive liquid (you can call me Japan now) and then sit quietly in said chair in darkness for fifteen minutes alone, so as not to distract your brain. Then be retrieved, only to sit in a bright waiting room (sunglasses helped) and listen to all of the young, ambitious doctors talking about the freak shows they had seen yesterday. *Shut up.* Some of us are trying to be *unstimulated here.*

So, some lady comes in to get me. Was her name Pam? I think she was Pam. And she notices my iHarem – iPhone, iPad, and MacBook Air all in my bag. And for ten flipping minutes she is asking me if she needs to get an iPad. I proceed to tell her it is the most necessary, unnecessary item I have ever discovered and that while I really don't use it for anything important, I could never live without one again. It was an intense conversation.

Then she strapped my head down with a velcro thing and told me to be still for the next hour. "And you may want to close your eyes. The camera comes eerily close to your face." Here's one, if you happen to be a medical technician: please do not use the word *eerily* with your patients at any time. So I think I fell asleep. I know I didn't move because my head was strapped down and I was in the Cuckoo's Nest.

Brain SPECT scan – *check!*

Brain SPECT scan – *fail.* (Diagnosis to follow)

The good times never end – now it was time to go to the New England Heart Institute to get a cardiologist evaluation to make sure I don't have pericarditis (fluid around the heart – *really?*). So again, armed for battle, I go in with my life history on paper and my meds list. And in comes the sweetest man. He was *so nice.* And he knew I was here for chronic Lyme. And he gave me *no flack.* He did an EKG.

EKG – *check!*

And then ordered an echocardiogram which I did a couple of weeks later.

Echocardiogram – *check!* And then, because I heave heart palpitations, get dizzy and sometimes cannot get a deep breath, we need to rule out heart involvement and so…

The thirty-day heart monitor. *Oh, yeah, baby!* I get to sport this thing for thirty days. I have it on right now. Maxi and I can have a blast doing just about anything, so as I was leaving the hospital with my brand spankin' new heart monitor I sang at the top of my lungs the most overplayed song of 2011: "I'm Sexy and I Know It," and we laughed so hard it hurt. Probably set the damned thing off.

So, there you have it. I am one sexy radioactive medical control freak with a bum gall bladder and a wretched brain SPECT Scan result.

Visit #2 with Dr. Jemsek

Back to DC

———◈———

Originally, Dad was not going to come on the second trip with me. The first trip was mostly a study of my history and we felt pretty secure that I could take on this next trip alone. The seizures, however, changed the game dramatically, and we decided he should come.

It was a hard appointment, but I felt so secure with this man as my doctor. His demeanor was very stable, calm, quiet, and confident. I am sure he is like this partly because most of us are photo and/or sound sensitive. I know I certainly am. I've had instances when there's been a lot of noise and action around me and I've just held my head, shaking it, as if to make it stop. Mini is working on her quiet voice. That is going very poorly, especially tonight, when she was acting like someone had given her a Red Bull. Anyway, Dr. Jemsek. Even-keeled. Good.

We talked about how the shots I give myself twice a week in my abdomen are causing huge red spots. He wants me to keep at it, so I will. We talked about my cortisol levels being dangerously low on the labs, but how they looked good after taking Cortef in the morning, so he does not think my mid-day crashes are adrenal-related. "It's just part of it all." He explained how when I get tired, I must sleep. I need sleep. To me, it was like rocket science. Huh?

One of my other concerns was my balance. I have become increasingly clumsy through the years and rapidly through the past few weeks/months. I am bumping into things, and falling over (kind of funny though). I am often dizzy. We talked about my sporadic *deep* depression that has arisen with the new meds and for the first time I was not only asked if I had felt suicidal, but when I replied no, it continued, "homicidal?" Holy shit. Um, no.

What was disturbing about this appointment was the result of my brain SPECT scan. Turns out, I had and still have encephalitis (which he now refers to as encephalopathy) from the spirochetes (Lyme bacteria) and cerebral vasculitis in my frontal lobes. This means by brain is swollen and it is hard for fluid to get through. The parts of the brain where this showed up are the parts that affect emotions, memory, seizures, disorientation, and everything else I have written about. In short, I have brain damage. *Fighting tears...*

I knew what this meant for me, but I had to ask, "So, what do you think about IV antibiotics?" He replied, "I think we have no choice." What he was saying, and the way he said it, was very clear: if I did not do this, things would get worse. Much worse. and the truth was, those around me knew it was getting worse. Apart from everything else you have read about so far, my vision was suddenly very blurry for the first time in my life. Until I went on the neurological meds, my pain was unbearable. I was pretty much a mess.

My poor dad. He just wanted some reassurance. "I just have to ask you if this is something you see a lot? Is this normal for your patients?" he asked. Dr. Jemsek replied, "We see it in many patients, but you need to understand, Andrea has been *very* sick for a *very* long time." And that was it for Dad. The floodgates opened and we realized together that this world specialist currently considered me one of his most severe cases. He made it clear.

So, he quadrupled the dosage of the seizure meds and spread out the Neurontin by adding a midday dose, and the plan was that on May 25, 2012, I would have my gall bladder removed. I would then recuperate and in the beginning of July, if I was neurologically stable on the meds, we would fly down on a Sunday, then Monday morning I would go to George Washington University Hospital and they would surgically insert what is called a PowerLine, *not* to be confused with a

PICC line. A PowerLine is placed in just below the right clavicle and can handle greater pressure than an ordinary PICC line. I am so glad we are preparing for extra pressure. *Yelp...*

It is a surgical procedure, so I will go under for the third time in three months. Not thrilled about that. Two incisions will be made. One is a little below the clavicle – this is where the line will come out from the body. The other incision is to place the line just above the clavicle. This line rests in the distal superior vena cava, which empties into the right atrium of the heart.

We were told that, after this, we could go have some lunch. *Burst out laughing...* Were we really talking about lunch? And that within a few hours we would then go to the clinic where I would have a regular appointment with Dr. Jemsek, followed by his IV team, who would instruct me on how to use this brand new atrocious device for the next seven to nine months.

And with that, all of our lives changed, once again.

Which Brings Us to Present Day
May 16, 2012

First things first, my gall bladder is coming out next Friday. I mean honestly, I am barely even thinking about this, as it seems the least of my problems. The only thing that concerns me is that this will be the second of three bouts with anesthesia in four months and, for a body that needs to stay detoxed, this seems like a challenge. I am also concerned about the extensive connective tissue disorder that turned my last surgery into such an ordeal.

Here's to hoping we can just pop this one out and call it a day. At the moment, this includes taking several measures to ensure my comfort during IV treatment. This week I bought a new sectional with slip covers so I can surrender to the pooches who, after six years of war, are now the ones sitting on the couch with Mini, as I sit in a chair; three against one. I lose. So, the sectional will have enough room for all of us, seating three on each side, but also has slip covers I can dry-clean the "dog" out of them. I am officially making the move from Ethan Allen to IKEA, giving in to all creatures under four feet in this house.

The couch is also very comfortable. Maxi and I tested it out, and I was able to sit up supported with my legs on the couch, but also lay down comfortably. It passes as an IV friendly piece as well. Part of me feels a twinge of sadness to be furniture shopping based on my future medical needs, but I am grateful that I am able to.

We are working furiously to gut my house of clutter and get it in order. I have hired a dog walker so the boys get enough exercise, and

I have Maxi, my personal assistant, to help keep my business running smoothly and help with Mini. I have also enrolled Mini in full-time daycare/summer camp for the summer. I may keep her home and take her to the beach on days that I feel okay, but I have no idea how many of these days I will have.

Why all the commotion? Because I know how bad my Herx reactions were on oral antibiotics, and these IV antibiotics are so much stronger. I need to be ready for this. I need to be comfortable and get through the days so I can be a good mom when Mini is home. I am just trying furiously to pull all of the pieces together. I like my puzzles to be complete. I can't stand it when I do a puzzle and a piece is missing.

———

This level of treatment is emotionally overwhelming, but it is also financially overwhelming on a whole new level. I can't even quite explain it. They were very careful to present the information about this process in parts and I think it was smart of them. Each piece is so mind-blowing that I think I really needed the time in between each bit of information to digest it all. This final piece of information, speaking with the financial division of the clinic in the car on my way home from the airport, just made it all so much of a reality and I could be strong no longer. I began weeping with shooting tears and howling noises upon hanging up.

It was explained that I have two options. I can try to get my insurance to cover the IV antibiotics, though no one has successfully in the past five years. Or, I need to pay for it directly to the clinic. I was expecting about $3,000 a month for seven to nine months. Wrong. It turns out, treatment costs $35,000. No insurance.

It was just all so overwhelming and felt unfair to me and to my family, who will obviously need to step in on a major level at this point. Thankfully, my family is rallying around me in every way possible and will be paying for the treatment. It's just, I *hate* being thirty-seven years old and taking this much money from my family. It's just not right. $35,000 to me translates as a new Volvo being injected into my chest. Angry.

What insurance likely *will* cover is the installation of the PowerLine in my chest, some oral medications (until I reach the insurance "ceiling") and maybe a visit each week from visiting nurses to redress the PowerLine. It's something and at this point, anything helps.

That's where things stand now. For the purpose of this book, keep in mind that I am sharing both the ups and downs, so perhaps you will be able to relate to the overwhelming logistics of the disease, or perhaps you can help someone in need of support of any kind. But mostly, I will be providing information so that you can share with others to make people aware that Lyme is dangerous, and that it's real. Understand I, and thousands of others, am being raped on a daily basis by the American healthcare system, which is corrupt and insists that chronic Lyme doesn't exist. Spend *five minutes* in my body and tell me it doesn't exist. *Climbing down from my soapbox…*

Starting now, together we will watch me unfold.

Invisible Illness
May 17, 2012

———◦———

I don't know when it became okay for people to decide that chronic illness comes with a forehead tattoo that says *sick*. While I write on my own behalf, my words come to me with not only my own condition in mind, but also those of a few friends in similar non-Lyme situations and the thousands out there who are also in the same boat. It is not only for myself that I address invisible illness, but for the others as well.

Lyme is not alone in being an invisible illness. Many people suffer physically, mentally and emotionally on a daily basis without others even being able to detect it. I am told several times a day, "but you look great!" and of course I appreciate it, because no one wants to hear, "You look so tired," or, "You look awful." But believe me, people do say those things.

You may not see it. I have some occasional balance issues. In fact, I ram into so many things that I have bruises all over my body. And you know, because I have such a problem with short-term memory, I can never remember where they came from. But, I can walk, even when you don't see the issues I sometimes have with standing up and getting my balance, pleading with my hips to cooperate with me. Yesterday, halfway down the stairs, my legs gave out from under me and I went tumbling down the rest of the way, covering my head with my hands.

I have had hallucinations, but you can't see me having them. I have joint issues, which unless I tell you or unless you were there with me when I dropped the $1,000 bottle of medicinal tincture on the floor at work because my right elbow gave out, you have no idea. And while I may walk more slowly at times, you probably don't know that some-times it feels like I am walking on shards of broken glass. Before I pre-viously mentioned it, did you know that I have had no feeling in my shins for twenty-three years?

You might notice I get grouchy or teary, especially when Mini is being a typical three-year-old and doesn't look happy to see me when I pick her up. Mini has a hard time making transitions. When she is in the middle of something, my arrival sometimes interrupts something she is enjoying, and when this happens, she throws a fit when she sees me. Which makes me cry in front of all of the teachers and other parents. But beyond my tears, can you see the war going on in my mind? I try to rationalize with what I know is true, that Mini's not unhappy to see me, but simply is not ready to finish what she is engaged in. And while some might find my state unstable, do you realize how incredible it is that I am as stable as I am? I am a rock when it comes to this illness and I do not intend on backing down.

I live my life with the belief that most people mean well. I choose to think people are, on average, good people, or at least try to be. But I also think there are some people who are inherently hurtful. In fact, some of my very best friends, who I thought were friends, have not even commented to me on social media or called me to see how I am. I have even reached out to some people only to be ignored.

I honestly don't think there is a worse trait in a person than narcis-sism and, sadly, I have seen some of that lately – which is fine. It just means more people get filed in the narcissist folder and are dismissed from my world. I am happy to do this because I have wonderful friends out there. People who care. People who are doing things to help. People who answer my calls. But there are those who I assumed would be there for me and they are not.

Which brings me to one of my favorite quotes of all time (I have no idea who came up with it): "*Careful*, or you might end up in my novel." Welcome…

Here's the thing, you learn who your friends are when you are invis-ibly sick, because unless you have the "OMG" factor, the big words like cancer, or if you clearly look frail or ill, or have had a dramatic event or accident, people don't see you as ill when they see you dropping your kid off at school every day or driving through town. When you have a visible illness, people rally around you. When it's invisible, many times you are left in the dust because even though people know you are ill, they assume you are feeling better because "you look fine."

Sometimes I feel invisible. Sometimes I want to scream at the top of my lungs, "*No, I am not fucking all right!*" Just begging the universe for someone to see me. *Really* see me. Beyond a few family members and friends I can count on one hand, there are very few people who really see me and even they don't know the half of it. And maybe that's my own fault. Maybe I have been too guarded for too long, since my return from Sweden really, to actually let anyone in on any type of profound level. My need for control is astonishing. I didn't used to be like that. Well, not to this degree, at least.

Mini really sees me. I think children have an incredible capacity to sense everything around them. Every time I leave her, I tell her again and again, "Mommy always comes back." Last time I went to DC, she held my face with her little hands and said, "And maybe this doctor make you feel better, Mommy." I hit my head a few weeks ago when I lost my balance and banged it on the kitchen island. I screamed. She came running and sat right next to me and said, "Okay, what can I do for you, Mommy?" She sees me even when my invisible symptoms are at full force. Says my rock, "Maybe we cannot have music in da car today, Mommy, so it don't hurt your head," without me having said a word about my head being ready to explode. What would I do without this child?

And so, here I write to you in a very vulnerable state, because I am surrendering to some of the control that I have held onto for so many years. I am putting words to what has been invisible for so long. I am pleading with you to understand that I am not lazy. I am exhausted. Always. Physically, mentally, emotionally, and spiritually exhausted. My tank is empty. I have had it and although I will likely greet you with a smile, I am not okay.

Through my journey, I have learned that I am responsible for what I put out there. And so, it is with shaky hands and great emotional discomfort that I let you in. I am letting you ALL in. Even those of you who I don't know, because if I can help other people with invisible illnesses feel validated, then I have completed what I set out to do with this chapter. To those people: *I know it's not in your head. I know you are not making it up. I know you hurt. I know you cry aloud and within. And while I will never say I know how you feel, I will say I see you and I care. To me, you are not invisible.*

Nighttime
May 17, 2012

—•◦•—

I never really know what the nighttime will have in store for me.

Up until last month, I still woke up at night and looked out my window to make sure no one was trying to get in. I walked around the house in the middle of the night and made sure, again and again, that all the doors and windows were locked. Was the alarm on? Until last month, I slept with my bedroom door locked, and I mean with a dead-bolt – the theory being that if someone got in the house, I could call 911 to get help before saving my daughter. Oh, the paranoia of the night.

Sometimes it's just a running mind. I have so much to do and I think frantically about all of the things that have to get done. When will I do this, when will I do that? *How* will I pull this off? Please let me go to sleep. I need sleep or I can't function. *No!* Don't let it be 4 a.m. *Please* let me sleep.

Or is it the sorrow keeping me awake? The sadness I feel from my illness. Maybe it's the fact that I don't feel independent anymore. I used to own a home. I was completely financially independent *and* successful, I might add. But now I live in a home owned by my parents, and my family must step in to help me pay for my healthcare. It just doesn't seem right. It can keep me up all night.

Maybe it's the excessive thirst. On any given day, I drink 64+ ounces of water and/or juiced vegetables. Still, at night before I go to bed, I feel a thirst within me like I'm in the desert. I frantically throw down three or four more large glasses of water.

Or maybe it's urinary frequency at night. God, I have to pee. Again. Well, that's obvious – I've been drinking all day. But why does it burn?

Is it because I am so cold I cannot get comfortable? Only after I get all ready for bed do I realize that I will have to scorch myself in a hot bath until my skin is bright red. Then maybe I can fall asleep, unless one of the other reasons gets me.

Is it the pain? My feet feeling swollen, like they might pop? Or my whole back tingling? Maybe it's a migraine. My stomach hurts from all the meds, perhaps? The sore throat that comes and goes. My hip hurts. I wonder if it will hinder my walking at work tomorrow? *Ouch!* What is that feeling of a needle being shot right into that same spot in my thigh that it did the other night?

Tonight it's a pain I know all too well. It's the one that I experienced as a teenager. When I told my parents, they called them growing pains. I thought it was strange that I was still getting growing pains at seventeen, but ooooh maybe I would grow another inch *(golf claps...)*, but ouch. At thirty-seven years of age, this pain isn't growing pains. I know now it's Lyme. The Bartonella co-infection is also active tonight, going after the bottom of my left foot, which feels hot and as if it is getting repeatedly stabbed.

By now, however, my new neurological meds have kicked in. The alarm is on, but my bedroom door is now unlocked. This is good timing since Mini seems to be afraid of the dark all of a sudden. I still look out my windows, but I wonder if it's more out of routine than paranoia.

But it is nighttime now. Time to sleep. And in my case, time to prepare for war.

My Mind Playing Tricks on Me
May 18, 2012

———— ◆ ————

It was Grandparents' Day at school today, but Mini really wanted me to stay too. I stayed for a couple of hours, then she said it was okay, that I could go. My eyes had been burning the whole time. I knew there was something going on today. The exhaustion has been unbearable.

I stopped at Dr. Steve's office, mostly for some social interactive comfort, but also to send a fax to Dr. Jemsek accepting and committing to the $35,000 cash treatment that will begin in July. That fax felt kind of like the start of the next stage and it freaked me out a bit.

I went home and, by then, Baba and Hoovie (my parents' grandparent names) brought Mini home after an ice cream trip. She was so excited. While everyone was saying their goodbyes, my dog walker arrived and took the boys out for their exercise, which I can no long offer them. There was some commotion as Baba and Hoovie went on their way. Mini went on and on about all they did, after the morning in school. With all that and the stress about sending the fax, I started to feel a little anxious.

I was so excited because it was naptime. At naptime, I have to close the blinds to keep the dogs from barking at every single car, biker, or grasshopper that may appear. So I did that. And then I went out to the back porch to call the dogs in. I called. They didn't come. And I didn't see them. So I asked Mini if they were inside. "No, Mommy, day not here." And my heart started pounding. My head was spinning. *Where are the dogs?* I rushed frantically outside and ran barefoot through their whole fenced-in space looking for them.

My mind was thinking of them going on an exploration that might wind them up in a fight with the black bears or the mountain lion I saw a few weeks ago. I started to cry. I was shaking. I called my dad, as I always do and yelled, "Dad! The dogs are gone!" and explained I couldn't find them anywhere. "Okay, we will turn around." "Bring tennis balls," I said, knowing that over anything in the world, Gunnar will come for a tennis ball, and Brody will always follow Gunnar.

I hung up and yelled to Mini to get her shoes on quickly. By now, she and I were both in a completely frantic state. I could not keep it together with her. I was going to get in the car and find my boys, but of course I had to get her ready first. But we didn't have time.

And then the phone rang. It was Dad. "Didn't Meghan leave to walk them just when we left?" And with a sigh of relief, I realize they were in fact on a walk. But with that relief, came The sob I had held in all day.

It's so hard to know that you are losing your mind. My short term memory is so bad now that my mind is playing tricks on me and, for the first time, my own mind is outwitting itself...

Thankfully, it was naptime and we both slept well for probably an hour and a half, but as you know by now, I prefer three to four hour naps. I woke up feeling okay, which is not always the case. My eyes burn still and I have an itchy swollen rash at the injection site on my thigh from the B12 shot.

I feel very lonely in my thoughts right now. I know I have many people who care about me, who are supporting and rooting for me. But right now, at this very moment, I know I am alone. I lay here in silence, wondering when this hell will end. I don't even long for a "Happily Ever After" anymore. I just want a "Peacefully Ever After."

I have removed so much from my plate, but I still feel like my plate is overflowing. I can barely sort my mind through five minutes, much less plan the coming weeks. I feel overwhelmed, and alone on a very profound level. I think anyone with chronic illness, no matter what his or her relationship status, can understand this deep pit of loneliness. It's a tough place to be and an even tougher place to dig yourself out of.

Road Trip
May 19, 2012

———— ◈ ————

I admit it, I cannot wait to get out of here. At the moment, my house and my town just feel like a cocoon of my illness. So, I am very excited that Maxi, my assistant/friend, Mini, and I will be headed to Camden, Maine, this weekend for my cousin's baby shower and a big old Irish family reunion.

I can also admit that I'm very nervous about how it will go. I am assuming I had some seizures in my sleep last night, because when Mini came in at seven, I could not pick my head up off the pillow. She climbed into bed with me and I got her happily situated with some cartoons and the iPad (yes, I have now become that mother, but of desperation). Finally around nine, I was able to force my head off the pillow and feed the dogs and Mini. I have spent the morning (three hours now) packing, which would usually take me fifteen minutes.

My phone has been dinging all morning with text messages. At one point, I wanted to jump out the window. Yup, my sound sensitivity is in full force. But off we go on a weekend of celebration. I am trying to create the reality that all will be fine, but I can tell by the way my head is working that this could be a struggle.

I am not even sure that all of my family understands or even "buys into" the severity of my invisible condition, which frustrates me because, by now, if they really cared, they would have said something. And when they see me this weekend, because I look normal, they will probably continue to think I am trying to seek attention. Most of my family gets it and supports me, and I greatly appreciate those who do.

I have to give immense credit where credit is due. My grandparents, my parents, my sister, and my aunt and uncle are all forming a shield of loving protection and support around me. And I need it.

It's hard to write about family stuff and maybe it's inappropriate, but we *all* have family stuff and again, I promised the real story here – the fact is, no matter who you are, your entire family may not all get it or in this case, even seem to care. I rarely think about it though, as many of my family and friends are all so amazing.

My vision is blurry today, and I still have no appetite at all. It seems I am hungry for one meal a day lately. I do make sure I get proper nutrition and am drinking protein shakes when I absolutely cannot stand to eat, but also juicing too. So, wish me luck. This could go either way. I could be relatively stable all weekend, or any number of Lyme-related episodes could occur.

Just as It Should Be

May 22, 2012

———◦◦———

The weekend in Camden was really wonderful. I was truly able to enjoy another incredible experience with my family. It's certainly different attending these events with three-year-old Mini, who was very busy beating balloons, chasing chickens, and getting splinters on her butt, making her *wail*. But the day was beautiful and my family is wonderful. I am so happy for my cousin and her husband who are having their first child. I have a memory of this cousin, caught in a photograph, of the two of us lying next to one another on our bellies, each with a slice of sour Granny Smith apple in our mouths, with one eye squinted. Her bleach blonde three-year-old curls and my "big girl" position in our relationship. It's really never left me.

It's so surreal to see her now as a mother-to-be in this really peaceful, balanced, wonderful marriage, which is everything I have ever wished for her. And seeing the ease with which they are welcoming this transition made me realize that all is well with the world, even mine.

In my mind, there are no accidents, surprises, or even luck. The time away, while pretty chaotic, did remove me away from my situation enough to be able to see how my life has unfolded into where I am today, and that I am exactly where I too should be.

For some reason, I was meant to contract Lyme. Perhaps it is to become a teacher, an advocate, or perhaps it is one of the lessons I have been presented with in this lifetime. All I know is that I was meant to contract this ugly disease; at the age of ten, we moved to Rhode Island, where one year later we believe I got Lyme. For some reason, I chose to go to an all-girls' Quaker school, which taught me confidence and independence, the kind of fierce independence that breeds mental and emotional strength. As you now know, Lyme had affected me enough in so many funny ways that it never occurred to anyone it might be the one single disease that had caused all of my strange symptoms. So, I pushed myself through school.

As a teenager, I went to the (then) USSR on multiple occasions, sometimes for several months at a time, for youth peace missions. I learned the language and learned to understand and love the people of what are now Russia and Ukraine. During one of those trips, on a flight from Toronto to Helsinki, the group I was traveling with this time, all girls, were on the same plane as a Swedish hockey team, all about three years older than us (a chaperone's nightmare).

On that flight, I met Christian, who would turn out to be a very important person in my life. Christian wasn't cocky like the others. He was very sweet and we spoke throughout the whole flight. When we got to Helsinki, we said goodbye and I went to my next gate. A few minutes later he appeared, I stood up, and in front of my whole class and my teachers, he held my face and kissed me. *Really* kissed me.

That was the beginning of a two-year committed, long-distance teenage, but very mature relationship that would bring me to Sweden several times and him to the US. We were monogamous and in love. Very in love. Eventually we broke up, but I'd contracted the Sweden bug and was not going to let it go. And so his role in my life was to introduce me to Sweden, where I ended up spending my senior year of high school.

My host family, which became like my own, had three boys; two grown and living out of the house and one boy my age. Daniel and I became best friends. We shared a joy for music and both had bands. I eventually joined his band too and my love for music was completely fulfilled at that time. "Mamma and Pappa," as I still call them to this day, were strong and supportive. I was truly happy living with them. It would later be their support and love that would give me the courage to return to Sweden for work after college.

⸻

College was a blast, but it was so dramatic. I was so dramatic. I learned to stand firmly for what I wanted – not physically, but conceptually. If I wanted something and decided it would happen, it did. I learned that my choices were my own, and that life would become whatever I made of it.

And so I went. Had I not gone to Boston, I would not have ended up in Sweden again. Had I not been unhappy in my first job there, I would not have gone to Miami and had the revelation that I had not yet completed what I set out to do for myself in Sweden. Had I not dared to set roots by buying the apartment I really wanted in Stockholm, I would not have met Gustaf. And had I not met Gustaf, I would not have lost him and would not have ended up back with my parents. Had I not wound up back with my parents, I would not have been able to function without help.

Because I was tested for Lyme in 2005 and testing was so unreliable that it came back "indecisive," I would have gone on living believing I didn't have Lyme. Had that 2005 Lyme test come back positive, I would not have adopted my daughter. Had I not started working for Dr. Steve, I would not have become as aware of my own body and as acutely aware of natural medicine and various illnesses. I believe that the clinic's Lyme surge came two years after I brought my daughter home so that we would bond appropriately to become a solid family that can withstand anything. I believe that same Lyme surge made me realize that I knew

I had Lyme and that the new reliable testing that had come out in the past year was something I just had to do.

I do not believe there have been any mistakes in the way my life has unfolded. I believe I was meant to watch *Under Our Skin*, because I connected with Dr. Jemsek's tenacity and conviction even then and knew he was my guy. I believe it was no mistake that my coconut-sized ovarian cyst was discovered and removed just in time for the surgery wounds to heal so I could clearly identify my Lyme symptoms from my now kaput girly issues.

I believe I had my seizure while driving because we had decided I would travel to DC for a trip alone, and clearly that was not what the universe intended, so my dad came on that next trip. Good thing, since the news was so astonishingly overwhelming. I believe Dad needed to be there to truly understand that this road is a very serious one. He needed to hear from Dr. Jemsek that I am one of his most serious cases.

So here I sit, gall bladder surgery awaiting me on Friday and I am not even really thinking about it. I mean at all. I keep having to remind myself not to make plans for Friday. Part Lyme, part peace. All is as it should be. I am still horrified by the whole IV thing, but I know it's supposed to happen now and the way we have chosen.

And so, I attack this next stage with vicious peace, knowing that I am currently strong enough to take what's coming my way, head on, but with the peace that all is just as it should be.

Chapter 31 — Alone
May 23, 2012

———— ◈ ————

I have always been known to be a little clumsy, but I have to say, with this new meds adjustment, it's a whole new ballgame. At the last appointment we had to adjust my meds to avoid further seizures. While I have not yet had any seizures since we changed the dosage, I actually feel drugged during my afternoon dose.

I take four large doses of multiple supplements, neurological meds, and detox support. The doses are different at different times of day. This new afternoon dose has made my vision blurry and I am very tired.

Today when I went to pick up Mini, she had been such a good girl (thank you, universe) and we were excited to go out for ice cream. She was playing outside and I needed to go into the school to gather her stuff. Right now my balance and positioning is off. I always think I am about two inches further to the left that I really am. That became blatantly clear when I closed the door to my car *hard* and slammed the tip of my right thumb in the door, splattering blood inside *and* outside my car. My thumb was gushing and now, two hours later, I am still not sure if it's okay.

I had my pre-op blood draw taken today, so I have my hospital band on already. Maybe if I still have a problem with the thumb on Friday, the surgeon can just fix my thumb too. *A two-fer!* I am frustrated. I need a break.

I am still in this place of "couldn't care less" about my upcoming surgery on Friday, but maybe that's because I feel like I am on another planet right now. I continue to be very focused on detoxing as much as possible. You just cannot even imagine the amount of *crap* that I am putting into myself with these medications. *Yes*, I need them, but there are always so many ramifications, so Dr. Jemsek and I are dead set on flushing out as much as possible, as consistently as possible.

I do this using the prescribed Deplin, which I take at night, the B12 shots (25,000 mcg), and by juicing massive amounts of cucumber, flat parsley, lemon, and apple. I also continue to use the entire non-toxic product line called Ava Anderson Non-Toxic. What you put *on* you gets into your bloodstream and affects your health.

Ugh, I can barely keep my eyes open. Maybe it's because I did about five hours of work today. Perhaps it was the massage. Maybe it's just Lyme. But right now I am wondering how I will even get through the bedtime routine with Mini tonight. This is the kind of exhaustion that no one understands unless you have experienced it. I just don't know how I will even stand up in five minutes when the show I have occupied her with is over.

Today I received a beautiful bouquet of flowers from a dear friend from college who I haven't seen in twelve years. She has been so supportive throughout this whole thing. As I mentioned previously, it's clear who your friends are when you are in a position like this.

At the moment, I just don't even know how to function. I feel very, very lonely. It's an incredibly common emotion these days, despite all of the love and support I receive from my friends and family all over the world, and despite a house full of dogs and a child, I feel very alone.

It's clear that at the moment, Lyme has control of my brain and, for now, it's got the better of me – but not the best of me. Tomorrow is a new day and I am ready to face it head on.

The Effect on Mini
May 24, 2012

Tomorrow is the day I have my cholecystectomy, which is just me showing off with a fancy word that means my gall bladder is going to kick
it tomorrow. But here's the thing – I haven't even given it a thought.
I seriously could not care less. In fact, several times this week, I have
forgotten about it. By now you understand that this is not shocking,
but still – isn't it strange? I feel like I am hitting a new level of weird.

The only thing that has me concerned is the effect all of this is having on Mini. She gets *very* upset when I have any kind of boo-boo, and
while it's nice to have an empathic child at such a young age, I really
sense a bit of terror in her when I'm not well that is quite upsetting.

As you already know, when I had my gigantic nine-centimeter
ovarian cyst, which they removed along with my left ovary, surgery did
not go as expected. The point is that I ended up staying in the hospital
for two nights, after which I was in bed and could barely move for a
week. I was unable to pick anything up for six weeks. This was really
hard on Mini and she acted out for almost a month afterward. She was
behaving in such a way that I didn't recognize her. She started having
tantrums, defying *everything* I said, and having issues at school for the
first time. I realize some of this could be a good case of three-year-old
acting out, but this was beyond typical.

I thought long and hard about it. My daughter is hurting. She has
seen me go away to the doctor. She knows I am sick. She's scared, and
it breaks my heart.

Tonight during tubby time, I explained to her what was going to happen. "Tomorrow morning Baba and Hoovie are coming to the house really early. Hoovie will drive you to school and Baba will take Mommy to the doctor." This started a slew of questions: "How many sleeps will you be away?" "Who will pick me up at school?" "Who's going to read my books at night?" I replied: "Well, guess what? Mommy has the *best* doctor in the *world* and that's why I pack a suitcase and fly far away to see him, because he is the best." Mini: "Like a Dr. Superhero?" *Swooooon...*

But it was hard for me to answer some of those questions because, the truth is, while a cholecystectomy is a common and easy procedure for most, the surgeon and I are prepared for the possibility of another ordeal due to adhesions. As a single entity, I feel fine about that. I am not scared at all. But as a mother, I am praying I will be able to do this as an outpatient surgery and at least be home and around this weekend for Mini.

And perhaps I should be taking things one step at a time, but *hello,* have you met me? I cannot get my mind off of how it will be when I travel again five weeks from now for tests for another procedure which involves me going under *again* to get the PowerLine installed for IV treatment. What will it be like for this little girl to see her Mommy, her only parent, hooked up to a scary thing attached to her chest? What will it be like for *her* to experience my Herxheimer reactions which, given the severity of my infection and the fact that it has taken over parts of my brain, promise to be on the severe side.

I have been very clear that the IV thing freaks *me* out. I have been thinking about where in my body it will hurt. Who will I yell at when the rage hits? How much will I cry when the depression hits? How will I walk when I feel the shards of burning glass on the soles of my feet? I am terrified, because after several months of antibiotics, I know what it's like to Herx and I also know that IV antibiotics increase the severity and torture of the

Herxes. Many may think, "Yay! She's starting antibiotics! She will feel so much better!" Well, that's just not how it flies with Lyme. There's a distinct possibility that I could become periodically debilitated to varying degrees.

How will that feel for Mini? How will she deal with it? How will we support her? I know kids are resilient and adaptive, but I fear for my girl that the next year will be tainted by Mommy's illness. I worry it might plant seeds of worry in her, perhaps codependent issues that will be hard to reverse. My mind is going a mile a minute right now and it's the mother lion that is coming out. What will we do? How am I going to pull this off?

Panic is starting to set in and it has nothing to do with tomorrow, but with what is to come when I next visit DC. I have felt panicked about my life twice. Once in 2004 when I moved back to the US unwillingly, and now when I have no control over what the next ten months will look like for me or, more importantly, for Mini. Because while I have a lot of help at my fingertips, all she wants is her mommy. She's just so little. And I feel so sad for her.

I won't be able to go to the lake with her this summer. I can't get the PowerLine wet. And there is no such thing as Mommy comes to the beach and grandparents or assistant extraordinaire play. If I am there, Mini wants me engaged. Fully engaged.

I am trying to think of things we can do together. Maybe a picnic. Maybe spend some time at my sister's pool which is so crazy that she won't even notice me in the lounge chair while her cousins run her ragged. The Children's Museum? A boat ride? Maybe I will even break down and take her to the dreaded "Chucker Cheese" that she's been begging me about. I don't know. But I can't control my tears. Consider the floodgates open.

Gall Bladder — You Are Dismissed

May 25, 2012

I had an awful night last night. Honestly, one of the worst nights of my life. This is something I don't want to get into, but let's just say my entire system was in chaos and I was a complete mess. The night was really quite traumatizing for me, but I was able to get back to sleep.

However, I woke up in a Lyme rage. Those who are close to someone with Lyme know what this means. It is unlike any other kind of anger I have experienced. I felt exhausted from the night though and my balance was off and I was just *very* clumsy when we got up.

Then I started packing a few things to take with me to the hospital and proceeded to jam my thumb (you know the CSI thumb that I slammed in the car door?) into *everything*. And wow, the pain was incredible, and it just set me off. Then the phone started beeping constantly with text messages wishing me well today, good luck, and I love you's. It was of course so sweet, but my cell phone beeping and my jammed thumb throbbing, and the dogs, sensing my stress, started barking.

My world started spinning around in my head and I knew where I was headed. I think, for the first time ever, I was able to identify my Lyme rage *while* in the midst of it, so I quickly texted my dad, "I am a fucking mess today. Please be warned. I am in a Lyme rage. I took an Ativan." It was all I could do. I knew when my parents arrived they would be all friendly and supportive, but that I wouldn't even open my mouth or look at them to talk, not because I'm mad at them, but because I don't have the capability of doing anything but lashing out, so the best thing to do is to look down, shut it out and remove myself from it.

My dad promptly texted back, "Thx 4 heads up." It's so nice that they understand these rages now. It takes a load off, because you cannot imagine how *awful* I feel after one of these episodes. There's a huge wall when it comes to me apologizing for something I do not feel I created. But, of course I do not want to hurt anyone.

Dad walked in the door a few minutes later to take Mini to school. Mom walked in a few minutes later. He quickly said, "I had left when you texted me so she doesn't know." So I told her, "I am in a wicked Lyme rage," and she waited for me to get ready to go to the hospital. At one point I couldn't find something and she said, "Take a *deep breath*," and then proceeded to take a really, loud deep breath out loud and it took everything within me not to flip out. She was only trying to help, but when I am like this, I just need everyone to back off and let me deal.

<hr>

It's not easy being around someone with chronic Lyme, especially while in treatment. It just isn't. I often feel sorry for family and friends because I can be so bitchy, unreliable in terms of planning, and so blunt. Everyone who is close to me knows that I have a heart of gold and that I am fighting a silent war within my body. Sometimes that war entails explosions that are seen by others; sometimes they happen at home when I am alone.

In any case, we got to the hospital and were greeted by the surgeon, who was very lovely and seemed to know that chronic Lyme really does exist. I had met with him previously, of course, and had, ahem, educated him a bit on the connections of various issues I am having and how virtually all of them are caused by Lyme. I explained to him that, in Lyme patients, the gall bladder acts as a toxicity magnet and creates havoc. Spirochetes *love* toxicity. I also told him that, because of my extensive Lyme infection, my gall bladder surgery might not be as straightforward as he might expect, due to the connective tissue disorder Lyme has also gifted me with. I explained what had happened during my last "simple procedure" back in February and that he should consider himself warned. Thankfully, he took me seriously.

Various nurses and hospital staff went through what was going to happen and I just kept nodding my head at the anesthesiologist like, "Dude, I was here seven weeks ago. We are practically dating. Hop to it." He was going to give me something in my IV to help me relax. *(Golf claps…)* Love it. As they wheeled me out, I saw this poster about the World Health Organization and said, "Oh, I love that stuff you gave me. Look at that pretty owl." And they started laughing.

I was wheeled into the operating room and I got to meet the team. I looked around because I love this stuff – all the spotlights, and scalpels, etc. A male nurse explained stuff to me, but I was so over it and in happy land by then that I just said, "You should just knock me out before I start bossing you around." And he did.

I could hear myself snoring back in my room after it was all done. The surgeon came in and gave me the pictures he'd taken at my request and told me that, as I had suspected, there were many adhesions and that the gall bladder was actually much sicker than he had anticipated and had "clearly gone through a few episodes." Whatever that means. Who cares? It's in the trash now.

I got home and was able to eat dinner at the table with my family. I am on a no-fat diet for a few weeks while my body adjusts, but that's no real change Mini gave Hoovie a hard time putting her to bed, so I finally got her down at 8:20 p.m. I do think she's stressed about Mommy, so I laid with her and she asked me how to say some things in Spanish, like window, sky and headlamp, because every three-year-old must know how to say headlamp in every language.

She gave me the cutest little kiss as I left and said, "Mama I hope you get some good sleep. I lub you." And with that, my gall bladder is out, Mini is asleep, and all is well with the world.

Happy
May 26, 2012

————— ◉ —————

It's so strange to feel the way I've felt this afternoon. It's a feeling I am not even sure I recognize, but here's the thing: I think I am happy.

I know this will come as a surprise to many of you who know me, and rightfully so, because I do tend to have a cheerful, sociable demeanor, but as I look back at the past *many* years, there have only been a few times when I felt *truly* happy, to my deepest core. Most of those happiest times were with or because of Mini.

I am sure there are many reasons behind this. It's clear that I have been through a lot on many levels and obviously have found myself in a place at thirty-seven that I *never* imagined I'd be. I haven't felt well and have found myself apologizing most of the time for being too tired or sick to do anything. People understand, but after a while they give up on you. I have felt lonely on many levels, even after bringing Mini home.

Dr. Jemsek told me that I would feel much better once my gall bladder was removed. I wasn't quite sure what to make of it because I really didn't know what gall bladder attacks felt like and, besides his suspicion, and the HIDA scan which was excruciating, I barely even knew I *had* a gall bladder.

Dad slept over last night to make sure I was all right after the surgery. I slept okay. He slept okay. Mini slept well. In the morning, Maxi came to take Mini to the beach. My three-year-old was *so excited* to get all beach fabulous and apparently played like crazy in the water. Dad also gave me the opportunity to sleep for three full hours this morning. It was amazing.

Maxi and Mini came home and Mini went down for a nap. A long one. When she woke up, I called Baba to come take the next shift. It was a gardening afternoon; they planted window boxes and watered the flowers and tomato plants. I am sure there was some kind of Fresh Beat Band activity involved, but I had a break. I wasn't asleep all afternoon. In fact, I was quite awake. I took a glorious shower and, beyond that, I forget what I did. Sigh.

We ordered pizza for dinner and, because Mini lives for anything tube meat related – *gag* – pepperoni pizza and Greek salad were on the menu. We sat outside on my newly decorated deck – new table, new chairs, new cushions, new umbrella, and new flowers – and we sat there like a family. I realize that Mini and I are a family in our own right, but there is something about sitting around a round table with more relatives and feeling like a – family.

Granted, we all spent most of the time trying to get Mini to eat, but she had to show us her "party tricks," get exactly three hugs and four kisses from Mommy, "give the dogs some love," and anything else you can think of. I finally bribed her to eat and while she sat and ate her ice cream it occurred to me: *I think I feel happy.*

I told my parents this and it probably felt very strange for them to hear it. It was a big deal for me. I mean, when was the last time I *had* felt happy? When was the last time I was entirely present and content with where I was, what I was doing and who I was with? When had I last allowed myself to be happy? *Was* this happy? I am not sure I remember what happy feels like.

Today was a big day for me. I am still a bit sore from yesterday's surgery, but no big deal. If I can enjoy this next month ahead, it will be a great gift to hold onto during treatment.

Lyme Rage
May 29, 2012

———— ◈ ————

It's an awful place to be. You feel yourself floating outside your body and watching your very own self with steam coming out of your ears. Your heart starts pounding, you fight back tears, but they gush anyway. It feels like a combination of fury, emotional pain, desperation, and confusion.

That is where I am at this very moment. I have mentioned Lyme rage in previous posts, but I wanted to dedicate a post to what it feels like to be in the middle of one. It can be about almost anything. Someone talks to you in a manner that you deem unacceptable (a way you would never talk to them), someone verbally attacks you, or someone gives you unsolicited advice (I will get into this later in this post, but *please do not give Lyme people unsolicited advice* – or at least not to me). The worst is when there is little reason at all other than the fact that you have Lyme disease.

Right now, I am coming down from a rage, which usually lasts for about an hour and consists of me running a situation through my head again and again without being able to control it. Eventually, you reenter your body, followed by about thirty minutes of sobbing, followed by a long nap (if I can get one in). It's miserable and exhausting.

Now that I am diagnosed with Lyme, the co-infections and the encephalopathy, which appeared on the results of my SPECT scan of the brain, it's easier for me. I'm a logical thinker who needs facts, to understand what is happening, but it doesn't *stop* it from happening.

But I can think about it scientifically, rather than emotionally. It's also easier for my parents to understand, who have, for all these years, been the targets of most of these rages, because they are those closest to me.

During a Lyme Rage, as I've said, I am especially sound sensitive and need to be in a silent place. I have to silence my phone because I am constantly getting text messages and it really just puts me through the roof. The phone is always ringing and I cannot handle it. Normally, I would do just fine with it. I mean let's face it, I am very successful at a job which involves 90% telecommuting. That means I spend my career on the phone, a given challenge right now.

But when I am in this place, I need to remove myself. So I walk away from everything and get to somewhere quiet and alone as soon as possible.

——— ✦ ———

Which brings me to something that I mentioned previously. You may have the best doctor or healer in the world who has worked out really well for you. You may see my daughter on a daily basis, but you do not know us. You may think you do, but unless you live with us, know the details of our life histories, you do not know what we live with and experience. Please *never* tell me what is best for me, when I should rest, when I should eat, when I should "take it easy." You will send me into a Lyme Rage, guaranteed. I appreciate your support and do not want to push you away, so I will often not answer or will just reply with something simple. But here, to the general public I am going to say it: it's none of your business and you do not, under any circumstances, know where I am at any given moment or what I need. You may say that I'm making it your business by writing this book, but I stand by my words as I experience this Lyme Rage – you do not know what it is like to be us or what is best for us.

This goes for my daughter as well. She may have a blast doing something with you, but the only thing my daughter needs is *me*. So please don't even dare to tell me what is right or wrong for my child unless you are prepared to meet the mother lion. Remember, this is me being authentic in the middle of a Lyme Rage. This is as flat out truthful as it gets, because I would never say these things when I am outside this bubble of hell that I am in right now.

Some of you may be nodding your head thinking you have seen me in a Lyme Rage before, but I assure, almost none of you have, with the exception of my very best friend, my sister, and my parents. I do get angry like a normal person too so, sorry, Charlie, you are still accountable for your own actions and cannot blame them on me because I have Lyme. It doesn't work that way. I can get angry like a normal person too.

I've stopped crying now and my neck hurts. It's stiff in the back and I feel the floating headache starting on the left frontal lobe of my brain. This is what I have come to know as a sign of an upcoming seizure, so now I will go take an extra Ativan to try to avoid it. If I have one, I will probably be asleep anyway.

I am going to try to take a nap now. This may have made you uncomfortable, but authenticity and honesty is the place I mean to come from right now, as draining and exhausting as it may be. And this is my ugly reality, so please bear with me. Tomorrow is another day.

"Yeah, This is a Big One"
May 30, 2012

It was quite ridiculous that three hours of driving was required to hear the following sentences from my (lovely) cardiologist: "Your echocardiogram came back perfect." (Yay, and PS, I knew this.) "If you need us again, just give us a call." And then we drove home.

On the way home, we had a bit of an adventure: we, meaning my friend and the Fire Department, saved a big snapping turtle that was crossing the highway. I had just gotten off a very difficult phone call and all of a sudden she threw on the brakes, pulled over, did a U-turn on the highway and went back to save the turtle. I was too upset to help, so I offered Mini's plastic putter from the trunk to get the turtle to bite it, then drag it across the road. Turned out the turtle wasn't interested in it. A fire truck happened to pull up behind us. They picked her up and carried her to the ravine, peeing the whole way. I was useless, but helpful in spirit. That's today's story.

At the moment, I am running on empty. I have an average of three medical appointments and one blood draw each week and soon I will have had three surgeries, one quite major, followed by a piece of cake, followed by the scariest, most foreign thing I ever will have had done to my body. All in three months. I am scared to death and I ask for your understanding.

We were talking about this tonight at Mom's birthday party (basically balloons and a cake), and party hats at Mini's demand, and Dad said it best with, "Yeah, this is a big one."

Blurry
May 31, 2012

The only way I can describe today is blurry. My thoughts are blurry. My emotions are blurry. And suddenly, for the first time, my eyes are *very* blurry. I know what this means: the treatment has set in. I am definitely seeing dangerously blurry, so much so that I told my parents today that I really cannot even drive to town anymore. For a woman who has built a life in another country, been to thirty-six countries, lived in the USSR while it *was* the USSR, spent eight years living in Sweden, traveled to Central Asia to have a baby on my own – for all of this, it is a very isolating feeling. I am trapped. I cannot even drive myself to the grocery store anymore.

It's blurry. Everything is blurry. I bump into things more than ever before. I have bruises all over my body. My memory is blurry and honestly, I am not sure if I took a shower today. I think I did, but just as I did yesterday, I will probably take another shower tonight before bed just in case. I don't think I have eaten today. I know I drank that iced fruit water and a protein shake this morning, but my appetite is gone.

I am looking down at my khakis, laden with teardrops. I am not used to this. I have always been such a happy person, but now that I know all that's happened through these twenty-six years, I wonder what being *truly* happy means. Do I even know? I have experienced *moments* of true happiness, like meeting Mini, like that walk in Stockholm when I was so utterly taken aback by the beautiful place I lived.

I think the happiest I have ever been in my life is in a summer house Gustaf had on Tjörn, an island on the west coast of Sweden. We made it there only once a summer for a week or sometimes two, but to me it was heaven. It was a perfect little Swedish cottage on the water with a well from which we pumped water. That's right, no running water. We did have electricity, but we only used it at night for one light in each room, and the radio. We'd listen to the news on the radio at night before dinner.

I loved it because it was *quiet* there. All you could hear was the soft crashing of the waves on the rocks. On Tjörn, we could just be. And we were our happiest when we were there. We picked cherries from the cherry trees on the property and made dozens of jars of jam. We drove to the farm up the road and bought Swedish *färskt potatis*, a potato that is found only in Sweden, and had lunch at the table outside with our potatoes boiled with dill, various types of pickled herring, *crème fraîche*, and a couple of shots of schnapps, followed by a dip in the ocean and a nap. It was like a dream.

There were rocks on the shore there, no sand. And there was this one rock – *my* rock – which had a dip in it that was perfectly designed for me to lay in comfortably for hours. The sun would beat down on the rock and I would lie there, sucking the heat into my body, from the hot rock below me and the sun from above. The feeling was amazing. Little did I know that it wasn't just my soul that was fed by that rock, but that the heat I was taking in was fighting the Lyme. Lyme hates heat. Perhaps that is why I have always been cold.

I've stopped crying now, because that is my happiest place. On that quiet, hot rock on the west coast of Sweden, listening to the waves, learning how to "just be" and not do anything. It's a skill that is learned and one that I, now that I have become Americanized again in my life-style, must fight to remind myself. For years it was hard for me to go to that happy place in my mind. You all realize why, having read about my experience with Sweden. But now I feel a bit freed from all of that and I hope that he doesn't mind that I often borrow that place, that perfect dip in the hot rock, as my own.

My life is nothing like I imagined. I feel like a prisoner. In my body, where I live, and now how I must schedule every single second of my day. It's devastating to me each time my prompt pops up on my phone (four times a day) reminding me to take my meds, but I have to, because otherwise I forget. And when your mind is blurry and your vision too, perhaps you can imagine how difficult it is to organize a week of meds – upwards of *four hundred* pills per week.

And now I just sit here, staring at the screen, barely able to see through my blurry eyes, and wonder: *Why?* With all of the good things I have done my life; with the people I have helped; with the students I have nurtured through their international studies; to the love I have shown to so many people? *Why* am I being tortured like this? I think I know what the answer is. It's to continue educating others. When I am stronger, I will be the one making noise. I know this is my purpose. Why does the universe have so much faith in me?

I've Been Preparing for This My Whole Life

June 1, 2012

———◦———

Today I had a very long call with the Jemsek Specialty Clinic. We went through the details and picked the date for the installation of my PowerLine. It has me thoroughly freaked out. It's not so much the apparatus – well okay, maybe a little – but mostly two other things. First, this will be the third time in three months that I get general anesthesia. Talk about toxicity in the body. It can take months to get anesthesia out of your system so three times seems like a lot to me. I can still feel it from the last surgery.

Secondly, I feel like this thing that is to become a part of my body for the next nine months is a symbol of how sick I am. I know that at some point I will come to peace with it and see it as a symbol of healing, but I am not there now. Please allow me to get there in my own time.

Dad and I will fly down to DC on Sunday, July 8. Very early on July 9 I will be at George Washington University Hospital where they will insert the PowerLine. (I will explain what that is in great detail below.) Then after I come back to consciousness and have some food in me, I will have a three to four hour appointment with the Jemsek Specialty Clinic's IV Unit, followed by an appointment with Dr. Jemsek himself. This feels *big*. Like the *biggest* step so far.

We have been told to bring an empty suitcase to bring home the IV meds. We will be given a special letter to carry them on rather than having to check them. All of a sudden, it all feels very real to me. It's really begun to sink in that my life is a movie. It's a book. It's been an incredible journey of joy, love, fear, and now great illness of the great unknown. I will bring these suitcases filled with a portion of the $35,000 worth of IV medication (not covered by insurance) with me each time I go back monthly or bimonthly for the next nine months. And the hope isn't even for a cure – it's for long-term remission. The *hope* is that in March 2013 I will be *able* to get off IV antibiotics and switch to oral antibiotics for about two years and then, quite certainly, continue at a lower dosage for the rest of my life. It's a big deal.

I will learn more about my IV schedule when I go to DC, but I do know that it will be something like this: I will do a thirty-minute drip of antibiotics morning and night, three days a week. On the off days, I will be doing a three-hour flush, which in this case will be mainly a strong detox process. In my mind, it's a lot of sitting, a lot of movies, and a lot of books. And a lot of loneliness. I have arranged a full-time summer daycare situation for Mini with her best friends. But the truth is, having a three-year-old as a single mother while sitting with a three-hour drip feels unbelievably impossible. I know it will work out. I know I am tough enough. But it's daunting. I have come to believe that all of my life's situations have prepared me for this.

———— ⚬ ————

At sixteen years of age, I stood in the bread lines of various cities in the USSR (where I stayed with families) with my ration cards for hours, only to find that they had run out of bread. So then I would hop on the subway and race to the next one to see what I could get. It was my chore. And I would get as much as I could for the whole month, because, when I got home, my Soviet mama would take the extra bread and run around the apartment building trading the fresh bread for things like toilet paper, fruits, and meat. Looking back, I was a tough broad;

unafraid, determined, and very dedicated to my purpose of creating peace between our nations, which was why I was sent there.

During those teenage years, I had been asked to be a part of a Soviet/American Peace Tour. We were a theater group which performed all over Ukraine and Russia, and the following summer throughout the US, with a performance at the UN and a spot on Good Morning America. The cast changed, but Natasha, who had become like a sister to me, and I remained part of the cast. We looked a little alike and could both sing and dance and, in the show, we were portrayed as the same person from different countries.

Our countries were so different and in political disagreement, yet *we* were so much alike. I visited Natasha and her family six or seven times during my teenage years. I was there during the coup when Gorbachev overthrew Yeltsin. It was dangerous to be an American in Moscow during the coup, but fortunately I had learned to speak Russian by then. So with a handkerchief over my head I would walk arm in arm with Natasha. My parents were worried. I was sixteen, and eventually I went home early. But again, I was fearless; I was a chameleon; I was adaptable. And I will adapt to this treatment the same way I adapted to life in what is now Russia.

I have already written of my years in Sweden and how they affected my life tremendously, but I haven't write about the summer I spent as an au pair on a rural cattle farm between my freshmen and sophomore years of college, which was a two-hour bus ride to the closest city of 100,000 people. The family lived in the farmhouse, and boy did they need me. They had an eighteen-month old girl and a three-and-a-half-year-old boy who was not potty trained. We built things all of the time and played in the dirt. Basically, I did all of laundry, and each morning as the children napped, I prepared the main meal of the day, which was midday for all of the farm hands. We sat together and ate, and I learned so much about farming that I know words in Swedish about farming that I do not know in English.

I lived in the grandmother's house, a mile's walk away, in a room in the attic. The house was very orderly, the grandmother very strict. I was miserable in that house. Each evening we both ate a light supper and then it was clear that I was to sit with her and watch the news. She also taught me to knit sweaters for orphans in Lithuania. We did this every single night until she went to bed. I was nineteen years old.

The baby got chicken pox while I was there and, much to my horror, only wanted me. It was a tough position to be in, because the child was in pain and had a fever and wanted me because I cared for her literally from before the sun went up. But I could see the sadness in the mother's eyes that the child was more bonded with me at that point and I looked at the mother and in my nineteen-year-old *old* soul told her, "This is just temporary. She is a toddler. She will not remember me." A couple of years later when I surprised them with a visit, we found that to be true. She didn't remember me was and neither did the three-year-old. Only the mom and I knew the impact I'd had on them. I taught them structure, how to connect with the family emotionally, and engagement.

Many times the cows got out of their pen. I'd find them standing on the road as I walked back to knit sweaters and watch the news. Straightening my arms out, my *Prince of Tides* book in hand, I'd guide them back to and through the fence and lock it behind them. I'd grown up a city kid. For me to have accomplished this made me a badass. I didn't realize it then, but now I know how amazing it really was and how it will affect my treatment that I so fear. On that farm, I faced my fears. I did things every day that I didn't want to do. I knitted those damned sweaters and sat there with that woman because although she was truly a nasty old bag, she was just lonely and I felt for her. So I just did it. And that's what I'll do now: I will just do it.

College was a Spanish soap opera. I fell in love with a total Colombian dreamboat and we had a rocky dramatic relationship for several years. We moved in, then moved out. We danced salsa, vallenatos, boleros, merengue, five nights a week at Latin clubs until four in the morning, when we were sweaty from the dancing and fully loaded from the booze. But when we had fun, boy did we have fun. We loved in Spanish, and fought in English. He gave me the gift of learning to speak fluent Spanish with a Colombian accent, now rusty, but still filed in the back of my muffled brain. One day he'd want to marry me, the next he'd hate me. When he cheated on me, and it had always been a given that it would eventually happen, it ended. We finally broke up and I moved to Boston.

He came to visit me several years later, however, while he was living Paris and I in Stockholm. He came up for a five-day weekend. Through the years we had let go of our anger and developed one of the best friendships I will ever know. That weekend was a passionate one where we relived many of the best times we had together. But it was very peaceful. My friends and my host brother, who knows me very well, all asked us why we were not together, that we seemed a perfect match. Everyone could see the connection.

That weekend was an incredible experience, because while we couldn't keep our hands off each other, without having to say a word, we both knew this weekend would be our closure. It was over. Taking him to the airport was very different from my airport experience with Gustaf. When I bid my friend farewell, I knew it was the end and he did too. And suddenly we were free to explore true friendship, the kind where you know each other to the core and when you go years without seeing one another, it's still the same connection. Two years ago, he actually rented a home ten minutes away from me on the water with his wife and two sons. Mini and I spent so much time with them that week. And his wife and I connected, too. She, in her incredible sense of security of her relationship, gave us the gift of sharing our families with one another. I cannot wait to see them again.

What that relationship taught me was to stand up for myself, even against the toughest opponents. He taught me that I deserve the best.

He may very well be the reason that I am thirty-seven and not married, because after him, I knew I would *never* settle. What that true, authentic friendship offers me now is the security of knowing that I could call him with any problem in the world and he'd be on the next plane. He taught me devotion.

———

In Boston, I became career-oriented. And I was aggressive. I made sure I was at the top of every sales list and that my region was the most stable and well run in the country. We also had a blast at that place. But I hated living in Boston. I wasn't well, and I eventually moved to Sweden. Boston taught me that I have an incredible business sense and that when I decide to do something, I will do it. I don't do things halfway. For me it's go big or go home. So as I go through treatment, I witness myself vigorously complying with every aspect of my treatment program.

I won't go back into my later years in Sweden through all of my twenties. It was the first time I became totally independent. I bought my first homes in Sweden. I did my first taxes in Sweden. I grew up into an adult in Sweden. I learned to "just be" in Sweden, and I learned emotional pain and loss to the deepest part of my heart. After many years, it has only strengthened me. I have understood that I can do this on my own. I redefined what family meant to me and let go of the fact that everything has to happen in a certain order. And because of that experience and the resilience, the sadness, the anger, I learned strength and bravery. I learned to say and do as I saw fit. I learned that I am in control of my own life and I choose how to live it.

And so, I know I am in control of this treatment. I am determined not to break. I am certain that I am capable of conducting the IV and flush procedures on my own. I am in control and I am organized. I will learn every detail and I will do it right. And the Herxheimer reactions are likely to be a hundred times worse than they ever were, but I know that even on the days I may have multiple seizures, on the days I can't walk or speak, on the days I may develop Bells Palsy, I will still have the determination to decide where my life leads. For that I am thankful.

———○———

I have had many nurses and friends ask me what the difference is between a PICC line, a port, and a PowerLine. Put simply, a PowerLine is a stronger apparatus that can take more pressure than a PICC line. Because so many people have asked, I am going to give you the information I received from the Jemsek's Specialty Unit.

PICC Line

A PICC line is by definition and per its acronym, a peripherally inserted central catheter. It is long, slender, small, flexible tube that is inserted into a peripheral vein, typically, in the upper arm, and advanced until the catheter tip terminates in a large vein in the chest near the heart to obtain intravenous access. It is similar to other central lines as it terminates into a large vessel near the heart. The upper arm is the area of choice. It is used for long-term antibiotic therapy, as well as other therapies.

Using ultrasound technology to visualize a deep, large vessel in the upper arm, the PICC catheter is inserted by a specially trained and certified PICC nurse specialist. Post insertion at the bedside, a chest x-ray is obtained to confirm ideal placement. The entire procedure is done in the patients' room, decreasing discomfort, transportation, and loss of nursing care.

A PICC line is not appropriate for all patients. Proper selection to determine the appropriateness of this device is required.

PowerLine® Central Venous Catheters

These are cuffed, tunneled, devices for short or long-term vascular access. Specially indicated for the power-injection of contrast media for CT scans, the PowerLine® Central Venous Catheter also allows for central venous pressure monitoring and administration of IV fluids, blood products, medication, and blood withdrawals.

Ports

Ports consist of a reservoir compartment (the portal) that has a silicone bubble for needle insertion (the septum) with an attached tube (the catheter). The device is surgically inserted under the skin in the upper chest. The catheter runs from the portal and is surgical inserted into a vein (usually the jugular vein, subclavian vein, or superior vena cava). Ideally, the catheter terminates in the superior vena cava, just upstream of the right atrium. This position allows infused agents to be spread throughout the body quickly and efficiently. To administer treatment or to withdraw blood, a health professional will first locate the port and disinfect the area. Then he or she will access the port by puncturing the overlying skin with a 90-degree Huber point needle, although a winged needle may also be used.

Surgeons, radiologists or physician assistants participate in the insertion of central lines. They are inserted using ultrasound technology or ultrasound with fluoroscopy, and may require sedation. Chest radiographs are also used to confirm placement of the central line tip if it was not inserted using fluoroscopy.

So there you have it, kids. Nine months of this – but thirty-seven years of preparation to get to this point. Game on.

Seizures

June 2, 2012

———◦———

Sigh. I just had the start of a seizure and got about halfway through it and was able to stop it with Ativan. I now know when one is coming on. I get a distinct headache, unlike any other, in the left frontal lobe of my brain. It's where my brain SPECT scan showed I have encephalitis and cerebral vasculitis. Anyone who gets migraines knows what it's like to feel one coming on.

For me, there is a sharp pain in my left frontal lobe of the brain, and then it feels as if I have grown a bubble outside that part of my head and it hurts there too. And when I say hurts, it stabs into my brain and grinds. My left eyebrow starts to strain and it is so painful. Seriously, who knew an eyebrow could be so painful. *Really?* When this happens, I always call my parents to let them know one is coming. We either stay on the phone or they come over.

As the pressure continues, my eyes start to twitch and my vision becomes blurry. My dad reminded me on the phone to take an Ativan. Today, I'd forgotten, as I forget most things these days. I lay in bed with the phone next to me, Dad listening and talking me through it, me describing each part of what was happening. This time my mouth seemed to be okay, so no issues with saliva or my tongue, but my *eyes*, my eyes. I worry about these suckers. Twitch, twitch, twitch.

And then it begins out of nowhere: the panic attack. And I start weeping and wailing and it's hard to talk. Dad asked me what I thought set it off and I knew. At about 5:00 p.m. today, I knew I had overdone it.

I was at my sister's house for several hours, and from about 4:00 to 5:00 I kind of felt like I was walking in circles. I didn't know what I was doing, lost my balance a few times, was slurring my words, and had a hard time processing things. So yes, I realized I had over-exerted myself.

About ten minutes after taking the Ativan, I was able to pull myself out of it. So, this time I did not have a full-on seizure, but man was it scary. My vision is still very blurry. This has happened a lot lately, so this week I will get my eyes checked, specifically to check the pressure of my retina.

It's quite a ride right now. I am trying to be a good sport and keep my family, especially my dad, who travels with me to my appointments, updated with very specific information, because honestly, I do not know where this is going. What if one of these episodes happens and I can't talk again for a while? What if I can't write? That's already happened multiple times when I have lost use of my right arm. What if I lose mobility?

So as usual, I share my inner thoughts as they develop, as they unfold. And right now, my thoughts have come to a stop.

Trapped

June 3, 2012

———◆———

I have good moments and I do have fun, so I don't want to be a super downer. But I want it to be real. Lately, I am not having much fun and am requiring a lot of help from my parents in caring for Mini. I am always here with her, but I can't play with her the way I usually do. I sort of have my place on the couch and about every fifteen minutes or so she will come racing to me, leap onto me and say, "I lug you stho much, Mommy!" in her little baby voice. She melts my heart.

We have a weekend routine now when we wake up. She tends to wake up around 6:30 a.m. With my new meds, I am just not functioning before 8:00 a.m. Of course, I am able to get up and help her if she has a nightmare or needs to go potty. I'm not unconscious, but I am wiped out. Last night, I was up from 2:00 to 4:00 a.m. with my French Bulldog, who was having tummy problems. Our new routine is that she waits for the "Good Night Light" to become the sun and she comes into my bed. She is so sweet when she comes in. She sort of stares at me about an inch away from my face until I feel someone looking at me. Sometimes she kisses me on the cheek. How did I ever get so blessed with such an angel?

Anyway, Mini sits quietly and either reads books, watches PBS Sprout, or plays a reading game on my iPad. She tells me when she gets hungry (and so do the dogs), and that is when I get up. We love our little morning routine now because she loves to snuggle and it has really helped her understand, in her own little way, how Mommy is feeling. She gets picked up for school by Mom or Maxi and then I'm here – trapped in my house.

I have a grocery list on my fridge, but I have to depend on someone to take me there. I have so many appointments, but I can't get myself to them, since I am unable to drive now. I cannot stand this. It's only been a few days and I feel panicked. I am putting all of my energy into hoping my eye appointment may produce some temporary glasses for me, so I can see more clearly. But who knows?

Throughout my battle during the last year since the beginning of treatment, I have maintained a pretty fun and positive attitude despite the pain, confusion, and difficulties I've had with the oral antibiotics. I've been able to grow and sustain an incredibly successful business, keep a solid public profile within the company, and portray my positive outlook.

But now I sit here, *trapped*. If I go somewhere, I have to be with someone. While I appreciate alone time, I have a hard time accepting anything that is being forced upon me. I love to drive alone. I love to just decide I am taking off somewhere. I love to take Mini on little adventures, just the two of us. This is the first time that I am feeling deeply depressed, deeply lonely, and deeply dependent. This lesson, whatever it is, is a tough one.

I Can See Clearly Now...
June 6, 2012

At my last appointment in DC, I complained that my vision has been getting increasingly blurry. I was pretty sure it was because of the change in dosage of the Neurontin and Lamictal, but had to ask, because I have *never* had trouble with my eyes. Dr. Jemsek suggested I see an optometrist to be sure that everything was okay with my retinal pressure.

Great, another doctor to see. *Sigh...* I made my appointment for yesterday. I showed up for the appointment at 3:00 p.m. only to find that my appointment was *really* at 2:00 p.m. Deep breath... Lyme brain. So I rescheduled for this morning and once again, had to depend on my friend to take me to an appointment. I acknowledge how lucky I am to have this supportive network around me.

I got there just before 9:00 a.m. and went through a very thorough exam. My retinal pressure is great and it seemed I had 20/20 vision until he dilated my eyes. Then he said it was very interesting to see that once they relaxed that eye muscle, I had a little more trouble focusing. All I could think of was, "There you go, Andrea. Forcing focus and perfect vision." Such a metaphor for my life. You get me to relax and I fall to pieces. *Rolling still dilated eyes...*

So the good news is that I will get some temporary glasses that will help with my blurry vision. Both the optometrist and Dr. Jemsek told me I can play around with the meds to find a balance where I can see clearly, but not be at risk for seizures. I think I know when the blurry vision started, so I will go back to the previous dose and play with it for the next few days. I hope to be driving again by the weekend. I need to get out of this house. Like, immediately.

So, my heart and my eyes are great! I'll take it! My gall bladder is gone, so that's great too! Now the eyes are taken care of and my schedule is clear of appointments for the next few weeks, unless something happens. A break feels nice before the next big step.

Still

June 7, 2012

———◆———

I am grateful that my ridiculous back-to-back doctor appointment schedules have come to an end and that I now have about exactly one month to focus on my daughter, my health, my business, and my home. My relationship with my dogs has gotten closer than ever. In the recent past, their spastic energy and barking at all things that move would send me through the roof, but now I am beginning to wonder how much of that was caused by my own anxiety and condition, because now, while they still bark at everything, they're much calmer. They both love the new couch and snuggling with us at night. I like that too. I think they're happier now that I am home with them. I've had a dog walker for some time now and that gives them the exercise I cannot provide them with, but honestly, it's very hard to wear these dogs out for any length of time.

I have many exciting things happening this month with my business. I am creating a solid foundation to keep things rolling once treatment starts and things become more unpredictable. I am able to put in a few hours each day, if haphazardly, to get what I need to get done, done.

But otherwise, I kind of don't know what to do with myself. Here I am, still unable to drive, which I hope will change very soon, possibly by the weekend. I'm tired, but I can't quite nap. I have *no* appetite, so I don't cook. I am mostly eating protein shakes during the day and then something unimpressive with Mini for dinner.

My friends are calling and writing, but I don't seem to have the energy to get back to them always. TV doesn't interest me for more than about fifteen minutes. I suppose I could take a shower today, but I don't really feel like doing *anything*.

I had a hard time waking up this morning and, when Mini woke me up, I was hysterically laughing in a dream that I will have to tell my mom about. It still cracks me up now and I have *no idea* where it came from. But I was *tired*. I went down and took my meds with a protein shake and hung out there for a while with the dogs and then came up to bed. And here I have been for three hours and have just kind of looked at the ceiling.

I'm not sure I feel depressed, but I do feel strange. I think the best way to describe it is that I feel *still*. Maybe it's just what I need right now. Today, I feel as if I am walking around as a shadow of myself, walking aimlessly around as if I need a map of my own home. But I'm not sad. It's the strangest thing.

I am reminded of what Dr. Jemsek said when I wanted an explanation and solution (this is how I work) for my midday crashes. Could it be that I needed to increase my adrenal medication (Cortef) at that time of day? He looked at me with some sympathy in his eyes and said, "I don't think it's your adrenals. I think it is your condition and something you just need to recognize. When you feel tired, sleep if you can."

And so here I am, Fifty Shades of Lyme, with no real plan for the next four weeks. The only other time in life when I have been in this type of situation was when I was on vacation for weeks at a time in Sweden. But that was vacation. That was sun, summer food, skinny dipping, love, fun, and purposeful relaxation.

This feeling of *still* is different. It's almost like a demand of stillness in my mind for what is to come. But a still mind and me are an anomaly. No comprendo. It makes me nervous.

I am finding that *still* is a very foreign, anxious place to be. I will try to embrace it and accept it as a message from my body as what I need right now, but I may have to add some Ativan to that thought process.

Moment of Peace
June 11, 2012

———◆———

As they say, no news is good news, so the fact that I have not written in a few days means I have been feeling pretty well. The eye drops have helped a great deal. I am able to drive again and, now that I have lowered my dosage of Neurontin, I am not as dizzy. So, I have found a moment of peace. A moment to be thankful. I have had a few migraines, which is a disappointment, because I had gone so long without one. Regardless, right now feels like peace.

Mini and I had a great weekend together, despite the fact that she had been bitten by some bug she's allergic to and her eye is swollen and closed shut. Today, with the help of some steroids from her pediatrician we were able to get the eye to open back up, but tonight when I picked her up from school, I saw a new bite on the other eye, so we shall see what I wake up to tomorrow. I suspect the other eye will be swollen shut. But I am so thankful for the day we were able to spend at my sister's pool, playing and truly relaxing. I am hoping for a few more of these days before my next trip.

I have so many scars on my abdomen now that I look and think, "*What happened to this girl?*" Today, the last of my sticky stitch adhesions came off. Rather than looking at badges, I am now able to look at the scars from yet another surgery. More importantly, I can get at those scars with some Ava Diaper Cream, which, for me, has miraculously cleared up scars, psoriasis, sunburn, you name it!

To be honest with myself, I have found that in these moments of peace – these few days of peace, actually – there's really never any sense of true peace. It's as if my guard is always up. Certainly, in the back of my mind, is the next procedure, more surgery, more scars, more of the unknown. But this bit of uneasy peace is much better than the chaos, seizures, loss of proper vision, etc. I am thankful for any taste of normalcy I am offered.

So for the next three weeks, I remain stitch free, until the next surgery on July 9. *Exhale...*

Welcome Back to Lyme Reality
June 16, 2012

I am thankful that I had a few days of peace and general stability. I do not feel I am in that place anymore. I am trying really hard now to keep it together, but I feel I am starting to fall apart at the seams. Against my better judgment, I have overextended myself this month. I'm burnt out. I also managed to pick up a horrendous upper respiratory infection, which has me basically coughing up a lung half the day. If you know anyone with Lyme, you know that even the smallest infection can take ages to get better.

Since Wednesday, I have been back in a place where I hate to be: three hours naps, heavy eyelids, depressed, and just trying to trudge through it all. I am trying to keep my business on track, planning two huge events scheduled for the week before I start treatment, while I should probably just be sitting doing nothing. But I am so passionate about what I do and I am so determined not to let treatment derail my business and success thus far. It's just not going to happen.

It's a perfect day outside. This is why we live here. People are out boating, biking, walking, and swimming. We spent a nice morning playing on my parents' deck, but I'm fried. I cannot move. And so now here we are at 2:00 p.m. and it's nap time. Mini is sound asleep and I, well, I should be too. But I sit here with so much to say and at the same time, nothing at all. I can't seem to make my thoughts into words.

I feel frustrated. I feel overwhelmed. I feel exhausted. I feel angry. I feel attacked. I feel I am not enough, ever.

So, it was a nice few days, but now I find myself back in Lyme with a side order of chest cough and sore throat. And to be honest with you, I just have no idea how I will pull the next three weeks off, much less the rest of today. That something I've learned is very common. I can plan and strategize all I want to about anything, but the fact is, I never know how I will feel at any particular time. It's hard for me to even plan a day in the morning because the afternoon may bring a totally other set of issues to deal with.

———— ⚫ ————

Lately, I have been approached by people who are "on the other side" of the whole IV treatment thing. And while I will never minimize their experience, I have to say, two months in the arm is not the same as nine months in the chest. And maybe I am just not open to hearing people lecture me about how I will get my life back because you know what? I need to deal with today. And I am so glad that so many people are feeling so much better, but I feel like shit and it's likely that I will feel like some level of shit for the next nine months.

If anyone understands the power of manifestation, it's me. I get it. But I am also being in the moment. And right now, *now* sucks. And it's allowed to suck. That's okay. I think as Americans we always want to present the best, to look on the bright side. As women, we want to nurture and give advice. It's really so Mars and Venus.

It's important when one is going through something like this that those around them allow the person who is struggling to experience authentic feelings. In other words, it doesn't matter what other experiences other people have had. It doesn't matter that *you* or your friend are/is on the other side. If you are hoping to be a truly healing presence in the life of a friend with chronic illness, you really need to listen and *hear* what is going on. As healers, we do not talk, we listen.

Listen. It's the best thing you can do for someone like me. It's really a skill that most people never truly learn. I don't need anyone on a soap box. Just be there for me. Just listen. Just notice me. And if it's too depressing for you, then don't feel you need to offer hope. Just walk away. Because that is what I need right now. I don't need people who are uncomfortable around me. I just need someone to sit beside me and get it. Play Scrabble with me. Just know that I am where I am and it blows and that's okay. It's part of my path, my lesson. I need a real friend right now. I just wish I knew who that friend was, because right now it's Mini and it's certainly too much for her to bear.

All I feel in my mind right now is sadness. Sadness for how I feel. Sadness from the loneliness. Sadness from the people who think they know it all, when really they know very little. Sadness that I cannot be all I want to be. Sadness that I am not sure I will be able to pull off the next three weeks for work. Sadness for my girl, for so many reasons.

In my body, I feel exhaustion. I feel like the tank is empty. My arms feel heavy and my shoulder muscles tight. My sinuses stuffy from my cold. My feet swollen. It makes me angry. Because there are people out there having an amazing weekend and I'm here in bed writing about my misery. I have tried my whole life to be a good person, to have a purpose. To do things that matter. To care for people. To understand people. To be selfless. And look at me now. I'm alone. It's not right.

I have so much more to say, but my thoughts are spinning around and around and it's not worth it. I choose instead to sit here in my reality and take it in. I choose to manage it. I choose to deal with it. I choose to prepare for the next step. And I need to rest, so I choose to do so. But today I wish I had a friend to sit with, who I could just cry with. All of my best friends are so far away. It's the hardest part of this, I think. To be so far away from the life I have built. To have so many friends in my life, but virtually all of them live far away, some on the other end of the world. And I can think of some of those friends who would instinctively know to just sit and be here for me. You know who you are. I miss you.

I'm sorry if you think this post was a total downer, but imagine how it must really feel inside me. Welcome to Lyme.

She Doesn't Deserve This

June 17, 2012

—◈—

I have been researching and watching videos of the effects of the treatment I am about to endure. I sit here in fear and in deep, deep sorrow for my three-year-old, knowing that for a long while, almost a year, she will not have the mother I have always hoped to be. I know now that I will need nearly full-time help. I know now that my life is about to be turned upside down. And so the goal is to keep hers as consistent as possible.

Any of you who know me, really know me, know that I am one tough broad with a fearless vigor for life. I have never turned down an opportunity to learn. Sometimes I even dive into my discomfort. But for the first time, I feel not only grounded in my fear, but weighed down as if I have a mountain of bricks on me. While I am walking around, it's as if I am in a zombie state. I am in a constant state of silent panic, periodically interrupted by streams of tears and sobbing. I try to do it when Mini isn't around, but today she saw some tears, several times and wanted to know, "Why is Mommy feeling sad?" As I write this, I realize that I need to talk to my old friend who has a husband, two kids and stage four colon cancer. I need to know how to talk to my daughter about this.

The clock is ticking. Three weeks until I start treatment that can and will induce incredible pain, swelling, migraines, seizures, immobility, loss of limb function, you name it. The worst part is that it looks entirely different in every person, so there are no "what to expects." I have MCIDS (Multiple Chronic Infectious Disease Syndrome), which for me includes Lyme, Bartonella, Ehrlichia, Babesia, encephalopathy, other co-infections, as well as adrenal insufficiency, and connective tissue disorder. People like me don't get a road map, we get airdropped into the war zone, not knowing what will greet us.

Knowing this has put me into purge mode, trying to get rid of everything in my bedroom and pulling together half of the toys/clutter in Mini's playroom which she has outgrown. Maybe it's just my way of trying to take control when I feel totally out of control.

Just now, Mini had a nightmare, so I went up and held her, and for the first time *ever*, she peed all over her *whole* bed *and* me. I even had to change the mattress pad. And as any mother would do, I carried her to the bathroom, cleaned her up, got her in new jammies, changed my own clothes, and then remade her bed. The bed is up against a wall, so it involved some climbing and reaching, changing of sheets, and normal things any parent goes through, all the while with a crying child.

As we snuggled our way back into a peaceful sleep, it dawned on me: *There is no way I could have done all that in the condition I will soon be in. I may have to have someone move in.* Deep breaths. All I can think of again and again is: She doesn't deserve this. I feel sorry for my girl. For the first time, I can't make it better.

"Different Roads"
June 19, 2012

———— ⚙ ————

She may be 3′4″ and weigh 38 pounds, but my three-year-old Mini sure does pack a punch. These parts are the hardest for me to write about because they are less about the science and logistics of it all, but get really personal into the emotional toll Lyme has taken on my family. I struggle with sharing these aspects because it is so painful, so daunting, and yet so important for me to share, because it is a very real part of the picture. If you or someone you love has Lyme, you may experience something similar, and it is for you I share this *very* private and sad puzzle piece.

We had a great day today. I kept Mini home from school/camp a little longer than usual because Maxi is back and yesterday was her birthday, so *of course* we had to have a birthday party at 9:00 a.m. when she showed up. We had balloons, party hats, chocolate chip muffins, tea, and even a tiny birthday cake. Mini was excited. My girl sure loves a party.

When she arrived, Mini hid under the comforter that is now a constant fixture on my couch since I am always home and always cold. When Maxi came into the living room Mini uncovered herself and jumped about three feet in the air and screamed "*Surprise!!!*" It was so cute. We had our little tea party, which included some wooden tea party toys, and then sang "Happy Birthday" with candles lit and everything. 9:00 a.m. = big deal.

At about 10:00 a.m. we took Mini to school. I picked her up early because she has been saying that her lower back hurts and "I need a justment from Dr. Steve," our naturopath. So off we went at 3:30 p.m. for our adjustments. And of course, she was right, her L5 was way out of whack and needed an anterior adjustment. I always believe my girl and take to heart what she is saying.

The evening was great. Dinner, tubby, and books. But in the middle of the second book, I noticed she was getting teary. Please understand, Mini has been practicing her tears in front of the mirror literally since she was eighteen months old, but I could tell from her breathing these were real tears. I asked her why she was crying. "I am upset," she replied. So I asked her to elaborate and she did. What she said stabbed a knife through my heart so violently that I am not sure what it will take for me to recover and fix this whole thing for both of us.

Between her sobs she explained, "When we take different roads it makes me sad. You go away too much and it hurts my feelings. I want to be with Mommy. I want you to take me with you. And it makes me so sad. And I feel angry at you because you leave me."

She's three and a half years old. The depth and articulation of her feelings astonishes me. And of course I talked to her about how I always want to be with her when I am away, but that I have to travel to see my doctor. How do you explain to a three-year-old what has been going on? My poor child. Her 2012 has looked like this:

January. Five nights away on business. February. What was supposed to be a minor surgery ended up being a full-on laparotomy that ended me up in the hospital for two nights with no warning, followed by a full week in bed, completely unfunctional.

March, I had to go to Palm Beach for our four-night Annual National Conference. At the end of March, I had my first appointment in DC with Dr. Jemsek. May, I had my gall bladder out (second surgery), and while I was able to come home, it was yet another few days in bed and more weeks that I could not pick her up. At the end of May, I returned to Dr. Jemsek for my second visit – another night away.

And now it's June. I spent one night away last week for work and will spend one night away on the June 29, also for work. And in July, I will return for this wretched PowerLine insertion procedure that promises to all but turn both of our lives upside down more than anyone ever expected. And I will be away for two or three nights for that procedure.

She's right. I am away too much. Every single month, it's been something. And guess what? I will have to return to DC every single month for the next year or two. It's breaking my daughter's heart and there is nothing – *nothing* – I can do about it. I know she knows how much I love her. But her needs are simple and what she needs and wants right now is for Mommy to be present and not sick and grumpy. I can barely offer her any of that. It hurts. I think it is the worst of any of the Lyme pain I've experienced, because there is no pill that can correct this.

On a logical level, I know she is a smart girl – I mean *really* smart. I know that we are lucky to have such involved and active grandparents in her everyday life to pick up my slack right now. I know that plowing through this treatment with the same determination I have used throughout my life for things I have wanted will bring me to a better, healthy place where I can be the mommy she wants me to be.

I get that. But it's all trumped by a feeling of inadequacy as a mother – of guilt, helplessness, and some level of desperation that I can't quite explain at this point. My baby wants her mommy, but her mommy is being consumed by a largely unknown, misunderstood, life-destroying disease that is currently leaving little of me in its wake. At this very moment, of all of the things I have been through in my life, I think I have hit my emotional rock bottom. There is nothing I can do about what is happening to my little girl while I do what I have to do to get treatment.

She is trusting me by articulating her feelings in a very mature manner, yet I will have to break her trust by continuing to leave her as I travel to DC. As I try to see the screen through my tears, all that keeps running through my head is: *Please do not let this disease destroy her as well. Please don't make her resent me. Please please please don't let her for one second think, at three years of age, that we are on "different roads."* It's just too much to bear.

We're Not Supposed to Talk About Money

June 22, 2012

We're not supposed to talk about money, but guess what. I'm going to.

I'm not even going to begin to try to come up with the amount of money my family has spent over the years trying to diagnose and treat me. I am afraid to even think about it. I am pretty sure I could buy a nice house in cash with that sum. But let's get a little real, just in case there is some person of influence out there who cares about how lives are being ruined by chronic Lyme.

As I mentioned, my treatment is not covered by insurance. Sometimes people with Lyme can get their PICC line treatments covered for a couple of months if their treatment is with the antibiotic Rocephin, but Dr. Jemsek skips that antibiotic completely and takes another approach.

Patients are indirectly encouraged to submit their claims, knowing that they will likely be denied, but hoping that when the insurance companies are eventually audited, the number of denied claims for this disease and treatment will become less easy to ignore.

By now, we have established that my Lyme is one of Dr. Jemsek's most serious cases, although I am thankful that I am currently moderately functional in that I can walk, talk, and get through most days without seizures. But let's face it, that's a pretty basic list of things to be thankful for and I am willing to admit now that I have been completely stripped of my quality of life.

By now, you have seen the physical, emotional, and mental toll that MCIDS has had on my life. But I think that it's important to know that the financial side of this is completely devastating. I don't remember what the statistic is for people with Lyme who declare bankruptcy, lose their homes, etc., but I am starting to understand now why it happens, and *man* does it happen fast.

I think Dr. Jemsek's prices are fair in terms of office visits. At this goes to print, the first appointment is somewhere around $700; subsequent appointments are around $350. I see him every four to six weeks. Once I start the IV meds, it will be every four weeks. Not covered by insurance.

The neurotrophic and pain medication expenses are, thankfully, largely covered by insurance due to my encephalopathy, but still, it's another $400-ish per month with co-pays and uncovered medications. As I mentioned, IV meds are not covered by insurance. In order to get a 10% discount, my family paid a lump sum of $30,000 put on account to pay for the IV meds. I realize that not everyone can do that, and I feel for *everyone*. While we were able to do this, please do not make any assumptions about our financial situation or anyone else's. It's private and one never knows how one funds such a sum. Many people take out home equity loans, other loans, or file bankruptcy. No matter how one finds the money, if they can at all, it's a major blow.

Then there's the travel. I just booked the flights for my dad and me to fly to DC for two nights. The cost for flights and two hotel rooms for two nights? $2,000. Usually we fly midweek for one night. That costs about $1,000, but this surgery happens on a Monday morning, and we need to fly in on the Sunday. *Ugh.*

So this month alone, we are pretty much out $40,000. The stress it puts on me to have to rely on my family to help me pay for this is torture. Of course, they are willing and everyone is stepping up, but seriously, it's just wrong. I cannot imagine what I would do if I did not have my family. Actually, yes I can. I would have to suffer with this disease, knowing my government is doing nothing to help me, a good taxpaying citizen. I am disgusted.

People with Lyme are already so tired, stressed and confused. To add this to the mix, to have to call my dad and let him know that this time the trip will be $2000 was like putting a needle in my eyeball. There are so many emotions involved in this whole scenario, not the least of which is intense guilt. I feel guilt that my parents and family are spending so much money on me. Guilt that my parents have to come over virtually every day to help me with Mini and maintain my home. Guilt that I really have no end in site because we just don't know how this will turn out.

It's a serious issue, and this $2,000 trip to DC is what made me break my rule of talking about money. I mean seriously, DC? It's like it thinks it's Dubai.

The Final Countdown
June 25, 2012

———◦———

Blame it on my many years in Sweden, but I cannot get the Swedish band Europe's song out of my head: "The Final Countdown!" So bad. So '80s. So… dramatic. But it's in my head and I am acutely aware that two weeks from today I will have had my first infusion.

I have mixed feelings about this final countdown. I can say with no uncertainty that I wish I had just gone in and done the procedure in June, as they requested. But I had this big idea that I would use June to build a solid foundation for my business and my field team around the country of over three hundred people. The problem is, I haven't been sleeping. I have been struggling. I have been scatter-brained and scared. It's as if I am walking around in a zombie-like state of panic.

So, to say the least, I haven't gotten much done this month, which was to be so productive. I haven't even really napped. I have tried, but it hasn't happened. Too much in my brain. But today I took an amazing two-hour nap and it completely changed my mindset and my demeanor. My parents came over with my nephew for dinner and I actually *enjoyed* an evening. Yesterday we spent the day at my sister's pool and I actually *enjoyed* the day. So, there have certainly been some good times.

The day before yesterday, my dad, Mini and I went to my parents' beach on the lake and while Dad watched Mini (a water demon), I was able to swim out a ways and was reminded of how much I connect with water. I feel so at peace when I am by or on the water, but most of all, when I am IN the water. It's as if I can let go of everything that is lurking within. I have found so much solace in that lake throughout the years I have struggled with this disease, which went decades without being named.

One of the hardest and saddest parts for me about treatment, besides the obvious physical and emotional effects this will have on me *and* my daughter, is the fact that I will not be able to go for those swims anymore this summer. I will have to spend most of the summer indoors. You may say, "hey, it's one summer and then for the rest of your life you will be there." But will I? There are so many unknowns. Will I *really* be done with IV treatment next summer?

It's kind of freaky going into this with no roadmap. As I said before, every person in my situation arrives with a different equation, a different set of infectious diseases, a different immune response, and different "others" such as, in my case, connective tissue disorder, degenerative disk disease, adrenal insufficiency, and who knows what else? So, there is no *What to Expect When You Are Expecting*. That would be nice.

We're preparing. We have changed Mini's playroom up a bit and added a twin bed so my parents can have a quiet space to sleep when they stay, which I expect will be a lot. My suspicion is that, after a while, I will become quite sufficient with my own situation but will really need them to take care of Mini, and of course, to be here to support me and hang out with me, if I can stay awake.

As I mentioned previously, most of my friends live very far away. This is a hard one for me, because so many people are asking me how they can help, when really all they can offer me is their support. I am an avid vegetable juicer. I make my own high alkaline juices to detox on an almost daily basis. But since my last appointment, I have been so overwhelmed and tired that I have dropped off the bandwagon. The benefits of juicing are amazing, but the work itself is pretty demanding and I suspect I will not have the energy it takes to *create* the energy that I will drink from my juicing.

In my writing, I continue to promise to share the whole picture on my personal level. I will tell you about the PowerLine surgery, what IV meds I am being given, along with the regular neurotrophic and pain medication schedule, and what happens in my next appointment with Dr. Jemsek. As I get information, I will share it. It's important to make some noise here and I will. I will post the ugly. I will write about my Herxheimer reactions so you can envision what Lyme looks like. I will tell you all the gory details. I will share the toll it's taking on my mind, body, and more importantly, my soul.

And with that dramatic soap box declaration, I return to *The Final Countdown* on repeat in my head. I kind of feel like I should go tease my hair now and wear rubber bracelets. Too tired.

Two Body Parts Removed, One Part Back

June 27, 2012

———◈———

I'm having a Lyme Day. There have been less of these since I started the neurotrophic meds, which have alleviated much of my pain. It's always there, but the edge has been taken off. Today though, I am "Lymie." My muscles are like rock, which Dr. Jemsek has diagnosed as "stiff man syndrome," I can actually *feel* the swelling in my left frontal lobe of my brain where I have encephalitis and cerebral vasculitis. My vision is blurry. I'm tripping over words, instantly forgetting what I have discussed with people. It's rough.

And I am tired. I don't think I can even explain the level of tired I feel right now. For several days, I have increasingly felt like a walking zombie. I can turn on "the normal" for brief periods of time, but I am now in a state where it's getting harder.

Yesterday, I spoke with my nurse from the IV Unit at Dr. Jemsek's office and it was confirmed that I will be starting my treatment with the antibiotic Meropenem via the IV PowerLine in my chest. This first part of treatment, as I understand it, will be focused on targeting the spirochetes in my bloodstream – the floaters, free agents looking for cells, organs, and tissue to plant themselves in and wage their attack. I kind of think of these as sleazy dudes trying to pick up chicks at a meat market bar. Yeah, we're going after those first.

It makes sense. Go for the ones who haven't implanted themselves yet before going for the big ones. This first part of treatment is unpredictable. It will be intense for sure because of the strength of the antibiotic and the usual reactions – seizures, migraines, nausea, diarrhea, excruciating muscle pain, general stiffness, convulsions, etc. I think the scariest part of this first phase will be learning to get used to and accepting this new part of my body, the PowerLine, which will be with me for the better part of the next year. In the last three months I have lost two organs. Now I will be gaining one, the way I see it.

After the surgery, we will have a four-hour appointment with the IV team to administer the first treatment, to check for adverse reactions, but also to train me how to administer the antibiotics and detoxifying Lactated Ringers solution. If something goes wrong, it goes really wrong, which worries me because I'm working with a brain that barely functions now, much less in treatment.

So if you really want to know how I am – I am freaking out now. I regret taking this extra month to "get things in order." Yes, I bought my new couch and the bottom up blinds have arrived so the dogs won't bark at every butterfly outside, but we'll still get some light in the living room. I wanted to spend this month getting my business stable, but really, it was already stable.

It's kind of surreal being in my brain right now. I think you can tell from the writing right now that my mind is all over the place. It's asleep, but highly functioning. It's thinking logistically about treatment, but panic-stricken at the same time. It's running a thousand mph working on the upcoming events and yet I sit here as a zombie. As you know, for weeks I was crying uncontrollably. That's not the case right now. At the moment, I feel I'm in a grey zone. It's as if I'm not even here in my own body. I am sure there are rivers of tears left to cry, but right now, I feel stifled, trapped, and wishing the days away until we just get this shit done. There you have it. Let's just friggin' do it and get rid of the fear of the unknown.

Decor Imposter
July 3, 2012

———— ◈ ————

What are you up to tonight? You know what I am doing? Assembling IV poles. This is not how I imagined my life, but then, is life ever how we imagined it? It's just that it never really even occurred to me that I would have to incorporate an IV pole into my living room decor. I'm sitting here, looking at this thing and it reminds me of the various drips I have endured over the past three months through my two operations. It also reminds me that I am about to have surgery yet again – in six days – only this surgery will change everything for the majority of the coming year or beyond.

That chrome stick. It stands there staring at me with its beady eyes, the loops where I will hang my medications. I can try to look beyond it, but the lights reflect against it from every direction, reminding me of its presence. I know I have a choice. I can either let this thing glare at me as a challenge or I can form some kind of an appreciative relationship with it. It's here to help me fight my war. It's on my side. Perhaps we will become friends. Perhaps it should have a name. But for now, it's staring at me and it's creepy.

I feel a bit relieved that the wait is almost over. I am honestly terrified of the unknown. I tend to let it all out at night when Mini has gone to bed. My parents have seen me break down enough and honestly, I know my dad has been getting more and more emotional and I just do not want to lay any more on them than I already have. And so, I cry in bed mostly. I cry alone. It's what I choose right now.

Six days and counting. Six days. *Deep, deep breaths…*

Rear View Mirror Art

July 7, 2012

—◦●◦—

I am not sure if anyone ever imagines that they will end up with a handicap sticker, but there's one on its way to me and let me just say, of the few things that makes me giddy at the moment, this is one of them.

Now, before I tell you why I am so excited about this, don't judge. I have heard no less than eight times this week the whole, "but you look great" thing. By now, dear readers, we have established rapport and you are aware that I have, in Dr. Jemsek's words, "been very sick, for a very long time." I will remind you that while I "look great," my neurological symptoms are the main reason I am getting this handicap sign. I have difficulties walking at times. I don't need to go into that.

But that said, Mom (who might be more excited about this than I am), is still wondering if it is or is not legit and has suggested that I might need to limp a little. *Rolling my eyes like I am fourteen all over again...* My final disclaimer for those raising a collective eyebrow with Mom: this is totally legit and I actually do need this, but have decided not to use it when there are regular spaces close by that I can use instead.

So yeah, totally helpful with my monthly visits to the airport, not to mention my, soon to be, weekly trips to the hospital for blood draws. This will also be infinitely helpful at the grocery store, since I am so forgetful and always lose my car. Okay, all great and practical, but let me let you in on a little bit of the ridiculousness of my mind – *wait for it* – I cannot *wait* to go to Target and park right the hell in front of that place! I'm serious. Every time I think handicapped sign, I think *Target*.

I don't know why, other than the fact that there are about a hundred handicapped signs at Target and I feel I could pay some needed attention to those spaces.

I don't know why Target firecrackers start to explode in my head when I think about this latest development, but I find it highly amusing. Do I desperately need to buy any of the pretty much everything that Target has? No. Is it my American consumerism alarms going off? Perhaps. But if I am really being honest, I think it's because it will be such a great relief, for the first time in *years*, not to have to walk up and down the parking lots aisles, sometimes for up to thirty minutes, trying to find my car. A sobering thought amidst all of the humor and excitement, but true.

And so, when you see me driving away from town with a huge smile on my face and my rearview mirror adorned with its new art, you will know *exactly* where I am headed.

Physical Manifestation of Emotions
July 8, 2012

———◦———

I am lying here in my bed at the Dupont Circle Hotel, just hours before my life is to change, first for the worse, but hopefully in the long run for the better. It's the strangest feeling. For months now, since Dr. Jemsek started me on my neurotrophic medications, I have been without body pain. Tonight, my whole body hurts. My muscles are hard. They ache. My joints hurt. I feel a headache coming on. And of course I know this is a physical manifestation of the emotional and mental aspect of this experience, because at the moment, I really do not know *what* I feel.

My body seems to know there is major chaos going on in my mind, but I think to protect myself, I have put up some sort of a numbing barrier to avoid the anxiety of what awaits, because the fact is, we have no idea what awaits me. This is the worst part of the situation for me. I like to know how things will play out from A to Z. I am not accustomed to this "watch and see" approach. The irony is not lost on me, because I feel I have become such an A-type personality as a result of my Lyme. It's been my survival mechanism all of these years.

But now, I lay here in bed, with my familiar body pains, about to enter a hospital tomorrow where I have never been, to meet a surgeon I have never met, at a time I am still unsure of, to have a procedure that is straight forward and quick, but will be followed by an extremely emotional four-hour appointment with Dr. Jemsek teaching me how to use my newest body part, my PowerLine, and how to properly self-administer and flush the tubing.

After we do that, they will administer my first antibiotic treatment to see how I react. I am not sure when the Herxheimer reactions will begin. It could be then and there, or they could begin a few days into treatment. We don't know. But we do the first injection there tomorrow to make sure I am not allergic to the antibiotic. Seems like the right thing to do. *Chuckle/ eyes rolling...*

We got stuck on the plane at the gate for two hours in Boston for a weather delay, but Dad and I did fine with our various forms of distraction and had a great dinner at the hotel. I am *so tired*, but I can tell you, if it were not for the sleep bomb concoction I take from Dr. Jemsek, and I mean an arsenal of sleeping pills, as tired as I am, there would be no sleep tonight.

I will try to write an update tomorrow on how things went, but don't panic if you don't see anything. One of my issues has been headaches and vision, so if I start to Herx right away, you may not hear from me tomorrow.

Act I
Surgery!
July 9, 2012

—◦—

So much has happened today that I am not quite sure where to begin. So, I guess I will begin at the beginning.

We headed off to George Washington University Hospital at 8:00 a.m. and after registering, waited two hours before I was taken back to change into my johnny. They brought Dad back and we waited for about an hour and played on our various diversion devices. I have to say, the entire staff was really friendly, upbeat and very informal. Right up my alley.

One of the fun things about waiting *hours* was the discovery of this awesome new system they have to keep families abreast of where their loved ones are in the surgery process. It's kind of like an arrivals and departures sign at the airport.

I was taken away to the operating room where I then waited for another thirty minutes in a freezing cold room for the surgical staff to come in. By now, it's 11:30 and my surgery has not even begun – and I have a 1:00 p.m. appointment with Dr. Jemsek for my first treatment. Chop, chop, kids.

I was laying there naked with a sheet over me in this freezing room and all of these nurses and doctors kept appearing three inches away from my face and introducing themselves and telling me what their role would be in this comedy of errors. Then each of them would yell for the white binder. The freakin' white binder. Another face. Yeah, hi. Where's the white binder? "Hi, I'm Doctor Who and I will be your such and such during the process. Where's the white binder?" Finally, I yelled too. "Guys, the white binder is right there on the shelf. Just make sure it's mine." I mean for Christ's sake, it was like an episode of Scrubs.

They finally got started and created some kind of tent over my head so I couldn't see what they were doing. Damn it. I wanted to watch. But then they gave me the happy stuff and suddenly I could not have cared less what they were doing. I was conscious during the surgery, but couldn't feel much.

This is basically how it went down. I was warned every time they were to do something and felt several of the things they were doing, but it wasn't bad. The PowerLine is like a thicker tube than you would see on a butterfly needle when getting a blood draw. It's designed to take higher pressure than a PICC line, for long-term medication, in this case antibiotics. They insert the line just above the clavicle and then into the jugular vein so it can empty directly into the superior vena cava. The result is a purple line hanging downward out of my chest, which is what I will use to administer my medications. It looks like a tiny little penis. *It's a boy!*

I'm going to be honest. I wasn't ready to come out of the happy place. The happy gas was awesome, but I am a busy girl and had places to be, so I only spent thirty minutes in post op, when it should have been an hour and a half, and actually made it to my 1:00 p.m. appointment by 1:15 p.m.

Act II

Appointment with IV Nurse
at Dr. Jemsek's Office

———◦◦———

I am always impressed by how on time this office is. We have really never waited more than ten minutes for an appointment. First, we met with my IV nurse, Christina. She's very laid back and soft spoken, and she certainly had her hands full with this Lyme-know-it-all, my non-stop questions and me. I am kind of known for that now, but I think they like it. I know Dr. Jemsek likes it. I can tell.

Anyway, she took my vitals. They always take my blood pressure lying down, then sitting up, and then standing up. Very interesting. And then all of the usual questions about the meds, etc. Once we got past the usual song and dance (and horrifying weighing in session; let's just say I am starring on a new show called *The Biggest Winner*), it was time to get serious and learn how to administer my IV antibiotics.

Holy crap.

Okay. This is complicated. Like really confusing with lots of steps and a bazillion tubes and caps, and syringes and IV bags and lions and tigers and bears, *Oh my!* Sterilize this. Sterilize that. Don't shake this. Pull this off, twist this one. *Oh… my… God…* That said, they give you a folder with explicit directions, so once I follow those two to three times I will be all set. But really, it was pretty overwhelming.

This month my antibiotic days will be Monday, Wednesday, and Friday, twice a day. On the off days, I still have to flush the line and if I am feeling poorly I do what is called a Lactated Ringers solution. This is a liter of a saline-like solution with extra electrolytes and other stuff. It's a two to three hour drip. You have five liters of blood in your body; this adds a liter of fluids to get things really moving and flushing out those spirochetes. So that's the plan.

Act III

Appointment with Dr. Jemsek

We did the first treatment to see if I was allergic to it. I am now armed with EpiPens, just in case. I am not allergic in this case, so here goes nothing! When Christina had done her part, Dr. Jemsek came in. Now that we've started building a relationship, he understands that we're the unusual fun Lyme people who pretty much joke our way through appointments as a coping mechanism. He also understands by now that I am a complete control freak, full of in-depth questions, and completely expecting to be spoken to as a peer at all times. So, our conversation today was fun.

After every appointment, my doctors and I are sent an in-depth explanation of what went on at my latest appointment. Dr. Steve calls it "The Press Release." In the last press release, Dr. Jemsek referred to my dad as my "husband." So, I clearly introduced my dad again as my dad and he said, "But haven't I met him?" and Dad explained that he had previously referred to him as my husband. He was very apologetic and started furiously correcting the last press release until I interrupted and said, "Relax. It's fine. I was moderately grossed out, but I have Lyme so I quickly forgot about it." He burst out laughing, as much as Dr. Jemsek bursts out, and that set the upbeat tone for the appointment.

Let me start by saying – this man is brilliant. He has an answer for every weird question I have. I complained of my recent foot pain. I have told him that I have had incredible inflammation and pain in my feet lately. I also told him that I feel that the shape of my feet has changed completely. He poked around and examined and quickly found that I have grown small nodules on the tops of my toe joints. He immediately diagnosed me with exotoses, which is when new bone forms on existing bone. It can be very painful, as I am beginning to experience, and is likely caused by the co-infection Bartonella. He has prescribed a compounded cream to apply on the area, which should help break it up.

So yay, another diagnosis. Exotoses. Super.

I then proceeded to show him that the undersides of my fingers have begun to peel within the last month. Again, he took a look, diagnosed it as acrodermatitis chronica atrophicans (ACA), a common Herxheimer reaction, and said this was good news. This kind of peeling of the face of the hands is a sign of Lyme and the fact that I now have this is a *good* sign. What it means is that the last months we have spent balancing my system with neurotrophics, supplements and detoxing has actually awakened my immune system. The peeling hands are now my body acknowledging the Lyme.

So, I actually *do* have an immune system in there, although you wouldn't know it from the freakin' SARS I contracted two weeks ago when Mini came home and sneezed *once*. I proceeded to cough up a lung for two weeks, but the peeling hands thing is apparently good.

I told him that I have been having some speech issues, squishing words together. His response was pretty much "get used to it." I also told him that I am rapidly gaining weight to which he responded, "There is a Fat Zone in Lyme and it has to do with inflammation. The good news is that you will eventually get to a place where you can lose it." So, basically, tough shit. I will get fat enough so I can lose it. *Laughing and bawling all at once.* It's only going to get worse.

Booooooo!!!!

We talked about what the next seven months will look like, what period will likely be the hardest and what we "might" be able to expect, although you never really know. At that point, we were pretty much done and Dr. Jemsek had left the building before I could pounce him for telling me that even though I drink kale and spinach juice all day I am going to continue to gain weight. Beat it, dude.

Act IV
The Handover

———— ◉ ————

So, Christina came back in with all of the things I will need for the next month. We had been told to bring a carry-on for these meds and supplies. The result was straight out of an episode of *Weeds*: When I received the entire suitcase of IV meds, all I could think was, "Mama needs a moment." Holy crap.

And next month we were told to bring a bigger bag. Yes, we have a letter to travel and carry the liquid medications aboard. *Ay ay ay*. So we rolled our way out of the Clinic after making our next two appointments. I need to be back in another four weeks, then again in four weeks. I wish I had energy and time to enjoy my city. I love DC. Maybe further down the road. I would love to bring Mini and go to the National Zoo, meet my DC friends (who I have not even seen yet since this has been so intense), and just reconnect with DC. Though perhaps not when it's 103°F with huge thunderstorms.

Dad and I chose to just do an easy dinner and get me back to the hotel. And here I sit. I feel fine. I am sure once the pain meds wear off I will be sore, but at the moment I feel fine and I will take it. We travel home tomorrow morning and I begin actual treatment on Wednesday. Game on.

56, Batter Up!
July 10, 2012

———◦◉◦———

We got home today with no problem. The flight was easy, although I was colder than I think I have *ever* been. Teeth chattering, shivering, etc. Dad said it wasn't really that cold, so I imagine it might have been a minor Herx reaction to the antibiotics the day before.

We drove home from Boston and stopped at my grocery store and pharmacy to see how many of the seven new prescriptions could actually be filled there. I came home with three, which I later found can be filled in town when ordered the day before. Score. I also bought Mini a huge Blue's Clues balloon and an ice cream cake to bribe her from torturing me for going away. It worked.

I got home about an hour and a half before my mom brought Mini home and I felt strangely energized. We took advantage of the time and dad brought a table into my room, which will serve as my triage area. I was able to organize all of my new goodies into super cute storage boxes, so Mini won't be hanging from the rafters swinging with an IV tube or popping Lactated Ringer water balloons.

We had a nice little welcome home party with Mini and my parents and, because I was feeling so well, I told my dad to just go home for the night. There will be plenty of nights when they will need to stay here, but this is not one of them. Of course, if I have any complications, I can call and they will come right over.

So, I grew some cojones and decided that since Mini fell right asleep and I have to catch up on my shows, I would mimic the way I operate in my business and "Just Do It," no matter how uncomfortable or unsure I am. So here I lie, with my first Lactated Ringer hanging above me on my IV pole. I feel comfortable and quite at peace. I know there's a long rough road ahead, but today I feel happy that the trip, the surgery, the appointment, and the homecoming all went so well. I am thankful and will take any kind of "happy" that is offered at the moment.

I continue to drink my high-alkaline Blue Print Cleanse juices and am thankful to have found them, as juicing is pretty arduous and my energy doesn't really allow me to juice the way I used to. I have had several friends buy gift certificates through my account with www.mealtrain. com, which is awesome. The juices make me feel good, but the costs add up, so it's been great that my friends from far off places want to help and can do so by helping supply me with this nutrition.

Tomorrow morning the plan is that my dad will take Mini to camp/ school and then I will have my first visit from my home care nurse. She will come here weekly to redress my PowerLine. I really need to figure out this whole shower thing. At the suggestion of Dr. Jemsek's clinic, I bought cling wrap to cover myself with when I shower. For now, I count my blessings. The trip went well. Mini did well with me away. I think I have a good grasp on how this whole PowerLine thing works. I was able to organize my vast medical supplies peacefully. My parents seem at ease now that I am at ease. I just feel like I am in the right place, and that this is a great way to start treatment. Good stuff.

Like the Nurse, Hate the Herx
July 11, 2012

———◦◉◦———

This morning I had my first visit from my visiting nurse, who was really just lovely. I am so thankful that this part of the treatment seems to be covered by insurance. *Fingers crossed...* She came in, explained to me how it all works, took my vitals, redressed my PowerLine, and then helped me (watched me) administer my first IV Meropenem drip. A thirty-minute drip, she sat with me the whole time, discussing Lyme and life and how our relationship will unfold.

Turns out that although she lives up the street and didn't know my parents were in town, she knew them in junior high. Her brother had gone to high school with my mother in Connecticut. Small world.

About halfway through the drip, I got a little itchy. Then my calves felt hot. My muscles started to tense up around my scalp. My neck became unbearably stiff, my eyebrows started to hurt, my teeth hurt, and my muscles tightened up. We said our goodbyes. She will be back each Wednesday morning, to take the blood draws at home (*Yay for no more hospital blood draws!*) and redress the PowerLine, making sure there is no sign of infection.

When she left, an incredible wave of exhaustion swept in. It's a nice day out, but I was cold, very cold. I buried myself under my comforter and almost fell asleep. I had a 1:00 p.m. conference call to attend so I rolled over and put the phone on speaker and laid there in what I can describe as an "out of it" state. I came back into it about an hour later and here I sit. I still have the headache, the one I have known for so many years. All these years I thought I was just prone to migraines. All these years it's been Lyme. And now I am on the attack.

I'm off now to pick up Mini. My mom will drive. I have some scripts to fill on the way and another iPhone to send back for replacement since my Lyme-clumsiness has been in full effect. Then we will go get Mini and take her to dance class. We'll see how I do.

Tonight I will administer another thirty-minute drip of Meropenem. I am not sure if I should have one of my parents stay here or not. On the one hand, if it were just me, I would say I'll be fine. But having a little one changes the equation, so I will weigh it out with them later on to see what they think.

I have now injected all I am going to inject for this month and will be able to do this day after day until we switch it in up week five. I can tell this will be a battle, but I'm going in determined and educated. I'm ready.

Blood in the Line!
July 13, 2012

———◦———

When I think of Tuesday evening and the first time I self-administered my antibiotics, all that comes to mind is someone yelling, "*Water in the hole!!!*" Except in this case, I was yelling, "*Blood in the line!!!*" The good times never end.

After my nurse left and the antibiotics set in, I had a rough day. It wasn't *awful*, but it made me uneasy enough to ask my dad to stay over that night. I had had a fever of 99.6° after the first infusion. They say to call when you have a 100° fever or higher. So, support seemed wise. He didn't flinch and brought over his office (computer) and just worked here. I was able to get Mini down pretty quickly and started my infusion. It went swimmingly. Like any other treatment of this kind, we use the acronym SASH – saline, antibiotic, saline, and heparin. The saline cleans and sterilizes the lines, and the antibiotics kill the little bastards – the floaters in my bloodstream (this month), then more saline to sterilize the line again, and then heparin to help avoid clots and all that good stuff.

Well, on this evening, you can imagine me as the patient contestant with half a SASH. I got through the saline injection and antibiotic hookup easily. Got the right pace of the drip going and settled in. Well, I guess thirty minutes goes faster than I thought because all of a sudden I looked up and the bag was empty, but there was blood flowing *into* my IV line. My instincts whispered in a screeching tone that this was probably not ideal.

"Daaaaaaaad!!!!!! Blood in the line!!!!!!!" *Clump clump stumble...* (My dad has the loudest feet *ever*).

Thankfully, I am actually *very* good in a crisis. In fact, I think I function better in a crisis than I do in a stable situation. Must be the spirochetes. I do well with imbalance. *Sigh...* Anyway, before dad and his loud feet got to my room, I remembered about the safety clamp, this tiny purple clip that I can use at any time which stops everything from coming in or out. What a smart idea.

So, I shut the safety clamp and was able to gather my thoughts. First thought was, "Okay there is only enough blood in there to fill one vial and seeing as I gave thirty-two tubes of blood on my first Dr. Jemsek blood draw, this can be considered one for the team. Chill out."

I proceeded to chill out. Okay. So there is blood in the line, but it won't come spilling out all over the place, because when I unscrew the PowerLine there will be no pressure, blah, blah, blah, just going through my logical process. In the meantime, we thought it a good idea to call the 24-hour IV Unit on call. While we were waiting for them to respond to the page, I pulled it together, removed the bag from Pol-ine, as my IV likes to be called, and threw it in the disposables. Then I took a bunch of alcohol swabs and wiped off the blood, etc. There wasn't much. Now that my purple penis, I mean PowerLine, was clean, I was able to crown myself an IV patient queen and finish the saline and heparin injections. Pretty sure after all of that, I didn't need to take my hydrocortisone/Cortef tablets (an adrenaline hormone called cortisol) the next day. Wow.

That said, it was a good experience and when the IV Unit called me back I had done all the right things. Yay for being an overachiever. Did I ever mention that ten years ago I fainted every time I had a blood draw? I mean, at this point, I feel like a rock star.

I slept really well that night, or so I thought. I remember going into Mini at 11:30 when she was having a night terror, but Dad said I also went in at 1:30 and 3:30 when she had them again. *No recollection* of that at all, but he said I sounded very coherent and got her back to sleep. Not bad. I've been sleep shopping too!

Yesterday, Dad took Mini to school, which is becoming easier. She knows one of the three of us will take her or pick her up and seems to be manipulating each one of us in a different way. I admired how she marched back in the house yesterday afternoon with a Hershey's three-pack of chocolate milk. Master negotiator.

While she was at camp/school, Mom and I tried to get a lounger for my back deck, to no avail. It was sold out. I was in an *atrocious* mood even before we got there. I don't do well right now with the un-expected. So when I met up with my mom and she started mouthing to me through two closed windows (pet peeve, because I so obviously have no idea what you are saying), suggesting we take my car because it's bigger, it was not what I had in my head and it set me off. Okay fine, my car. No, your car. My car is bigger. Okay, my car.

I *hate* having to make any decision right now. But I had to, so I finally decided that we were going in her car. I was in a *foul* mood after that. Of course then we got into this discussion about whether I wanted to go or not. *Again*, when I am like this, please do not make me make a decision. So for ten minutes, it was, "Do you want to go?" "No I do not want to go, but we are halfway there, so go." Starts to turn the car, "I said go!" It was bad.

We stopped at the pharmacy on the way home, and I dropped an-other $314 in meds for this month. On Tuesday I will go get my supple-ments. It's amazing how I am just writing checks here and there. At this point, after all this time, I could never do it without the support of my family. It's ridiculous. I do not know how people do it when they do not have the support system I have. *Shudder...*

We got home, and I decided to have my mom sit with me for my three-hour Lactated Ringer. We are watching a British drama series, so that was a nice distraction, but I felt *awful*. I mean *awful*. Obviously when you are doing a one liter flush you have to pee a lot, so I rolled Pol-ine back and forth to the bathroom several times. I just felt *exhausted*, which was how I felt the last time I did an LR. I thought these were supposed to make you feel better, but in my case they wipe me out.

In any case, once the drip was done and there was no blood in the line, I was all set, but before I knew it, Mini was home with her damned chocolate drink. My non-toxic organic detox alarms were blaring. I can still hear my dad saying, "*Get over it!*" So I did.

And today, I got up at 5:30 a.m. because Gunnar was barking and had puked all over his crate. I spent forty-five minutes trying to clean it all out of the plastic wicker, but will see if he rejects it tonight or not. I had to clean his beds three times to get it all out. *Gross.*

I did one injection and felt quite well. My mom took Mini to school early this morning so I could get my drip done before my 9:30 massage, which was brutal. My muscles have *never* been like this, and they are always a challenge. I came home to a clean house, thanks to my wonderful housekeeper and went to take a nap. I managed to sleep a bit, but for some reason, naps are hard for me these days. I would like to be taking more of them.

I just finished watching six seasons of *Weeds* that Netflix has on Instant Queue. I'm not quite sure where to go next. I'm thinking *24*. The show started while I lived in Sweden, so I never got into it. It sounds pretty addictive and a great reason to sit on my couch with my dogs.

In all, I would say I am doing pretty well. It's almost an hour-by-hour thing right now. An hour ago, I called my mom to say I could pick Mini up. Now I regret it because my eyes hurt. Which reminds me, I really need to go get a pair of glasses with that prescription I got over a month ago.

Unfolding
July 16, 2012

———◦———

I have now begun to unfold. Today I did my fourth antibiotic day (two doses via IV each day) and, as of right now, I am just coming down from a complete freak out.

To begin, Dr. Jemsek has told me I need fourteen to sixteen hours of sleep. I am currently getting six if I'm lucky. Part of this is because I have a three-year-old who is waking me up multiple times a night, probably precisely because I ask her not to. After begging her, yelling at her, reasoning with her, etc. to no avail, we created a sticker chart. When she fills the sticker chart by letting mommy sleep, she will get the big-girl blue bike she has wanted. It's sitting in my closet and I am dying to give it to her, but I feel that this is my bargaining chip right now and I want to reward her for good behavior rather than be frustrated all the time. And I want to sleep. Yeah, well that worked for four nights.

My French Bulldog has been throwing up a lot. Lately it's been happening around 3:30 a.m. and he barks for me, knowing I will always come at the first bark. We went to the vet on Friday. I was hysterical, as I always am now with my Herxes. We did X-rays and found nothing. His stomach was enlarged to three times its normal size because of all the air he's sucking in when he wheezes before he pukes.

This really does get me Herxing…

So this morning, I did an antibiotic drip and then set off to take him to the emergency vet (they are amazing) where I planned to have an endoscopy, a biopsy and an ultrasound. This place is an hour away.

We got halfway there and I thought, "Shit! He obviously needs to be fasting." And I had fed him this morning. I confirmed with the vet that it was a no go.

When I got home, I made him some rice. Time to switch to plain rice and chicken for a while. Of course I couldn't find my rice cooker and then I couldn't find the top to it. Then it was the measuring cup. And you can imagine the panic starting to set in. I proceeded open the cabinet of pots and pans and everything came falling out on the floor, and the crashing noise made me scream, the sound igniting a rage in me like I have not experienced in several months.

I started wailing, that kind of sobbing that comes from deep within your belly and you can't stop, the kind where you can barely speak. And I was screaming. You know, the kind where you are weeping so uncontrollably that you forget why you are crying. I talk about this like everyone knows how this is, but truthfully, I'm not sure if this is normal for everyone or just my normal. In any case, I knew right away it was a Herx. These kinds of episodes have been some of my worst neurological symptoms of Lyme.

So I am raging, wailing, sitting on the floor in a lump. But then I get pissed. Why is everything so friggin' disorganized and cluttered? So I grab a black trash bag and start throwing away everything in my kitchen island. That huge bag was full in thirty seconds. In the middle of this, I realized I will probably put myself into a seizure so I asked my mom to bring me an Ativan, which eventually calmed me down.

Now I can feel the swelling in my left frontal lobe. I feel exhausted. I feel sad. I feel so angry. I feel like I want to be a different person. I feel helpless.

Thankfully, since Gunnar's appointment didn't work out, I have nothing else on the roster but to sleep. I will try, once again, to take a nap. Maybe this time I'll be able to.

And so, my friends. the Herxes have begun. It's time to watch my layers unfold.

When Two Become One
July 19, 2012

I always dreamed that my "when two become one" would be with a soul mate. I believe in that stuff. I have a very romantic heart. Currently, my very romantic heart is plugged into a purple wire and, to be honest, we're kind of friends now.

It's been a learning curve to administer the meds and Lactated Ringers. The other night, I was so comfortable with the process that I was kind of nonchalant about it. That morning, my nurse had come to do a blood draw (through the PowerLine = so cool) and redress, which is done weekly. Well, the cap of my PowerLine used to be purple, but she put a white one on it. Not really paying attention, I finished my drip, screwed off the white cap and slowly walked over to my "triage table" to administer the saline and heparin injections.

"Hmmm," I thought to myself, "That feels kind of wet." I looked down and saw that there was blood all over my nightie and in a trail across the floor. Had this been last week, my reaction would have been to panic, grab my green folder, read furiously about what to do, call the emergency IV unit line at Dr. Jemsek's, etc. This time it was a little bit of "Here we go again."

I clamped the safety clamp to stop the blood flow and went and got the damn cap. Of course I had to ridiculously sterilize both the cap and the catheter itself because they had been exposed to the room and yeah, you don't want that stuff going straight into your jugular. Anyway, my line and I had a chat. I put on the new cap and then flushed the line again.

At this point, the long three-hour drips kind of fly by. I've figured out a schedule and it's working. In all, I feel pretty stable at the moment, but as we all know, it could change in a heartbeat. Literally. Tomorrow, I do two doses of antibiotics and then I have the weekend off. Next week, I add 500mg of Flagyl orally to the mix. That ought to be a good time.

My French Bulldog dilemma continues. I spent a total of sixteen hours this week at the emergency vet an hour away. Poor Gunnie. It's been stressful watching him be so sick. Yesterday he had an endoscopy and they found an issue that we are trying to correct with meds. We came home yesterday and he finally ate something tonight, only to puke it up thirty minutes later. That has me on edge.

My blood work came back perfect today. It's drawn every two weeks here at home to make sure my liver and kidneys are not taking a beating from the meds. Good blood work = good news. Me feeling okay = good news.

So, *let's take it!* I feel okay. I am currently *okay*, and that is a blessing. If only Gunnar would get better and if only I could get enough sleep, I'd have a really successful first month on IV meds. It feels surreal that, two and a half weeks from now I go in for round 2 and change the whole thing up just as I get into the groove. That will be interesting…

Tanked

July 21, 2012

———◈———

Betcha loved all the happy happy joy joy of the last post, huh? Get over it.

I feel like crap. I am grumpy. I am angry. I am exhausted. I think I was in pain this morning but I can't remember, because I can't remember anything. I can't find anything.

Let's break this down a little. I have been on IV treatment now for two weeks. I was told that I might not feel anything the first week, and I didn't, really, but during the second or third week, it might start to hit me. We know all of this.

There's a lot that you don't know, and I am going to share the nitty-gritty with you because, let's face it, I am not shopping for a boyfriend here and I promised to be honest. There are others going through this treatment or who are about to, so I want to keep it on the real.

———◈———

Let's start with hygiene. They told me I would be able to take showers as long as the PowerLine isn't steadily under the stream of water, so basically stand backwards. Okay, I can do that. And when I did that, my entire sterile dressing came off and I had to call in an emergency VNA visit to quickly clean up and redress the area. This is no "my Band-Aid fell off" situation. This is more like a

I-have-an-opening-right-here-to-my-heart-so-any-of-you-floating-bacteria-that-linger-everywhere-can-feel-free-to-hop-in-and-wind-me-up-in-the-hospital situation.

Okay, so no showers. What does this mean? Well, first of all, I am sorry if this grosses you out, but I can never remember if I have taken a bath or not. I think my routine is to take a shallow bath in the morning and get the job done, but I am not certain that happens every day. It depends on what's going on for the day I suppose.

Then there is the whole hair debacle that I am still trying to figure out. I was traumatized since the last open dressing event, so here's where it gets gnarly: until tonight I hadn't washed my hair in eleven days. I know. I'm sorry, but I don't want to sleep with you either, so get over it. In my downstairs bathroom I have a claw foot tub with a handheld showerhead. So it seemed logical to give it a shot.

So, I went and got dressed for my shower. Yeah, you heard me right. I got dressed to wash my hair. No way in hell was I going to allow that dressing to open and send me into a panic again, so I put on a white t-shirt to cover the dressing and figured if I got the shirt wet, the solo white t-shirt contest would indicate exactly where I would need to use sterile gauze so as not to open the bandage.

This might sound like no big deal, but I have a lot of thick hair, so washing my hair takes some time. I gave it a good go. I bent my head over the edge of the tub very uncomfortably, got my hair wet and began washing my hair. Ouch. My back hurts. Scrub, scrub, scrub. Phone rings. It's mom. "Is my Kindle in Mini's beach bag?" Me, "My head is over the tub." Click. So as I am washing my hair, I notice the water is not draining. Why? Because I have just shed half my hair into the tub. No lie, I have never seen anything like it. Yup, now I am losing my hair.

I quickly conditioned it and rinsed it out, tried not to get too choked up about my hair in the tub and searched on the floor to find my towel and then wrapped it on my head so I look like a "Mom-Mom," as Mini would say. My shirt remained dry, as did the dressing, but when I stood up, my lower back was *screaming* in pain and I could barely make my way upstairs to put my pjs on.

———◊———

Let there be sleep. I am been ordered to get fourteen to sixteen hours of sleep. I think that's what it is. I can't remember. But I am definitely not getting enough sleep. Today I was able to take a nap and it made all the difference in the world. It brightened my mood, it made me think more clearly, and I felt generally more peaceful. But the day had gotten off to a chaotic, unexpected start and I wound up driving around with Mini in an unplanned pursuit of stuff I didn't know we needed. By the time we got home at 1 p.m., I was completely spent. My plan had been to do my three-hour Lactated Ringer drip in the morning so after naps we could go to the little circus that's in town. It just didn't happen that way. I knew I needed a nap as much as Mini did, so we went straight to bed. Then Dad took her to the beach and I did the drip. By the time I was done it was 6:30 p.m. and they had ordered pizza. I went over there and brought her home around 8:00 p.m., an hour past her bedtime. So, clearly today did not work out as planned. Now I am tired but wired. Not a good combo.

———◊———

TMI – the female stuff. You may think I'm out of my mind for sharing all of this, but again, there are women going through this out there and I don't want them to think they're alone. I am also out of my mind, as we know. If you have read this far, you know that Lyme took my left ovary in the form of a 9cm endometrioma that wound me up having a C-section in February. So I only have one ovary. I also have a Mirena IUD, so I have not had a period in a couple of years.

Well, as if Lyme hasn't given me enough crap to deal with, it turns out that every time I take a dose of antibiotic, I spot a little bit. *Seriously? Really?* I have *one* ovary and it's working that hard every time I do an antibiotic drip? Yesterday I got a terrible sharp pain in my right ovary and all I could think was, "That's what's next."

The truth is, as much humor as I may find in all of this, it's really very depressing. At this point, I don't even really want to be around myself. I don't want to sit here watching TV while my parents entertain my daughter doing the fun things that I want to do with her. I don't want to be around my unshowerable self. I don't want to play dumb games on Facebook. I just want my life back. Right now, I just want my life back.

Eyebrows? Really?

July 23, 2012

My eyebrows are killing me. *Really.*

Mondays and Fridays are the days I go for a physical therapy-type massage with a massage therapist who understands Lyme. Her massages are really very different than any I've ever received, because they are perfect for my condition.

On Mondays, my dad picks up Mini at 8 a.m. and takes her to school/camp so I can fit my thirty-minute drip in before my massage. As I get further into treatment, these massages may end up occurring at my house, as it's unpredictable how I will unfold. I am thankful to have these breaks twice a week where I am forced to lay on a table and have someone care for me. Because when you are a thirty-seven-year-old single mother of a three-year-old, with two dogs (both of whom are on their own very complicated meds schedules), there is no such thing as a full night's sleep, taking a break, taking a nap for as long as you need to, much less getting fourteen to sixteen hours of uninterrupted sleep.

As I sit here, halfway through my first of two thirty-minute Meropenem drips today, I know that I have begun to Herx. I have been having some emotional responses to the treatments, the worst being on antibiotic days. I definitely am having restless leg issues, headaches, etc. But this morning I really wanted to document how I feel as the drip occurs. What changes immediately? What comes as part of the aftermath?

Now I am about twenty minutes into the drip. The worst pain I feel – and this may sound minor or weird to you, but it's no joke – my eyebrows hurt so much I feel like I want to rip them off. I feel a great increase in post nasal drip. My eyes have started burning and my vision is getting increasingly blurry. I am now getting a headache in my left frontal lobe, where they found the encephalitis on the brain SPECT scan a couple of months ago. My arms are itchy. I am starting to cough a dry, but deep cough. Most of all, I feel exhausted – to the bone.

Today, I am hoping to get a real nap in. I have gotten a taste of how solid naps have an incredible effect on my well being, but am never really able to nap into completion. I will try to buckle down and do that today. Just drop everything and sleep. Seems like the right thing to do. Sleep and let the battle occur to make way for some healing.

Lights Out!
July 24, 2012

———◦◉◦———

Tuesdays are the days that my nurse usually comes to redress my PowerLine. Again, I didn't have my usual nurse today. The one who came today is the same one who came when the dressing had completely opened last time. She is very nice, but not used to this apparatus and just sends off nervous energy. Which… makes *me* nervous.

So, she took my temperature and my vitals, as usual. And then began tugging and tearing the dressing away, albeit gently, *really* going after this thing. I have noticed all week that my skin has been itchy under the clear part of the Tegaderm. Well it became blatantly apparent that my skin *no likey* the Tegaderm. So, I am now looking for an alternative.

Tegederm reaction after two weeks – can you imagine what this will look like after nine months? The area was covered with hives. As she was cleaning that section with sterile alcohol swabs (*agony*) we heard a huge thunderstorm boom and, just like that, we were redressing the PowerLine *without* power. That's right, as if we were in a yurt, we were now forced to work using my electric lantern that I have for such moments, although when I bought this lantern, I never envisioned myself having a nurse at my house redressing a little penis-like apparatus attached to my chest.

Well, Nervous Nelly got even more high-strung and shaky. I suggested we move into the bathroom because of the skylight in there. That was much easier. My skin irritation was a real problem. I emailed Dr. Jemsek's office looking for an approved alternative. Of course, the control freak that I am, I had already done vast research all day on the subject. Seems I am not alone.

Of course, as soon as the nurse left, the lights came back on. Whatever. I then began my three-hour Lactated Ringer. These Ringers are supposed to provide some relief, but I am finding, to the contrary, that for me they seem to provoke issues. Today, my feet started burning so badly. They felt steam hot, like sausages about to burst. I didn't see much of a difference in them, but man could I feel it. So, an hour into the Ringer, I had my feet in an ice bath. Literally, a bathtub full of ice water and my feet, with me hooked up to a Ringer.

I knew then this would be a tough one and it ignited the first full-on migraine I've had in months. I called Mom, barely able to talk or think through what I wanted to say, and asked her to pick up Mini so I could try to take a nap. She could hear the strangeness of my voice and asked me if she should come over. "I don't know," I replied, which is my usual answer when I am in any kind of Lyme episode. Being such a decisive person, it puts me in a very vulnerable state to have to acknowledge that I have no idea what I need or want, and it makes me sad because I feel helpless. I don't do well with helpless.

I have found that the rest I've been prescribed is really the key to surviving this treatment. Problem is, it's hard to find or make the time to nap. I'm working more at making it happen, but the fact is, I do have to work because when all is said and done and this treatment is over, if I haven't maintained what I've spent two years building, I will come out of this with no job or income. That's just not an option.

It's also hard to fit in the naps between drips and appointments. I have now figured out a way that my hair stylist can wash my hair twice a week without me having to lean so far back that I jeopardize the PowerLine. So that is a plus.

At this point, my brain just feels tired. It's overwhelming how much there is to coordinate when you are so unable to function as it is. And then the fact that as soon as you get into a rhythm, it's time to go back to DC to change it up, add more, take away some, change days for Ringers and antibiotics, and you have to start all over again. My brain. It's just… fried.

Let the Games Begin!
July 27, 2012

———◦———

Yeah, I am soooo not talking about the start of the Olympics today…

As I lay here in bed at 6:30 a.m. with scorching feet, screaming eyebrows, and a raging migraine, I can report that I am pretty miserable. Yesterday I added two doses of orally administered Flagyl to the mix, and this morning I'm getting a taste of what a ride this next month is likely to be. I only have two more doses of the Meropenem drip and Flagyl today and then I start my ten-day "antibiotic holiday." I still have to do the three-hour Ringers every day, and will stay on all of my other oral meds, but I am looking forward to ten days of manageable eyebrow pain, headaches, upper cervical pain, sinus pressure, photosensitivity (just had to make a visor with my hand to find something in the fridge for Mini) and vision. I need the break.

I have had to call in the nurse again this morning, as my Tegaderm patch over the line was very bloody when I woke up. It's also been so itchy because I am allergic to it; I've been scratching it in my sleep. We are going to do one more dress with what I have and then hope the other samples arrive ASAP so we can make a switch. In the meantime, I've added Benadryl to the mix. Can you say "face on the floor?"

I have a massage scheduled for 2:30 p.m. today and, I have to say, it feels daunting to have to drive the eight minutes to get there. At this point, having anything on my schedule feels rough. My best days are the ones where someone else takes Mini to school; I take a sponge bath, then switch into fresh jammies. Kind of sad, I guess, but that's the best kind of day for me.

And then there are my special needs dogs. It seems I have finally found the right dose of Prozac for Brody, so he is no longer anorexic. Brody is a rescue who came to me as a puppy with major emotional damage. I worked with him for five years to rehabilitate him and make him feel more secure, but he will never be exactly "right." Anyway, I avoided going the Prozac route for all of these years until I found out I needed to go on IV. Then I gave in. Apparently he was on too high of a dose for a while, which made him anorexic. That's what the vet said. Not "no appetite," but "anorexic, as it is one of the side effects of the drug." Okay then. I have an anorexic Puggle.

And then there is my Gunnar. He's my dude. I've had him since he was ten weeks old, and he might just be the happiest dog on earth. As I mentioned, he had an endoscopy last week because of chronic vomiting and yesterday I got the results of the biopsies. Turns out he has *H. pylori* and is going on Flagyl, just like his mama! He is also going on amoxicillin and Pepto Bismol for, get this, Diffuse Chronic Lymphoplasmacytic Gastroenteritis and Inflammatory Bowel Disease. Yes, my friends, we are officially the special needs unit.

So here is the thing: I have amazing friends who have been taking care of my meals via mealtrain.com because I really do not have any sort of energy to a) go grocery shopping or b) cook. That said, I now have to cook for Gunnar, which means Brody too because he has to do everything Gunnar does. They have been on a frozen raw diet for some time now, but Gunnar is so fragile that he now eats mashed potatoes (nothing added), shredded chicken breast and like this morning, shredded organic nitrate-free beef hot dogs. *Are you kidding me?*

That is all.

Quarantine
July 27, 2012

——◦——

You thought I was done for today. No such luck.

As I mentioned this morning, I had to calmly invite the visiting nurse to come check out my very bloody, very itchy reaction to the Tegaderm – a sterile patch that protects my PowerLine from outside bacteria. If that bacteria were to get in, it would go straight to my jugular, and it could land me right in the hospital.

My nurse rearranged her schedule and put me first, getting to my home around 9:00 a.m. She removed my Tegaderm to find a pile of hives and skin conditions caused by the allergic reaction to the dressing.

Well, apparently this was a pretty serious situation. In fact, she said it was the worst she has seen. I'm such an overachiever. We sat down and talked about what to do. Having seen this brewing a few days ago, I called Dr. Jemsek's office and they have alternative dressings on their way, but we needed a plan to keep the area sterile *today*.

She decided to cover the area in sterile gauze and paper tape so the irritation can get some air. The kicker was that I had to stay in my room and upstairs bathroom all day. I was not to go down to the dogs at all. If I had to let them out, I was to cover with a tight t-shirt that would protect the entire area.

I promptly started pounding Benadryl and quercetin, a plant-derived flavonoid, and sprayed the exposed area with Benadryl spray. I have no words for how itchy it was. I emailed a picture to Dr. Jemsek's office and they responded that the nurse did the right thing. The plan was that she would come back in the early evening to figure out a more long-term solution. Dr. Jemsek had instructed us to cover the entire area that's exposed by the clear part of the tape with sterile gauze; then we should be able to tape the sides shut. We've done that and a large part of the irritated area is now able to breathe.

Once my skin calms down, the nurse will remove my sutures and we will use a stat lock to secure the line. It was comforting to hear from Dr. Jemsek's office that my nurse had done the exact right thing.

So here's what happens when I am quarantined to my room for a day:

1. I text like a teenager on her iPhone at the food court at the mall
2. I scratch my wounds
3. I take some meds
4. I watch reality TV, knowing I'm killing the few brain cells I have left
5. I drink massive amounts of electrolyte-infused drinks, mostly to have an excuse to leave the room and pee
6. I yell at my dogs to stop barking
7. I take more meds
8. I take a nap
9. I call Mom six or seven times for no good reason
10. I play dumb computer games
11. I harass my colleagues with emails
12. I worry about unnecessary things
13. I take more meds

I was so happy when my nurse returned I almost knocked her over with a hug, but that would have been human contact with my wound – a definite no-no. I don't do well with being locked in a room. Let's not have that happen again.

I have now taken my fourth and final dose of Flagyl and my final Meropenem IV drip for this round. This means this time I now get an eleven-day antibiotic holiday. *Yay! I do* have to take my neurotrophics and supplements, as well as the three-hour Lactated Ringer each day to flush, flush, flush, but this will be a much needed break from the Herxing I have been experiencing, and a time for me to gear up for my next trip, which is a week from Sunday. I have a Monday appointment for an introduction to the second, much more aggressive round of treatment.

So, here I lie, in the bed I have been in for twenty-four hours now. *Over it.* Maybe I should sleep in the playroom in protest. At least we learned something today: I am not a good candidate to live in a bubble, although I might actually need one soon.

Holiday! Celebrate!
July 28, 2012

—◦—

Today, I start an eleven-day antibiotic holiday (*Woot! Woot!*). Just in time, because this morning my stomach just started to protest that wicked Flagyl. Despite all that I have gone through during the past week, I would give myself a B on the scale of horrendous experiences. This past month the focus was on killing the free agents that were traveling in my bloodstream. Because I did eight months of oral antibiotics, I think I may have already taken care of a good portion of that.

My worst experiences have been the headaches and foot pain, but worst of *all* is the pain in the eyebrows. *So weird*, but, Lyme is known to throw curveballs at you. I do know from the introduction of the Flagyl these past two days (which has been horrendous) that this next month will pose a challenge. I foresee a lot more nights of my parents having to stay here. Another terrible symptom I have had since starting the Flagyl is incredible night sweats. Despite the A/C set as low as it would go and the ceiling fan blasting, I woke up soaked several times last night. It's a sticky, yucky kind of sweat on my whole body, but especially in my hair and neck. This is a common symptom of Babesia, a co-infection we will target this coming month, I believe. It promises to be a very rough month, but I am already feeling strong and ready to go after this.

Mini seems to be getting used to allowing others to do things Mommy usually does. That's a load off. But one thing that has been really hard for me personally is that my parents have been so great at taking care of Mini, but that no one was really taking care of me. This past week, I have felt very sad and lonely. A lot of tears have been shed.I need someone here to help me get through this. I need help with the dogs, with organization, running errands, maintaining my business, grocery shopping etc. Most of all, I need the company. And so, we welcome my new assistant into the mix. I have nothing but wonderful things to say about her. She only has two bad qualities: 1) she is terrible at merging on the highway and 2) she doesn't play Scrabble. I will have to ask her if she plays Monopoly. Other than that, she has quickly become one of my best friends and confidants. I am so happy that she will be working with me five days a week.

Okay, back to my antibiotic holiday. Even though I am off antibiotics, I am stuck at home each of these days doing three-hour Lactated Ringers, because I still need to keep up the detox flow. So, I am actually more stuck at home than I was before. Thankfully, the Olympics are on, so I have something to glue myself to the tube with.

It is amazing how much my rash has cleared up overnight from airing it out and using paper tape. The sterile area did open during the night, but I noticed it was open in the middle of the night, promptly sterilized it and closed it back up. No more itching, thankfully.

Toxic Waste Dump
July 30, 2012

Who called it a holiday? It may be an antibiotic holiday, but when I think of the word holiday, I think of fun, joy, freedom, and pretty much everything *but* what I am now experiencing.

It's strange to me that now that I am on this so-called holiday, having completed Phase 1, that I feel absolutely shattered in every sense of the word. I am so exhausted that I don't know what to do with myself. My speech is slurred and I am missing words. I have pain on the bottoms of my feet, right at the back of the arch. It is like walking on nails every time I put my foot down. My muscles were so tight today in my physical therapy massage that I could barely feel when she was digging. I am waking up with my hair sopping wet from sweats. And I'm angry. I'm so angry and miserable. I feel trapped. I want my body back. I want my mind back. I want my life back.

This week, I'm still somewhat housebound because I have to do the three-hour Lactated Ringer drip each day. So, I drop off Mini, come home and spend half my day on the drip, which means no nap, which I *really* need. I mean, I could use like a four or five hour nap each day. Not happening. Because when I get off the drip, then I have to cook for the dogs.

And the irony is, I'm not eating. I don't have any food here that I want to eat and there is nothing to eat, except what Mini eats, a regular rotation of the usual fruits, veggies, organic chicken nuggets, nitrate-free hot dogs with no "parts," or organic shepherd's pie (which I used to make for her, but now buy frozen).

Tomorrow I am going to have my hair properly washed at a salon. I can't stand feeling like this dirty unabomber-esque sloth for another second. Not only does it hurt me to hang my head over the tub to wash my hair, it makes my line insertion bleed and we all know that's no good. I'm tired of bathing up to my belly button and pretending it feels good. So, maybe I will feel better with a good hair washing twice a week. At this point, I'll try anything.

I am swelling up like a balloon and I don't know how to release all this shit that's been put into me. I feel like a toxic waste dump. I know it's all to kill the bad guys, but I can't help but feel right now like my body is a graveyard for millions of spirochetes.

And believe me, from the pain and symptoms I am feeling now, the spirochetes who are left and embedded in my tissue, muscles, bones, brain, heart, you name it, they are attending this funeral and are on high alert. These fuckers are going to fight back hard. I hope I can get through this and still have the same spirit that's always been within me, that fun, happy, smiley girl with a wicked sense of humor. That girl is quickly becoming a faded memory.

I will be relieved when I go back to DC on Sunday. I need a Dr. Jemsek fix. I need something to hold onto.

Schmoliday

August 2, 2012

———◦◦◦———

Holiday, schmoliday. I feel like crap. I had a pretty good day yesterday, but yesterday afternoon it all took an abrupt turn for the worse. I started slurring my speech and almost seeing double, and my feet were *screaming* in pain. My muscles tensed to stone and I had a headache. I couldn't keep my legs still.

I had to call my dad to bring Mini home and help me with the evening routine. Last night, I was completely worthless. As soon as Mini went to bed at 7:45 p.m., I was out like a light. Today I woke up with the same migraine, but managed to get her to school. I used to be a morning person. Now I am grumpy in the mornings and everything is very challenging for me.

I returned from dropping off Mini and hooked up immediately to my Lactated Ringer, hoping for some relief, but my eyes began to burn and my exhaustion continued. In fact, although I never was able to fall asleep today, I was in bed until 5:00 p.m. when my dad brought Mini home from playing, grocery shopping and general errands to keep her busy. I feel like every ounce of life has been sucked out of me. And the thought of having to wake up tomorrow morning just terrifies me.

I emailed my IV nurse at Dr. Jemsek's and let her know how miserable I am and said: WTF, this is supposed to be a holiday!!!????!!! Her response was, as always, very nice and reassuring:

"It's very common that when people start out on IVs they feel really bad on their off weeks. Eventually those off weeks will be when you feel the best, but your immune system isn't to that point yet so it ends up feeling like a continual Herx reaction. Resting will help the most, as will the Lactated Ringers. Make sure to do one every day while you feel like this.

"Hang in there, you're doing great. Remember to not expect anything of yourself – you just lay in bed and make everyone serve you. Your body is very busy and worn out fighting on the inside, so the less stress you can place on it the better. Hope this helps!"

So, it turns out that this holiday is like the one you find on TripAdvisor.com that looks so awesome, but when you get there it's a dump with a light bulb hanging from the ceiling and a thirty-year-old, hard mattress and a smelly, rocky beach with broken beach chairs. Yeah, this is that kind of holiday. Pretty right on, actually. This kind of holiday almost always ends up with Flagyl and Cipro.

I never thought I would say this, but I am looking forward to getting back onto antibiotics, although I know next month will be much more aggressive. Just get me out of this nearly unconscious state, *please!*

The Day of the Dragon
August 2, 2012

———◦———

So here's the thing: There's a dragon living in my esophagus.

I am pretty sure it will be the end of me. We all know that I am not the hottest piece of ass on Main Street right now. In fact, I think that 87-year-old woman I saw at the hair salon today might possibly have more swag than I do at this point. I mean, because I am sporting and unable to hide the gigantic patch above my right boob, and I am kind of limping around town in various odd ways, kind of like Ichabod Crane, only what's causing it is a crap shoot.

It could be the fact that my feet feel like they are cramped and curled into a circle, but have to walk flat. Or it could be the soleus muscle in my calf cramping. I can barely walk because of the shards of glass under my feet. Maybe my hip is out. Am I covering my eyes to create a visor because even with my sunglasses on the sun is too bright for me to see? I have never in my life felt so unattractive, or crazy for that matter.

But recently, my most bothersome symptom is certainly the gross-est of them all. Besides the unbelievable fatigue and dizziness I have experienced during this week of good times they call an antibiotic holi-day, it turns out that my esophagus is on *fire*. I am not kidding, there is a dragon in there and the most torturous part is that I take Neurontin, a neurotrophic, three times a day and I cannot take any antacids until two hours after I take the meds.

Now, my iPhone, iPad, and MacBook Air, otherwise known as my iHarem, are constantly popping up with reminders of the medications I have to take. Beep. Beep. Beep. Seven different times a day. Handful after handful of meds. And even though it's always beeping, I stare at the clock on my iPhone waiting for the two hours to have passed. At that time, I start popping TUMS like M&Ms. This has been going on for months.

I have been reading a lot about the importance of complete detoxification during this process and take it very seriously. For a couple of months now, I have been religiously drinking high alkaline juices which help to balance acidic issues that come with taking forty to forty-five pills every day. The reason I order juices from BluePrintCleanse.com is because I am too tired to juice myself. I am a juicing snob – a bit of a juicer slut, really – and have kissed many a juicer to find my prince. I love my sexy juicer, but right now it sits neglected on my counter. When I read Blue Print Cleanse's slogan, "We think. You drink," I felt I had found my soul mate. Since we all know I can't think straight, I like that they do that for me.

I am also incredibly diligent about using completely non-toxic products on my body and in my home. I have been passionate about this since even before my diagnosis. In the past two years, as I've said, I have been fortunate enough to represent a company called Ava Anderson Non-Toxic (www.AvaAndersonNH.com), a company that educates the public about the shocking lack of regulation when it comes to putting harmful chemicals in personal care and household cleaning products in America. In Europe there are 1,342 toxic chemicals banned from personal care products. In the U.S.? Just *nine*. Think about that. So while I sit here with my ball and chain "Pol-ine" (my IV pole) and do a Lactated Ringer seven days a week to detox, you bet your bottom dollar that I will do *nothing* to further the burden on my body by putting toxic products on me that instantly go into my bloodstream.

Anyway, I have been looking into what I can use to bind the spirochetes to gather them for excretion and get them the hell out of my poor body. When I ran the naturopathic doctor's office, one of the supplement lines we used was a Chinese herbal line called Zhang. I knew from that time, and was recently reminded by Dr. Steve, that Zhang's Circ P

would be a good binder and would help with my Herx reactions. And through my reading, I decided to throw chlorella, a powerful algae into the mix. Its purpose is also to bind the bastards and get them out. It's crazy powerful stuff. If you use the powder, it will turn your teeth green. Since I am not trying resemble Shrek any more than I already do, I chose the tablets.

And let me tell you, this morning I woke up and almost filed divorce papers against myself. I will try to describe this as best as I can. You will be disgusted. So, imagine waking up with this film on your tongue – I mean waaaaay back down your long tongue – that feels like wall to wall shaggy carpet. I hate wall to wall carpet in general and now it's crawling down my throat. Then, imagine that it tastes like bitter fermented fish. *Hurl…* OMG make it stop. I literally jumped out of my bed, raced to the bathroom, grabbed some mouthwash, and gargled and swished multiple times. I used my electric toothbrush, then my regular toothbrush. It wouldn't go away.

I tried to drink it away with a BluePrint Cleanse drink that I love. *Yack…* No way. Couldn't even drink a second sip. I tried some green tea. *Nothing* touched it. It changed the taste of everything, and blew wind on the fire in my esophagus. I mean clearly the chlorella has been dismissed, but it still lingers. Gunnar, my French Bulldog with severe upper GI issues, and I are sharing the Pepcid and Pepto Bismol tablets now (because someone is laughing *very* hard at me up there). I just think that's really funny. But step off the TUMS, dude. Those are mine.

On Sunday, we go back to DC for an introduction to the next round of antibiotics. This past round was the rookie, "get used to using the IV round with a single drip of Meropenem three times a week and, toward the end, the introduction of two oral antibiotics. This time, if my snooping serves me well, we will be testing to see if I am allergic to Clindamycin and assuming I am not, the next phase will likely involve two antibiotics IV drips and three or four oral antibiotics. I am about to get my ass kicked, but at least I will have slayed the dragon by then.

"Now We're Going to Stir Things Up"

August 8, 2012

———◦◦◦———

I don't know where to begin. My mind is so jumbled and I have wanted to write since we got back, but I have to say, things are different now. I feel it. Now I am really in treatment.

I realized last month, at the end of treatment that while I was definitely feeling the Herx reactions to the IV meds, that that month was really designed to get me used to using the IV and to my newest body part, my PowerLine. So, I knew this was coming.

Since I don't know where to begin, I will just start from the beginning.

The trip was awful. Dad and I left promptly at 12:30 p.m. to get to the airport two hours away. We had already checked in and only had carry-ons, so we expected to be up and away at 4:00 p.m. You may remember last month when we boarded that exact same flight, Sunday at 4:00 p.m., and we got on the plane, buckled up and then they announced that there was a ground stop and we ended up waiting on the plane for an hour and a half before taking off. Well, this time we boarded the plane, buckled up and were then told the same thing, although this time they let us off the plane.

We waited an hour, then another hour. After four hours we finally left, at 8:00 p.m. It was miserable, but we both got a lot of work done. I have to say that it took a very hard toll on my physical and mental state.

By the time we checked into the hotel at 10:15 p.m., I thought I wouldn't be able to take another step. Another fifteen minutes and I think I would have collapsed. And that is exactly what I did when I got to my room.

My appointment was at 10:40 a.m. the next morning, and it was completely magical for me to sleep through the night until 8:00 a.m.

The next morning. I need to do more of that, ahem, Mini. So we went to breakfast, packed our suitcases and made our way to Dr. Jemsek's Clinic. It was as if the hotel stay never happened. I was completely unconscious there.

As usual, they called us in right on time, which still amazes me every time. The first thing they do upon arrival is weigh you. *Miserable.* You might remember "The Fat Zone" Dr. Jemsek mentioned in the last appointment. Well, I know all about that. I had gained two pounds, better than the four I had gained last time and the sweet nurse's assistant who is used to patients dreading this part just said, "You gained two pounds with your clothes on." She was very sweet.

They took my blood pressure lying down, sitting up, and standing up, all of which were fine. Then my infusion nurse, the sweetest, most even-keeled person I have met, came in and we got right to it. She noticed right away that my PowerLine area was a war zone. "Okay, we need to do something about this," she announced.

She hooked me up to the new IV medication I am adding to the cocktail – Clindamycin. Thankfully, I had no reaction to this medication either. During the infusion, she removed my gnarly and very bloody dressing, and then removed my sutures, which I had reacted severely to for some reason, giving me hives at each suture site. It then took her fifteen swabs to clean all of the blood off the line and my skin. Once she removed the sutures, she attached a stat lock, as predicted. It is *much* more comfortable and stable. I kind of regretted the tunic I was wearing, as it wasn't easy enough access. To any of you who may be going through this, I highly recommend buying breastfeeding shirts, which make it very simple to access the line without having to strain or get undressed.

She then dressed the sterile field with the new Sorbaview dressing which I can tolerate, thank goodness. So, right now, I am much more comfortable with my line. We commented to the RN about the office and its calm, stable environment. She explained that it is very much intentional, that their patients have a lot of trauma and many of us (like me) are very sensitive to sound. For that reason, there is no real expression of emotion. No belly laughs. There are smiles and support, but above all else, there is monotone stability. And I love that. It makes me feel very safe and comfortable.

We chose this appointment date based on my father's work schedule and knew I would not see Dr. Jemsek this time, but the Physician's Assistant who joined us at my first appointment. She is a very smart, very adept woman, clear and concise. It is easy to communicate with her and she is a fantastic listener. Just like Dr. Jemsek, when I explain symptoms to her, she is able to give me actual explanations for these reactions and often diagnoses as well.

Since I am sharing it all, here is the list of things I wanted to discuss with her:

- Forgot to add Septra at end of cycle (it *was* on my calendar)
- Severe Tegaderm reaction – better with Sorbaview
- Sticky sweats, mostly at night but daytime too; especially face, neck and head
- Very hot, swollen feet –severe
- Acid reflux in esophagus – severe
- Full body muscle tension – severe
- Skull muscle pain – severe
- Eyebrow pain – severe
- Anger – periodic
- Depression – constant in varying degrees
- Blurry vision – moderate
- Trouble with balance – occasional

- Trouble napping (decreasing morning Cortef from 10mg to 5mg seems to help) – always
- New ACA on bottoms of big toes, very painful, now gone. Hand ACA continues – now gone – was like they had been on a cheese shredder
- New exotoses found by massage therapist under right middle finger on palm side – mild issue
- Extreme exhaustion – severe and constant
- Fifteen minutes into Lactated Ringer, my eyes itch and I have to poop
- Restless legs – day and night – moderate
- Headaches in left frontal lobe – feels like swelling outside my skull – moderate
- First weeks every time I've started an antibiotic drip started to spot period
- *Very* sound sensitive and I often cannot finding things – both can set me into a rage (I guess many of these things sounded like regular Herx reactions.

She wrote everything I said down, but one thing she touched on was my depression. She asked, as they always must, if I had had suicidal thoughts. I answered no, but that I have often thought and even said, "Just wake me up when this is over." It's a sad, but not dangerous thing to feel.

I told her that I have been crying *a lot*. I mostly cry when I am in a parasympathetic position, lying down. But I can be sitting on the couch, perfectly fine and then all of a sudden tears start streaming down my face. I told her that I don't know that there is anything that triggers it and that I don't necessarily feel sad until the tears start and then *that* makes me sad and it gets worse. I was amazed to hear from her that she believes I have been having limbic seizures. In fact, I had had one during the beginning of the appointment when the aid asked me to lie down to take my blood pressure. My tears just started streaming out of nowhere. My dad looked at me lovingly, thinking it was sadness and stress, while I lay there wondering why there were tears flowing. So strange. It was kind of shocking to hear it was a seizure. When my dad heard that, he went, "*Whooooa.*" But all of a sudden it made so much sense.

Limbic seizures are anxiety-based and obviously that has been an issue for me my entire life. My mind runs on high-voltage and when the batteries run out, I collapse. This all makes sense to me. Now I am just sitting on a drip all of the time and my mind is finally able to react to the war going on in my body. I do see it as a kind of neurological mourning. It's strange that there is a physical diagnosis for what has been happening, but as always, I believe that health is physical, mental, emotional, and spiritual, and it is all linked.

As a result of this, my Lamictal and Neurontin doses have been increased. Dr. Jemsek increased them before and I felt extremely drugged, so I decreased them on my own, with their consent. Now that I have been on them a while, I can tolerate the higher dose.

Then we began to discuss the next phase of treatment for the next four weeks. As you now know, Dr. Jemsek uses an approach called "pulsing" so that the antibiotics aren't as harsh on the body as they might be if you attack the body with them daily for months at a time. It's supposed to be easier on the body, but the IV treatments are enough to make side effects noticeably severe. In Dr. Jemsek's approach to pulse treatment this month, my antibiotics days are Monday, Wednesday and Friday, just as they were last month. On the "off" days, I do the three-hour Lactated Ringer, which is supposed to help flush out the toxins by adding a liter of a saline-like solution only with less sodium and more electrolytes. I thought these would make me feel better, but honestly I feel like a truck has hit me when I do the Ringers.

This month, we begin to address the Babesiosis, also known as Babesia. From my work with Dr. Steve, I know that Babesia causes a lot of neurological symptoms: anger/rage, sadness, hallucinations, etc., many of which I experience. It also can cause severe sweating, especially night sweats. All of these symptoms can and tend to *increase* during treatment, in addition to the joint pain, muscle tension, headaches and exhaustion. Babesia is hell.

I will also add another antibiotic infusion, Clindamycin, which is a thirty-minute drip that I infuse *after* my thirty-minute Meropenem drip, which I have been doing since I started IV therapy. This means that my antibiotic treatment will lengthen to an hour, twice a day. This of course affects both my morning and evening schedules, as on two of the days I have my physical therapy massage at 9:30 a.m., so my parents will need to take Mini to school so I have time to do the drip before my appointment. It also complicates the evenings, because Mini is now falling asleep around 8:30 p.m. after I put her down at 7:45 p.m. She often gets up, as any three-year-old does, and wants things. I really need to be still when I do the infusions, so I have to wait until she is asleep to do it, which keeps me up later than I am often able to stay awake.

We also added the oral antibiotic Septra to the three-day schedule for this first week and for the rest of the month. Next week I will add Mepron, an anti-malarial drug which has been shown to be very effective in treating Babesiosis, but is also a pretty brutal drug that can cause chills, hallucinations, paranoia, etc. Many people cannot tolerate it. I have taken a similar drug in the past and had to stop it because my body completely broke down. We'll see how it goes this time, now that my neurological state is more balanced and my immune system (while still pretty much non-existent) is waking up. I'm a little reluctant about that one.

And finally, during the last Thursday and Friday of the third antibiotic treatment of this round, I add the dreaded Flagyl, sure to help me lose a couple of pounds. Not a good time.

It's a lot, and it's overwhelming at first, but now that I'm in my fourth month of taking so many pills, it's kind of second nature. I have finally accepted now that my situation reaches beyond the scope of naturopathic treatment and I gotta do what I gotta do.

Once we discussed the meds and what was going to happen, we thanked the Physician's Assistant. After our intentionally monotone, calm appointment, she looked us dead in the eyes as if to relay a *very* clear message and said, "Now we are going to stir things up." Dad and I looked at each other.

When she left, Dad said, "Well, that was a loaded statement." We knew that the month ahead was likely to be very ugly. That was our warning.

After she left, we proceeded to engage in Season Two of "The Real Weeds." That is, as always, we brought another empty suitcase, which we proceeded to fill with all of my IV meds, tubing, dressings, new prescriptions, and a letter for the airline screeners to let me through with my atomic liquids. It was way heavier than last time and my dad was once again my Sherpa.

With that, our time in DC came to a close, much earlier than expected. When we got to the airport, we had a twist of fate and actually got onto an earlier flight. *Yay!* The trip home went swimmingly, and I got home in time to put Mini to bed.

After she fell asleep, I knew I had to ignore my exhaustion and get organized right away while the information was fresh, as my new antibiotic schedule would begin the next morning. I proceeded to create documents to help spell it out for me when my mind is blurry. Which is almost always. Which is sure to get worse on this intense treatment.

I did my first August antibiotic treatment and, I can tell you right now, my whole body felt so heavy from my head down. It was truly like one of those fun house compartments where the roof is coming down on you, only this roof didn't stop. I felt so *heavy* all day and my muscles all scrunched; I could barely walk and I got my first migraine in months.

And so, the continued fight against Lyme and the commencement of my war against Babesia has begun. The battleground is my body. I am not scared about what's to come, but I am worried. And once again, even though I have so much support from everyone, only I know how this feels. I feel *very* alone.

Expect the Unexpected
August 12, 2012

———◦———

I was told to expect the unexpected. This phrase symbolizes my whole life. I've always been a "fly by the seat of my pants, Type A" kind of girl, an oxymoron, I know. While I have been comfortable, or even motivated by this phrase in the past, right now I just want a list of what's going to happen. Anticipation and surprises are no longer on the menu of fun.

So, as usual, while expecting the unexpected, I came up with some expectations. *Sigh...* I anticipated having to race to the bathroom all day, constant body pain, and exhaustion. While I have had some of that, just one week into the treatment and with three antibiotics still to come in the next two weeks, it's been pretty easy – with a few exceptions, of course.

My massages and physical therapy are excruciating now. My entire body is like a rock, but so far I am so lucky to have an intuitive, effective massage therapist who has Lyme herself and knows where to go and how to deal with it. My soleus muscle on the bottom part of my calf has been a major source of pain, especially on my left leg. It's extremely painful when she works out the muscle, but I have learned that when the spirochetes die they gather in the feet and calves – *gag* – which would explain the extreme swelling and change in muscle texture.

A muscle at the bottom of my skull that attaches to my trapezius muscles is also hard as a rock. It's so hard for her to get in there. We have been using hot stones, which seems to help. Lyme doesn't like heat, so we use it a lot. I wish I could use the sauna in my basement right now, but it makes my sterile dressing fall off and that leaves a risk for serious infection. So, my twice weekly hour and a half massages are no luxury. Believe me, this is not a massage to be envious of.

My feet continue to be a problem, but they are not as hot as they have been in the past, mostly just swollen and hard to walk on. Some days are worse than others; I am not sure why that is. I am trying to figure out a pattern to it that corresponds to the meds schedule, but because I have Lyme, I always forget to make note of it.

Mostly I feel the weight of a thousand elephants sitting on the top of my head, weighing me down in exhaustion. I feel no motivation to do anything, except sit in the corner of my couch under a blanket (it's been 85° and humid here) with my three little creatures around me. Iced Earl Grey tea motivates me. It's always exciting when I make it to the kitchen to create one of those masterpieces.

So yeah, I am tired. And my speech and memory are greatly affected. I am finding it much harder to type, often hitting the wrong letters on the keyboard, which has never happened before. I am also losing vocabulary. There are many times that I can't remember what I want to say. What some of you may call a "senior moment" is a senior state for me. In a sense, I do fear some level of dementia. I have to rely so much on my phone reminders that it's concerning. The one thing I never forget about is Mini. Thankfully, somehow I am able to continue to be a good mommy.

My anger seems to be better, I think. I think this is because we increased the Neurontin and Lamictal as a result of my limbic seizures. So, happier mood makes for a happier mommy, which makes for a happier kid.

My biggest concern at the moment now lies with the diagnosis I got two visits ago, when Dr. Jemsek told me I have Acrodermatitis Chronica Atrophicans (ACA) a potentially serious skin disorder. I currently have it on the palm side of my hands, mostly on my fingers, but it's starting to appear on the palm as well. The Wikipedia explanation of this condition totally freaks me out. Here's one of the jewels of the definition:

"The course of ACA is long-standing, from a few to several years, and it leads to extensive atrophy of the skin and, in some patients, to the limitation of upper and lower limb joint mobility."

OK, let's discuss this for a minute because I kind of fear that this could happen to me on my hands. Since I first noticed the peeling and painful cracking of the skin, it's quickly progressed into a thicker, larger, and certainly more painful state.

The area can swell, creating a thicker layer of skin, which makes it stiffer to move and when I extend my fingers, the skin is actually starting to tear, as if I have cut myself to the bone. The level of pain this induces in indescribable, especially on the new split of my pinky finger, which is becoming a deeper and deeper sore.

It can start by looking like a paper cut, but it's really bigger and deeper than that and, let me tell you, every time I go to wash my hands (which is about every five minutes) I literally wince in pain, and squeeze it until the pain stops. It's brutal. I have emailed my assigned RN to see if there is a cream that can help me with this. My Clobetasol cream that I once used for psoriasis, which has since cleared up since my neurological meds treatment began, does not help at all. It seems from Wikipedia that the way to treat it is with antibiotics. Um… I happen to have some of those handy. Not working.

The other thing: bruises appearing all over the place, likely from the nighttime when I am bouncing into walls trying to get Mini back to bed or if I am going to the bathroom. Thing is, I never have any idea where they come from. I look like I have been mugged and beaten. I have deep, dark, black bruises the size of my fist popping up on my legs and around my body.

My loneliness has been somewhat alleviated by my assistant (who we have now decided needs a better title so we very tongue in cheek refer to her as the "Director of Operations") who is here fifteen hours a week to help me with everything, especially keeping my business going. But we also just hang out and talk about *US Weekly* stuff too, which for me is really nice. I really can't go out right now and I appreciate the company.

My Gunnar is doing much better. He has successfully one-upped me with four doctors – regular vet, specialist/surgeon, nutritionist, holistic vet, and a veterinary compound pharmacist. My father asked me the other night if he has a spiritualist yet. *Snort!* He's been on his new meds for three days now, and I have been making him a potato and chicken meal until yesterday, when I received his new diet from his nutritionist. It's pretty amazing how much food I am to prepare for him. When you make homemade food, the quantity is honestly more than I eat and he only weighs thirty pounds. But he likes it and he's not puking, so that's a good thing.

Here's the problem: my hands are cracked in half and the dogs eat a bag of potatoes every other day (no joke) and 450 grams of ground turkey per dog per day. I have to peel these potatoes before baking them, which is a pain in the ass itself, but to do it with the ACA, it's just torture. I have taken to wearing latex gloves, which helps a bit, but I bought a potato peeler from Amazon last night and am anxiously awaiting it arrival. I will also be getting a big freezer for the basement so I can make the food three weeks at a time. Really?

In all, I have to say that I feel moderately stable at this time and have no issues with my infusions. It's second nature now and I just get it done and move on with my day. If only I could get more sleep. And hire a potato peeler.

"There Better be Diamonds in This Bottle"

August 15, 2012

I'm serious. There better be diamonds in that frigging' bottle.

I posted a provocative status on Facebook yesterday which seemed to wake some people up to the absurdity that chronic Lyme disease is not acknowledged by the ISDA and, as a result, many of my meds are not covered by insurance and I will say, I have the best insurance I think one can get!

Here was the status:
My Lyme experience since August 6, 2012
Travel to last appointment = $1000
Actual appointment + IV meds = $6500
Prescription medications picked up today = $2000
Total in the past week: $9500
Can you afford to have Lyme?

That's right kids, I have spent nearly $10,000 on this in a week. It's astonishing really. Now it makes sense that so many people have to choose between financial ruin and/or suffering unnecessarily. Does that piss you of as much as it does me?

So, on Monday I asked my assistant to drive fifteen minutes away to the big pharmacy/grocery store and pick up some groceries and my meds. I knew this would be a big one, because I am now on the anti-malarial drug Mepron. Unfortunately, I know from past experience taking a similar drug that insurance tends to cover about five days of a malaria treatment and I will obviously need more than that, so I was prepared. I forgot to tell her that. When she got to the pharmacy, she called and said, "It's $568. Is that right?" And I said, "Oh yes, I was ready for it to be some ridiculous amount. Go ahead and give them the check."

And so she came home and put away all of my groceries (love her) and after a while I hobbled down the stairs on my feet which have those shards of glass beneath them again and went to open the bag. Mind you, I had already missed a dose of this because the prescription never made it to the pharmacy, so time was of the essence to stay on track for the next visit.

I opened the bag and saw a bottle of Abilify, which has been suggested to add to my toxic waste dump to help stabilize my mood. Although now that we have upped Neurontin and Lamictal (epilepsy/neurotrophic meds) I am actually quite positive these days. Anyway, *Abilify*, not Mepron. "Shit, they forgot to send home the expensive one." And then I started looking at the receipt. Holy crap. This IS an expensive one. I called the pharmacy right away and said, "There should be some Mepron waiting for me there too." Response, "Oh, yes, it's here and one other thing is waiting for you. I should tell you the Mepron is going to be $1229." *Whaaaaat???*

Such a cliché, but I am not often speechless.

Here is my reaction: "…" Then, after an uncomfortable many seconds of silence, I said, "Okay. Well, I need it, so I will send my assistant back to get it," and so off she went and, just like that, I had spent $1900 in one day on oral meds.

So, rather than go into an unpleasant Lyme rage and bring you all down, I decided to think of things that I could have injected into my jugular or swallowed for the same price. I did a little research in a slight Lyme rage.

Here are some ideas:
Mepron $1229

- I could've booked two round-trip tickets from Boston to Stockholm.
- Oh! Oh look! I could stay for *seven nights* at Canyon Ranch.
- Here's one! Mini and I could fly *and* stay at Disney World for six nights.

Okay, so that sucks.

But let's check out the cost of the last appointment?
I wonder what we could do for that?
Ahhhh – there we go. $6500 worth of IV meds and related supplies.

- I could get a 2012 Hyundai.
- Oooooh, look! I could go to Bali with my secret (nonexistent) lover!!!!
- This sounds appealing: Nine Day Indonesia Culture and Beaches: "Be immersed in an exotic land of coconut palm fringed beaches, golden temples, ancient traditions and ancient ruins with this private tour of Bali, Yogyakarta (Java), Borobudur, Surakarta. Enjoy spellbinding dance ceremonies, colorful markets, hot springs, private guide & driver & luxurious hotels." Flights not included.

But hey, there's always the Mepron/Diamond Water I could sell on the black market to pay for the airfare.

Namaste

So, when I hook myself up tonight, I will try to appreciate the feeling of the Hyundai being shoved into my jugular. Hyundai has come a long way, after all. And it's fuel-efficient. We like that.

And when I take my oral meds tonight and get to the Mepron Diamond Water Collection part of it, I will just smile, knowing that I have just swallowed Mickey, Minnie, Goofy, Donald, Daisy, and the whole gang in one magical experience for my Mini.

Halfway through IV Phase Two
August 18, 2012

I was afraid of this stage of treatment. I feared that my system would be overloaded with so many antibiotics that I would not be able to function, would be in great pain, and a neurological mess. I was afraid that I would be stuck in the bathroom with terrible diarrhea for a month. I was afraid I would be depressed and cooped up.

Now that I am halfway through this phase, dare I say I actually feel good? Because I think I do. When this all began, my parents were fully prepared to have to sleep over often, yet through the whole thing, I have managed to get by with only three nights of them being here. I am still too tired to cook and I spend most of my days on the couch working when I am not in appointments, but I actually feel okay. I think I could say I even feel positive at times.

My hands are still peeling, but I have figured out that an antibiotic cream and a moisturizer followed by Band-Aids is a great help.

I can credit all of this to a few things. First, I think having jacked up my neurological meds seems to have done wonders. Now that I am on them, I am honestly not sure how I ever functioned without them. It seems all my life I have had limbic seizures and interpreted them as sadness and depression. I think I can even recall some times in my life that could actually have been a-typical seizures, like the time I got stuck in the middle of the road in Stockholm. I now believe many of my anxiety attacks, though not all of them, have been seizures. I think my brain is so happy to have help now. That makes me feel very, very happy.

I also credit my relentless determination to follow Dr. Jemsek's orders. The Lactated Ringers are not required, but I do them on *every* off day when I am not taking antibiotics. This three-hour detox drip keeps me hydrated and keeps things flowing. They cost $36 for twelve, so it's an amazing way to flush. They make me tired and make my feet hurt a lot and sometimes I experience other body aches, but I would suggest to anyone going through IV therapy that you request your doctor to prescribe the Lactated Ringers to do on your non-antibiotics days.

Next week, I add in two more antibiotics, totaling two IV and four oral antibiotics. Then on the last two days, Thursday and Friday, I add Flagyl. That's a lot. But the week after I have another ten-day antibiotic holiday before I travel back to DC to begin Round 3. The last holiday was a nightmare. I felt worse than I had when I was taking the Phase 1 antibiotics.

Right now as I write this, I am halfway through a Ringer. I'm experiencing restless legs and have to stretch them a lot, I feel tired and my muscles feel tight, but I'm okay. And I will happily take okay.

Lymeopolitan
August 21, 2012

———— ◈ ————

"Now we're going to shake things up," said the IV nurse as she ended our last appointment. She was right. Though I glided through the first two weeks of Phase 2 with relative ease (relative being the keyword), I now find myself in a heavy pit. And I mean heavy.

There should be a drink named after this. I am not sure if I have been shaken or stirred. It seems to be a combination of both, but I am pretty sure that this Lyme cocktail of forty-seven pills a day and nine IV bags a week should have a name. The Lymeopolitan, perhaps? All I know is it makes Harry Nilsson come to mind. The theme song in my head is, "You put the Lyme in the coconut and shake it all up." Seems kind of apropos.

It began last night at about 6:30 p.m. I had not even taken my evening IVs yet, but it swooped in and took over with a vengeance. I looked at my three-year-old and said, "Mommy is so tired, Mini. *So tired*. We need to start your bedtime routine now." It was an hour earlier, but my girl saw that I needed to do it and gave me no resistance at all. She watched me for the first time as I went through my own evening process; giving the dogs their various medication in meatballs, with their stuffed animals; closing the blinds; turning everything off, etc. And then we went up and she was no problem to get to bed.

I believe my last bit of adrenaline got me through that bedtime routine. Once I got out of her room, my vision blurred, my arms and head felt noticeably heavy and I recognized what was to come.

I took my temperature. It was 100° F, which is when I am supposed to call Dr. Jemsek. I decided to wait until after my IV drip to see if anything changed. My temperature was back to normal after the two drips.

You know it triggers me when I can't find things and of course, at this worst moment, I could not find my iPhone, which has all of my notes for my schedule, all my numbers, etc. I looked everywhere. Even in the garage.

When I gave up, I called my dad and told him how I was feeling. and right then and there I began a limbic seizure. Tears from nowhere turned into uncontrollable wailing and distress. Dad asked if I wanted him to come over and I answered the usual, "I don't know," because in that state there is no possibility of making a decision. So he came over and sat on my bed and rubbed my knee as I sat through an IV. "I don't want to do this anymore," I said. "I know. I know," he replied.

He went to find my phone, knowing it was driving me crazy. He found it deep under a sofa cushion – where it always is, by the way. He asked if I was ready for him to go home. I said yes, but I really wanted him to stay. I took my evening meds, had several more seizures, and finally fell asleep. I vaguely remember bouncing into the walls and losing my balance sometime that night, but I can't remember when or why, probably to go to the bathroom.

Today I lie here completely shattered. I can barely move. I continue to have periodic limbic seizures, crying all day. My nurse came today to change my dressing and, for the first time, we had to do it with me lying down. My legs are numb, and I can barely walk. My eyes are blurry, so I am not seeing well. I am completely and utterly exhausted beyond any description I can come up with.

I haven't been able to sleep yet, because the nurse was here and that takes a while. Then I had to do the three-hour Lactated Ringer drip, which I just now finished. Now I am having trouble taking a deep breath, I can barely see, and I am definitely not walking well. Thankfully, my parents are helping with Mini today.

This is a very unsettling, but not unexpected part of this journey. As Dr. Steve said this morning, "It's all good. It's a battle and you are winning. That bacteria is fighting back – and dying."

Nice to Meet You!

August 24, 2012

Wait, who are you? *Ohhh*, my best friends. Right. Well, nice to meet you. Where am I again? Wait, what is this I am writing? *Oooooh*, a book. What's a book? Why am I writing it? Oh, okay. Thanks.

That's pretty much how I am right now. *Zero memory*. It's pretty scary actually. I remember a movie like this, although, ahem, cannot remember which one, but it was about a guy with amnesia who got flashbacks and put the pieces of his life back together with those flashbacks. Okay, so I'm not *that* bad, but my short-term memory is *zilch*.

If Only I Could Remember What They Were

I have a full and detailed memory of my life, it's just the here and now that has me totally baffled. What to do when, who I should contact for what, etc. I put it all on my phone calendar, but a lot of things change in my business and when they change, I write in the new time, but often forget to erase the old one. I can be in the middle of a sentence and completely forget what I am talking about.

And then there are the really personal moments that I find kind of devastating. I am never really sure when I have bathed last. I try to do it every morning, but even when I remember to do it, I can't remember if I did it later on. I definitely cannot remember if I have eaten anything, except when I am taking Mepron, because I was told to eat Nutella with that because you need to eat something fatty. As an unpaid spokesperson for Nutella, I can attest to the fact that one does not forget when one eats Nutella.

In any case, my weeks are jumbled. My days are jumbled. My timing is fine though, because I have alarms set all day to remind me of things. I will have full-on conversations with people and then vaguely remember them. A good example of this happened yesterday when Mini asked if she could play a PBS game on the iPad. "Sure," I said. "But I can't, Mom. You took it away." "No, I didn't." And right then I had a flashback to a tantrum she'd had and that I had, indeed, taken it away. Thank goodness part of that flashback included where I put it, so I found it and all was well with the world.

These types of things were occasional occurrences that led me to start testing unsuccessfully for Lyme in 2005, occasional instances. Right now, they are happening dozens of times, a day. As a result, I have called in the reinforcements and my parents are now switching off to stay with us overnight or stay until bedtime and come when we wake up.

I am finding it hard to keep up with my business at the moment, which is scary because my work is commission-based. I am just not able to manage a team of hundreds of people the way I once did. And this is very sad for me because I have worked very hard to create a solid business for myself. While it continues to move along nicely, it really should be skyrocketing by now. And although I feel very fortunate to have a job that I can do 95% in my pajamas in bed or on the couch, it's still hard for me to swallow the fact that things don't come as easily to me anymore.

The other glaring (pun intended) symptom that is getting to be unmanageable is my eyesight. I need to go this afternoon to get my glasses. My vision is getting increasingly blurrier by the second. I've had 20/20 vision my whole life. And now… glasses, but hey, if they work, I am all over it. I can't read right now and I am having a very hard time typing. Typo after typo and I miss keys I never used to miss. I can't really even see the TV in my room anymore. I certainly can't see the menu if I pull that up. I have to walk right up to the screen to see anything at all. Books are out, although I can magnify the text on my iPad, which is working, for now, but I am sure the electronic reading is not good for me at the end of the day.

I have people around me showing me they care at every bend, and I know many Lyme patients don't have this. I really feel for them because, even with all of this support, I feel completely isolated in a world of my own, staring out my window at the trees. My parents want to understand my "mood," my anger and sorrow that comes barreling out of me at any given moment, but they just can't seem to get it. I am lovingly offered "ways to communicate my emotions," but they just don't get that I can't modify my reactions. It just comes out in its raw form, no matter how hard I try. I am fully aware of how things are coming out, but even then, I have no filter. It is what it is.

Sorry for this downer, but it's real. And it will likely get worse, if I am able to write at all.

Just "Poopin'" It All Out There
August 25, 2012

Yes, my friends, this is where we get to the *really* TMI (too much information) version. So far, I have tried to spare you, but guess what? If it's happening I have to write about it, because that was my commitment to you. We're going to talk about poop now. My poop. So if this is an issue for you, skip ahead. I know my friend Katherine in Germany will love this. She loves to talk about poop.

We all know I am *undateable* right now. If you read this and don't want to date me, don't worry – I get it. If you don't want to date me, much less *marry* me, then the feeling is probably mutual, because I have to say, in retrospect, this is pretty bad ass (pun intended).

Holy crap. And I mean this literally, because only such a vast amount of crap could be holy. On the "gut front," I have done very well, thank you. Yes. I have seen a change in my bowels throughout treatment, but I am like the spokesperson for probiotics, so I have been *really* good about taking all of my supplements, which includes high-dose, prescription-grade probiotics. Let's be clear, yogurt and kim chee are not touchin' this.

I had glided pretty well through the first two weeks of the month. I mean, I felt pretty positive. I was able to a have clear thought or two, I wasn't completely miserable, and my weekly blood draws were coming back perfect. Then I started Artemisinin about a week ago, which immediately knocked me on my ass. And I stayed there. What a nightmare of a week it's been. I have written of the memory crisis and all of the other stuff that came along with that *sixth* antibiotic I was taking this month, but it was the addition of the *seventh* that got me *off* my ass, several times…an hour.

I am not going to go into some crazy Poop Chronicles descriptions, but I can say it's been obnoxious, annoying, painful, confining, and… amusing. There have been times when it has come so fast that I have not been sure I would make it. Thankfully, I have. But you know me, always looking for ways to crack myself up, and so now every time I am in a "questionable" situation of timing, running through my house, sometimes with an IV pole in tow, I can't help but welcome my newest theme song into play, the theme song to *Chariots of Fire*.

Good night, all. I will think of you during the many times tonight that I will be running barefoot through the crashing waves.

Lesson in Asking For and Accepting Help
September 1, 2012

———◦◦◦———

This is the longest I have gone without writing. I have to say it's scary, as it's because I have forgotten, for several days, that I am even writing a book at all. I've found that during the last two to three weeks, I have close to no short-term memory at all. I can tell when I ask people questions that I have once again forgotten something. They either look at me with surprise or pity. I forget things all day, even the basics. I forget if I have bathed. I forget if I have called someone. I can't remember what I did during the morning, if I have already done my drips or taken my meds, etc. For me, this is becoming rather devastating because my sharp mind and wit have always defined me. I told my father yesterday that I feel like I have dementia.

I know this started the moment I took that first dose of Artemisinin during week three of Phase 2. I am still able to walk, but often it's *very* slowly and my balance is way off. I find this to be especially true when I am getting out of the car. Because I was so inconsolable last month, once I was into the halfway point of this phase, I added Abilify to stabilize my mood. Thankfully, it seems to be working. While I am sometimes having trouble walking and getting around and cannot remember my own name, I'm not as much of a witch in the morning, and that is a great relief.

This disease manifests itself differently from person to person. Some people lose mobility, others lose their cognitive functions. Many of us have symptoms of lupus, MS, rheumatoid arthritis, etc. No two Lymies will ever experience the same symptoms or treatment. Now that I'm into treatment, and taking into consideration what I learned working in a Lyme clinic for several years prior to diagnosis, I am able to see what would probably have happened to me as a result of the Lyme. I believe that because of the raging onset of my symptoms again last year (they've come and gone for twenty-six years), I was on Lyme's path of destruction. One thing is for sure: if I had not gotten diagnosed and begun to immediately treat this disease properly with a Lyme-literate doctor, I believe that by the time I would have turned forty three years from now, I would have some level of actual dementia and certainly an incorrect MS diagnosis. A scary thought, but one that makes me feel lucky as I struggle through this treatment.

I have been on antibiotic "holiday" (yeah, right) for a week now and I can say it is truly horrendous. I am *so tired* I can barely pick my head up sometimes. Some days I can't drive. I'm able to decipher right away which days those are. My hands, which had gotten a bit better during the first two weeks of Phase 2, are now peeling horribly, on my fingers in particular, which are starting to look like sausages that might pop. The skin has gotten very hard and red. I have actually gotten a couple of migraines this month, one of which I feel coming on now. My legs have been very achy and my feet feel swollen and hot. Sometimes I soldier through it and sometimes, like today, I just look at my mom and cry. And then I know it's a limbic seizure, because I don't feel sad. But then I *get* sad because I'm crying and am aware that I am having a seizure. It's a strange "chicken or the egg?" puzzle that I don't bother to try to figure out anymore. It is what it is.

I have always been a very proud person, self-sufficient and independent. This has somewhat changed over the past few years as my disease progressed without diagnosis. It's been incredible to see who has stood up and reached out to help me with words of love and support, meals, visits, and many other things.

This week, one of my best friends left her husband and one-year-old behind to come and stay with me for two nights to help me out and give my parents a break. I think it was amazing of her to do this and I am so grateful that my parents had even a few days to exhale. Red, as I call her, is Mini's godmother and we really haven't seen much of one another in the past year or so, because we live four hours from one another, and I have never been well enough to make the drive, especially with a three-year-old. But she made the drive and took right over, which she's been trying to do for fifteen years, but I would never let her because, my friends, in case you haven't noticed, I am a control freak.

This time was different. I actually asked her to do things, get things, and play with Mini. They went to the beach, to the playground, rode Mini's bike, etc. We also managed to go out to dinner, something which made me feel human again. Mini loves refried beans, so we went to the "Taco Place," which is actually a really authentic Mexican restaurant. I mean, we went at 4:30, but we went. I felt so well cared for and knew Mini was having a blast in great hands, bonding with her godmother.

And what I learned from this was the culmination of many recent experiences: allowing people into my life on a level I have rarely been open to. I have always been the one to help. Beyond allowing my parents to help sometimes in a very controlled manner, I feel I have now surrendered, pocketed my ego, and become very honest with myself about my current situation and my needs. It's been very humbling, but I feel that once I decided to go all in and admit I need all kinds of various assistance, it came to me.

I do not see this as my own lesson, but a lesson for us all in identifying our vulnerabilities and opening our arms to embrace them. We are all human. We have different needs, backgrounds, and beliefs. We will all accept and reject situations differently. I've found great emotional power within by letting others in to see a part of me that many have never known existed. I am not embarrassed anymore. I am learning a lesson, which is my responsibility to share. I urge you to lean into your discomfort and give it a try. Acknowledge what is blocking you. Is it fear of being *truly* seen? Is it because you are protecting your heart? Are you hiding behind your own busy schedule? What is it?

I believe I have truly just watched a layer of myself unfold. As I break my way through these layers of pain, sadness, anger, fear, frustration, control, gratefulness, trust, and everything else that can and probably will arise, I vow that while I may forget right away what I have learned about myself, I will allow myself to further unfold and accept my discomforts with open arms of acknowledgement.

I hope that this lesson in learning to ask for and openly accept help has been a lesson for us all and will serve a greater purpose than just mine alone.

Phase 3 — IV Treatment
September 7, 2012

———◦———

I am still sort of overwhelmed by all of the information, reactions, and travel. I took a stab at putting my jumbled thoughts into words last night, to no avail. I will try again today.

And now five minutes have passed and I, once again, stare at my screen.

In the past, I have come home with a lot of detailed information. I will share some element of detail, whatever I can recall and articulate, that is. What it all came down to is two things: 1) I clearly have a worse case than Dr. Jemsek seems to have originally thought and 2) I am a neurotoxic waste dump.

I feel lost right now. I don't know what to write. It kind of feels like my thoughts are careless smears of paint that are meant to be a detailed portrait. But as I babble on, I will once again, give it a shot.

I was feeling very chipper on the way to the airport. While talking my dad's ear off, I started to feel like I had a minor sunburn, especially on my arms. I thought it might just be the sun shining through the windows. The plane was on time for once and the flight was okay, but the feeling of the sunburn was getting worse. I asked my father several times if it looked like I had a sunburn. The travel was fine, hotel was as usual, and weather sticky.

We got to the hotel and I told Dad right away that I was not up to going out to dinner. He went out and bought some salads across Dupont Circle at Panera. Kind of generic and boring, but that was just what I wanted. We ate together and I began to get tired and snippy so he went to his room. It took a while for me to fall asleep and once again, I was awake at 6:17 a.m., even though I could have slept until 9:00 and still have had plenty of time to get ready, have breakfast, repack and get there in time.

I stopped writing about eight hours ago. I think I am game to write a little more.

We headed to Dr. Jemsek's office after breakfast and were welcomed in, as usual, by Monet. I saw that doctor's scale there staring at me as I walked closer to that pit of doom. I stood on it. And then I wanted to snuggle with it – I had lost seven pounds since my last appointment. Thank you, Flagyl.

Monet took my vitals, asked me a few question about my reactions in the past month, clearly to prep my infusion nurse who would then get more details to prep Dr. Jemsek. It's kind of a tag team effort, but I like that there are multiple people involved in my treatment and that every time I ask a question, I get the same answer.

This time I had a new infusion nurse, Erica. I had briefly met her before and quite liked her. She has short dark brown hair and strikes me as a serious nurse by day, fun party/dinner girl at night. She has a great smile and was engaged and listened just as well as sweet Christina. As soon as she came in and was making small talk, she went straight for my chest and hooked me up to the test dose of Zithro.

Erica explained that, during this next phase of IV treatment we will eliminate IV Meropenem, which will apparently come back at a later time. I will continue the IV Clindamycin twice a day and add one IV Zithromax after my nightly Clindamycin drip. The antibiotic days continue to be Monday, Wednesday, and Friday, starting next week.

Erica explained that IV Zithromax at this dose and by IV can really tear dramatically at the stomach lining. I was strongly urged to take the

Pantoprazole tablets each morning right when I get up, before my other meds, to prevent this from happening.

She looked through my emails to Christina during the past month and saw that I had had two nights of difficulty falling asleep. I had correctly correlated it to the two days of taking of Flagyl twice a day. I was told that if I continue to have trouble falling asleep with my knock-out meds, that I should add the second Klonopin that I have not been taking because what I have is sufficient to knock out Mike Tyson. My theory is to just expect to get less sleep when taking Flagyl and spend more time telling you about my poop chronicles. Good times.

She asked me to tell her about how things were going. By the time I had finished telling her about the first week, she seemed surprised and said, "Wow, you are having a really hard time." Well hold on, sister, that's just week one. So I went on to tell her about the rest of the weeks and how, for the past two weeks, I have pretty much had dementia. She took her notes after asking several questions and left me on the drip, probably to go have a briefing with Dr. Jemsek.

Dr. Jemsek came in and welcomed us again. I always feel so relieved to see him. Every time we go there, I know for certain that I am in the right place. I have written a lot about how even-keeled they are there. And they are. But both the infusion nurse and Dr. Jemsek reacted the same way once I told them of my Herxheimer reactions during the month and while they didn't say it outright, Dad and I both agreed later that while they have seen this before, we both got the feeling that when people have the illness as severely as I do, they usually come in wheelchairs or completely disabled. This was sobering and I think more terrifying for me than my dad took it. While he listens carefully and is realistic, as a dad he is always listening closely for that, "What I need you to tell me is…" so when the doctor says there will be blue skies ahead, Dad is doing *tour jetés* while I am more focused on the hell I am in right now. Yes, it's getting better and I need to create a positive reality for the outcome, but the way my brain functions right now is one thing at a time. Let it all take its course. Right now the course sucks. I see blue skies of summer every day right now, but from behind the blinds in my long-sleeved shirts dragging an IV pole around, it's hard for me to be positive about this one.

Anyway, Dr. Jemsek was very clear that I am "so toxic now, you are going through complete neurotoxic chaos." The treatment is never meant to be unbearable and I can pull back at any time, but so far it's been manageable and I soldier on. He surprised me by saying he wants to double the Lactated Ringers, those three-hour drips, to twice the amount, not dripping but on a constant flow. At this point, he spoke a lot with his hands and motioned how the constant flow of the flush will rush through my six to seven liters of blood and force the spirochetes to move, even the stubborn ones. And so I will do that. I will do whatever I am told at this moment.

He explained that I am still in the grunt phase, so it's to be expected that it's rough. You may recall the first dose of the natural antibiotic Artemisinin knocked me on my ass for the rest of the month? Dr. Jemsek said that if these double Ringers do not alleviate some or most of that aggravation from my system, that I will switch to Artemisia, a Chinese herb that I am familiar with from working with Dr. Steve and from my original treatment with him and working with other patients. In that case, I would take the Artemisia at 500mg twice a day, five days a week, a switch from the three days of other antibiotics.

Dr. Jemsek asked me if I have had any muscle cramps that wouldn't let go. I am glad he asked this because I hadn't made the correlation between the two such instances I'd had during the first week of my antibiotic "holiday." He wanted me to let him know if this continues, as this would indicate a basal ganglia issue, which would indicate a big inflammatory cloud on a compromised cerebral cortex. From Wiki, which is certainly more articulate at explaining this than I am right now: "The cerebral cortex plays a key role in memory, attention, perceptual awareness, thought, language and consciousness." Um, hi. I recognize this. All of it.

Dr. Jemsek then requested that I look for joint pain on holiday weeks. Okay, *please* stop referring to this as a holiday, unless it is meant to be in Somalia *or* unless I will have emergency evacuation travel insurance, because this, my friends, is no fucking holiday.

Anyway, back to looking for joint pain. That would indicate mycoplasma. Read that and then recall my February love affair with a coconut-sized ovarian cyst. Hmmm… Any indication of a mycoplasma would result in treatment with a member of the tetracycline antibiotic family called minocycline.

Moving on, I explained that I am a writer. I love to write and I write a lot. I am writing a book. I live for Excel, I work from home, etc. I explained that I have a great deal of trouble writing by hand and typing and that this has been especially disturbing to me, as I have never experienced this at this severe level. He explained that dysgraphia is to be expected, which means there is a brain issue going on that is blocking my ability to write by hand and to read (also an issue right now), and is not correlated to intellectual impairment. Okay, we can do a *tour jeté* there, Dad. However, I will say that it sucks.

I explained that my speech has been affected in that I have had trouble speaking clearly. Words get jumbled, I sometimes stutter or slur, I forget words, and I get lost in the middle of a sentence. This was interesting. He explained that speech and balance (also an issue) are controlled by the cerebella and basal plasma. He said that I am not ready for it yet because I am still too exhausted and fragile, but that core training will help with this and he will prescribe physical therapy for core strength down the line. Dad, this is where he first said, "I need to see the blue sky first." Context, Dad. Context.

At this time, I noticed the strange thing that had happened on the way down with the sensation but absence of a sunburn. I knew when this was happening that it was a Herxheimer reaction and I knew it was one I *did not* want to have, as I know where it can lead. Burning skin is central pain. I have had episodes of central pain for a while now. For a long time I have complained of the sensation of a needle being stuck straight through my left thigh, always my left thigh in the same place. I have complained of headaches that felt like a swimmer's cap of needles, and now the sunburn, which I experienced again today. According to Dr. Jemsek, this indicates that the thalamus is in the middle of a storm. The way to treat that is with medical marijuana or Marinol. I am a mom, so if it comes to this, it will be Marinol, which will double as an anti-nausea med.

We concluded by going over my new antibiotic schedule (which is separate from the neurotrophic and natural supplement regime I take daily), that I'll be taking approximately forty pills a day, before the oral antibiotics. This time around, it will be two cycles of two weeks on antibiotics, and one week off antibiotics. So, I will be back in six weeks for the next phase.

We then started to discuss this current antibiotic holiday and how it had been twelve days so far, rather than seven, as we had to travel when it would suit my dad's schedule. I explained that I had been in complete hell for ten days, even worse than when on antibiotics, but after the past two days I seem to have come out of it. This was the second time that he mentioned blue skies. He said these last two days had been bluer skies which is an indicator that I *can* come out of it and that what we are looking for is for the bad holiday days to become less and the blue sky days, where I feel moderately human, to increase.

We again spoke of my excruciating foot pain on the tops of my feet due to exotosis, the formation of new bone on an existing bone. It's truly torturous to have this on your feet because you cannot take a step without experiencing inexplicable pain. I have been given a compounded cream that I had thought was just to numb the pain, but the concoction, made of Ketamine, Clonidine, Gabapentin, Imipramine, Mefenamic and Acid-lidocaine not only numbs the pain, but will break down the new bone with time. I am also okay to take over-the-counter painkillers or Vicodin, if necessary, for pain.

He began to wrap up and explained that we are now hammering the co-infection Babesiosis, and also working on another co-infection called Bartonella. We are keeping the Lyme at bay, but not really treating it beyond keeping the spirochetes stunned for the moment.

I was told that I need not expect a more intense reaction than last month and that I may see some blue skies (that's three, Dad) on my antibiotic holidays. He explained that there would be no new oral antibiotics at this time. If things go well for my next appointment, then my next appointment after that will be seven weeks out, which would be the first week of December.

We went straight to the airport around 1:30 p.m. and, upon getting to the gate, managed to weasel our way onto a earlier flight, which had been delayed, and we boarded immediately. This got us home about six hours earlier, which was nice. About halfway home, I was feeling funny. My legs were numb and I felt like I was floating out of my body. I was completely exhausted and all I could think of was, "How can I ask Dad to stay over because I just can't do it alone tonight." I felt I just couldn't ask him after taking yet another trip with me. And then the weight came down on my head. My vision blurred. And I slurred slowly, "Dad, I feel really funny. I am not okay. My legs. I am not okay." And then I started to feel the tears coming from nowhere and I knew I was having a limbic seizure. I told him and grabbed my Ativan. After some tears and several minutes, it went away. Ten minutes later I was talking his ear off again.

Now, this may be a little too cosmic for some of you, but hear me out. We turned onto a short road that leads to my road home. As we drove ahead, I saw that there was an enormous crow eating some road kill face to face with a smaller bird that was doing the same. As we got closer, I saw that this crow had a long, skinny neck. It seemed to wait much longer for us, and it felt like it was looking me dead in the eyes, for the car to approach before it broadened it wide wings and flew away. "That's a raven," my dad said. "I have never seen one around here."

At this very moment I knew I needed to look up the spiritual/Native American meaning of the raven. Mind you, this is not common practice for me, to feel the urgent need to look at the Totem symbolization of an animal, but I felt drawn to look it up. So, I grabbed my iPad, looked it up and found the following:

*"The symbolic meaning of the Raven in
Native American lore describes
the raven as a creature of metamorphosis, and symbolizes
change/transformation... Often honored among medicine
and holy men of tribes for its shape-shifting qualities,
the Raven was called upon in ritual so
that visions could be clarified...
The Raven is also called upon in Native
ritual for healing purposes.
Specifically, the Raven is thought to
provide long-distance healing."*

Well if *that* wasn't one hell of a message!

Phase 3, Part 1
September 18, 2012

———❦———

I would say the first week of this treatment went relatively well. I am still pretty emotional, exhausted, and experiencing weird symptoms. The new routine seems to be that I fall asleep around 10:00 p.m., wake up at 6:45 a.m. with Mini and get her ready for school. I drop her off and pick her up when I can, but some days, like today, I am not able to do either. This morning I felt okay, but I had to fit in an antibiotic drip before my physical therapy, so my dad took her to school. I planned on picking her up, but at 1:00 p.m. I became so exhausted that it almost made me panic. I had to ask my mom to pick her up.

As a reminder, I am now on two weeks of IV Clindamycin, twice a day, on Monday, Wednesday, and Friday. At night, I add another drip of IV Zithromax. This one is pretty brutal for me. When I took Zithromax in tablet form previously with Dr. Steve, I tolerated it with no problems, but this time, I take two anti-nausea medications before that drip and sometimes again eight hours after. I have also been told to eat before *and* during that drip. So I do. I eat a lot. Problem is, I have no appetite.

On the oral antibiotics end, I'm taking Septra, Artemisinin, Mepron (liquid), and Flagyl (my weight loss plan of choice – *wink wink*) twice a day at the end of each two week antibiotic cycle. I also continue to take my myriad neurotrophic medications. It's a lot of pills to take – about fifty a day now. Today was the first day that I just couldn't take everything in my first dose, so I took only the prescription meds and then spread the supplements out throughout the rest of the day.

My sunburn sensation continues, although I am as white as Mr. Bean right now. It's a vague kind of pain; it's there but it's not. I feel it mostly on the backs of my legs, face, and chest. There is no rash to speak of, just pain.

My feet continue to be a major issue and this is a tough one. When you have pain in your feet, you never stop thinking about it because every single step you take reminds you that it's there. Strangely, the pain has migrated to the tops of my feet.

I am experiencing some sinus issues, which press down on my cheeks and the tops of my teeth, so that's also bothersome. My eyebrows still give me some trouble. But most prominent is the feeling that every ounce of energy has been drained from me.

All the while, I work my hardest, mostly from bed, to make sure that I keep my commission-based business thriving. As such, I packed up my meds and my pole and headed to Rhode Island this weekend to an executive meeting. It was an extremely jam-packed meeting and while I came home full of ideas, I am also *whipped*. My eyes are barely open right now and I am not sure I will stay awake for this drip.

Today I got my "press release" from Dr. Jemsek. Here is part of his impression:

> *"The patient was able to incorporate Mepron and Artemisinin on her last cycle, but seems to have a lot of neurotoxicity... she does mention some interesting description that she feels things 'bubble down' on her and she has dissociative and perspective issues. She is also having some seizure activity. This is indicative to the enthesopathy, dysgraphia, speech disorder, and dystonia that she has already discussed..."*

I am now doing two Lactated Ringers per day to intensify the detox flush. I do think it has helped. I seem to be tolerating the Artemisinin this month. I realized yesterday that I have only been taking half of the prescribed Mepron for the past month and a half. According to the infusion nurse, *"It is unclear that the dose you have been taking is effective. I cannot tell you how that will affect of your treatment. From now on, please take the Mepron as prescribed."* Excellent!

As you can tell, my creativity has been sucked out of me a bit. I am better now than I was last month in terms of many symptoms, but the exhaustion is indescribable. I just wish I could go to bed and sleep until Friday, then wake up and go to bed again for another three days. It's rough, but it is what it is. I know it's working, except for whatever reason, I've screwed up. *Rolling eyes…*

Give a Girl a Break

September 21, 2012

———◦◉◦———

This week has been very up and down. As predicted, I have been very exhausted. That said, I have had some okay days. I'll take okay.

I continue to cry a lot, pretty much out of nowhere. And at times, I am completely checked out. Today, I came home from physical therapy and getting my hair washed, and I could feel something wasn't right. I felt like a zombie. I knew I had no color in my face. I could tell my eyes were glazed over.

I walked in and literally dropped everything, went upstairs and did a face plant right into my pillow. It was noon. I slept until 3:30, when I had to get Mini to take her to dance class. I have been exhausted all night and now, for the second time in a row, I lay here panicking about whether I will be able to stay awake.

My eyesight is worse. I can't really see the screen and am typing without being able to see the keyboard except for some white blurs, so if this is illegible, I will just have to rewrite. My sunburn sensation continues, mostly on my limbs, sometimes on my face. It's worse when I am actually in the sun, like in the car. I am not supposed to let the sun hit me at all with all of these antibiotics I am taking, but life happens.

I am falling asleep. Must stay awake for drip.
Anyway, my symptoms have been as expected.
Oh wait, there's that…

I have a green tongue. And it feels fuzzy even though it's not.
And the tongue itself is dry, but my mouth isn't.

Okay, I am sorry but this is so friggin' disgusting I can't stand it. I googled green tongue and it came up as a disease of farm animals or lizards. *Really???* That's just *rude*. So, I am trying to find some humor in this, but once again, I think I am in the part of treatment where most things are a downer. I mean, my feet are screaming in pain, I can barely keep my eyes open, I cry all the time for no reason, and my tongue is green. Oh, and I am in "The Fat Zone," as Dr. Jemsek calls it. *Not* a fan.

I stopped by Dr. Steve's today and made my way back to his office after asking if he was with a patient. Since he wasn't, I barged in and stuck my tongue out at him. Nice greeting, right? We don't think it's thrush, but definitely a liver reaction. That said, my labs are flawless, go figure. But my tongue is green. Something is *not right*.

And so, as I finish this drip, I dread the next eleven days of my antibiotic "holiday." I think we should rename it "helliday."

Helliday #3
September 25, 2012

—◦—

I am now halfway through my week. In my last appointment, Dr. Jemsek doubled my Lactated Ringers to two liters per day. That's *a lot* of liquid. He did this because my neurotoxicity was at such an unmanageable level that we needed to increase the intensity of the detox flush. I have to say, this helliday, while no holiday, is much better than my last one.

That said, I still have many issues I am dealing with. First, you heard about my tongue. I thought perhaps it might be an indicator of thrush or some other liver issue, but having sent that picture to my infusion nurse, the office agrees that it is a Herx reaction, my body responding to myriad antibiotics I am taking.

I continue to have sporadic bouts of a feeling of severe sunburn, where there is none to be seen. It's mostly on the backs of my calves, but also occurs on my arms. I foresee this being addressed with something funky at the next appointment. Hang onto your hats, kids. I know what they do about central pain issues…

I have noticed a few things about the two days I take Flagyl. My ACA (severely peeling palms and fingers) get dramatically better and then begin to worsen about four days into the helliday. I have also noticed that it throws my back out of alignment in almost every single vertebra. Especially stubborn is my C1, the top vertebra up in your skull area. This has been the cause of headaches for nearly my whole life.

As for the Lactated Ringers, my eyes burn as soon as I begin and I get restless legs to an incredible degree. About fifteen minutes into the Ringer, I have to go to the bathroom. And when I come back I stretch uncomfortably for the duration. My eyes get blurry and I get that weighty exhaustion again. I have also noticed that when I start these IVs, I instantly get very mucousy and begin to cough deeply. My sinuses clog up (and remain clogged up), and this time I have a sore throat and constant post nasal drip.

Of note this month has been my confusion with numbers. I cannot seem to get timing right, phone numbers, addresses, you name it. I am numerically challenged at the moment. It's strange reading a phone number and pushing a completely different set of numbers. Other than that, I would say that I am functioning at an acceptable level.

I am still unable to read a book. My vision is impaired for the moment and glasses do not help. My feet just kill me every time I stand up. Sometimes they crack in a million places. Other times, I just walk carefully and wince at the pain I am experiencing on the tops of my feet.

My skin is very dry. But amazingly, the psoriasis on my elbows, which I first got when I was eleven, is now gone. I mean, I used to use steroid creams on this and now it's gone while treating Lyme. Pretty incredible. I noticed yesterday that even though I have not been in the sun at all in the past five months, my chest is *very* dark, like I have a rockin' tan. I will need to ask Dr. Jemsek about this for sure. I also need to talk to him about this incredible pain I get in my thigh, where it feels like a large needle is being jammed right into it. Same place every time. And now the same sensation has me feeling very itchy, especially on my arms. I also need to tell him that I am getting muscle spasms that do not let up. He had said to keep an eye open for it and now that I know that it is also Lyme-related, I am more conscious of it and notice it happening a lot.

I finish this helliday on Sunday, so ten more Ringers to go before I start my next two weeks of antibiotics again, the same course I took this past time. I then get a five-day helliday, then a trip to DC for Phase 4. So, that's the update. I can barely keep my eyes open.

This is Your Brain. This is Your Brain on Lyme.
September 26, 2012

———◦———

In addition to being an emotional outlet, writing has also helped me dramatically in preparing for my appointments in DC. Every month I start a log of symptoms, but since one of my biggest issues is memory, I have forgotten that it exists every single time. And so, even though I filled you in yesterday on how I am feeling, I want to write today about a few random things I have noticed which have (*duh*) just now occurred to me that may be, or obviously are, related to my treatment.

I am losing things on this helliday. I lose everything. Today I thought I left my phone at Dr. Steve's when, in fact, it was in the very pocket in my bag that I had looked in three times. I forgot Mini's lunchbox today, which added another forty-five minutes to my driving schedule today. And here I lay at 11:30 p.m. – *awake*, despite my knock-out meds. I have been experiencing a lot of "growing pains" in my quads this helliday, something that I will mention at my next appointment. I am feeling itchy all over, and like small needles are being poked into me on random parts of my body at this moment as well. And while I lay here, it feels like my muscles are being pulled and not releasing. Sometimes this can be my most painful and annoying symptom because it often stifles movement.

The two days of Flagyl at the end of each cycle seem to make my ACA (peeling palms and fingers) go away. It starts to come back about four days into my holiday. I can feel it happening – the skin thickening through the course of a day or so, start of the peeling, topped off by the skin cracking to the bone. It's excruciating.

In the past, I have mentioned that I have had headaches all my life. Between treatment with my Dr. Steve and Dr. Jemsek, I described those headaches as swimming caps with needles in them. What I experienced today was the headache I have had almost every day since I was eleven, until March when I began my neurotrophic medications. I get two kinds of headaches/migraines. The first begins as a consistent twitch in under the top of my right eyeball. Twitch. Twitch. Twitch. I know that when this happens I have a twenty-minute window to take Excedrin Migraine or I am shot for the rest of the day. The headaches make my head feel like it will explode altogether. It's as if my entire brain swells so much that it could break my skull.

The second kind of headache, the one I had today, is one that I actually haven't really thought twice about, because I am so used to it. This one starts at the base of my skull, in my upper cervical area, specifically the vertebra C1 and C2. When this happens, my neck starts to crack, again and again. Certainly chiropractic and naturopathic adjustments have helped with this, but at the end of the day, it is a consistent problem I've had since I first contracted Lyme, in 1986, we believe. This kind of headache begins in the upper cervical area and then climbs up and around my head. It creeps up the back of my skull and then splits, migrating to both sides of my skull up to my temporal lobe area. I have always thought of these as migraines, because that was what I was always told. But tonight, I had a revelation. I now believe I have had temporal lobe epilepsy for almost three decades. That means, these headaches were yet another type of epileptic seizure I have experienced my whole life without knowing it. I realize that I am self-diagnosing, but at this point, with all of my background and my in-depth knowledge of my own body, I am seldom wrong. This makes me…very sad. I am sure my parents will hurt hearing this too. All they ever wanted was for me to feel well. None of us had any idea. I will run this by Dr. Jemsek and Dr. Steve at our next meetings.

This morning, I had one of these headaches and nipped it in the bud with Excedrin, but I now know I need to take this up with Dr. Jemsek and make sure all of my meds are correct. Thankfully, I have been on several epilepsy medications since March. But something must be missing.

Late this afternoon, I began violently sneezing. I counted fourteen times. It just would not stop. And once it did, I started coughing *very* deeply. This was followed by a heavy exhaustion that made it hard to function at all. This is something that I have also experienced on and off through the years and so tonight it occurred to me that I should Google it. Sure enough… Temporal Lobe Epilepsy is what popped up. I was not sure whether to gasp or sigh. I continue to unfold layer by layer.

In some respects, I feel stronger for having the knowledge of what has happened and why for 75% of my life, but I admit, I find myself mourning the loss of so many years. The loss of many important things and people in my life, so many possibilities. It's not easy to let these thoughts go, especially when your mind is *beat.*

My arms itch below my elbows now, when they do not feel sunburned. I have the periodic sensation of a large epidural type needle being inserted straight through the middle of my left thigh. Sometimes it lasts an hour or so and sometimes it lasts for days. It is excruciating. I have always known it was nerve pain but, um, I never correlated it with Lyme. *Sigh…*

I have also had a similar sensation near my belly button for many years. It was as if a thread was being yanked down and pulled so badly I would sometimes wince out loud. Thankfully, I have not experienced that since my C-section for the endometrioma in February. I am quite simply hoping they cut through and killed that nerve. I wouldn't miss it.

I am getting muscle spasms that get stuck and impair movement. The usual places are my lateral muscles on the tops of my shoulders, my trapezius muscles under the wings of my shoulder blades, and my calf muscle. I also experience carpel tunnel-like symptoms in the arms. This will certainly be a topic at the next appointment.

Yesterday I received an email from my nurse that I am now to double my Hydrocortisone (cortisol pills), as my adrenals are not co-operating in the slightest. I was diagnosed with adrenal insufficiency in 2004, so this is no surprise. Currently, my pituitary gland seems to be joining in the fun by not participating either. Both my ACTH (adreno-corticotropic hormone) and blood cortisol levels are very low, despite my steroid supplementation, which means that my pituitary is now not even sending the messages to my adrenals to create the cortisol and DHEA I need to function and to live. My body has been beat up now for over twenty-five years without a diagnosis. My adrenals have definitely taken a fatal hit. There are many natural supplements and glandulars I can take to help increase adrenal function and build them back. I have been taking them for years. It would seem though, at this point, that I am beyond that. I will continue to take them, but the truth is, I will likely add hydrocortisone to the list of medications that will probably be with me for the rest of my life.

So, while this is very much a chapter written for my own notes for my next appointment in four weeks, I hope it may help someone, be-cause honestly, these strange symptoms on their own seem like nothing, but when you compile them into a list, you may very well have Lyme on your hands. Pay attention. Listen to your body. Be persistent. And trust your instincts. One of the most important things that Dr. Steve ever taught me is that you *must* be your own health advocate. You must question things, be suspicious, pay attention, and seek second opinions. I have done that every day since I first met him in 2004 and it has been one of the greatest lessons of my life.

It's Getting Hot in Here
September 27, 2012

———— ⋙◉⋘ ————

I lay here with my hands periodically rubbing my eyes and down my face in distress. Then they lay on the keyboard wondering what to write. I lay here on my second Lactated Ringer of the day, unleashing the detox hell within me.

This morning I was doing really well, and then I did the first of two one-liter Lactated Ringers today. And wow, did it wake something up in me. It brought on a flu-like situation. I always feel exhausted after a Ringer, but today, I started to burn up. My sunburn sensation has spread to more of my body. It's still on the back of my calves and on the fronts of my arms, but now on my chest and face. My cheeks look like tomatoes. I am running a fever of 100°.

My nurse, who came to see me today to redress my line, was very concerned. My fever was at the point where we need to consider calling Dr. Jemsek, and my blood pressure was 126/92. That bottom number is higher than it's ever been for me, when I've had it checked. I have had heart palpitations all day, which explain it. I feel like I have the flu. I itch everywhere. Very itchy, but not pronounced itches, just little ones. My face itches. My arms itch. My knees itch. I just itch. It's like slow torture.

I am confused about many things. I have walked downstairs several times today and forgotten why. Then I go again and forget again. My balance and spatial relations are *really* off. I have stumbled several times and bumped some walls.

Last night, I didn't sleep at all. This is exactly what happened on the sixth day of helliday last month too. On the fifth day my ACA peeling hands come back and on day six I do not sleep at all, waking up every thirty minutes.

My left knee is bothering me. I have the sensation of needles there too and in my left thigh as always. And it itches in that spot too. Thankfully, the sensation of a urinary tract infection goes away on day two of helliday. And I am tired. I am very, very tired. But I am hot. My whole body burns. I want out of this skin. My right elbow is very sore and I feel like I have carpel tunnel. My left frontal lobe is aching, warning me of a seizure or a headache.

It's so strange. I have so many miserable symptoms and yet I still feel kind of "with it." I am okay. But what is okay? Do I even know? Would okay for me be miserable for you? I just don't know. I am aware that I seem completely incoherent, because I am. But I am still here. And I take things minute by minute, because things change so quickly. So I just move forward through the easy and the tough. I just soldier on.

Now Hiring
September 29, 2012

———— ◦◉◦ ————

I have never been accused of having a lack of emotion, that's for sure. While I am still the emotional puddle of mush that we all know, yesterday and today I have had little to *no feeling* at all in my calves and back.

It started at my Friday morning appointment for physical therapy/ massage. My muscles often get so incredibly hard that we have to use hot stones for her to even get the muscles to budge. This is not unusual for me. My muscles have been like walls of granite since I was a teenager.

But yesterday when she put the hot stone on me, I didn't feel it. I knew something was there, but I didn't feel the heat. I thought she had just put her hand on me. Then, a few minutes later she said, "You're usually screaming by now. Are you okay?" To which I responded, "I must not be okay because I barely feel that you're there at all." It was a very scary thing to hear come out of my own mouth.

She continued to work on the backs of my legs for about a half hour. She got a lot of work done, probably because I couldn't feel anything. And then she got to my back and I felt…nothing. It's worrisome for sure.

I have mentioned the feeling of a sunburn I have had on the backs of my legs. I believe this to be correlated to what I am now still experiencing: a lack of physical sensation of any kind on the backs of my legs and a tingly feeling all up my back, as if it is asleep. I do not feel numb, it's just… I don't feel anything. I am walking okay, if slowly, but it is strange to ram into something while walking and having no idea beyond the fact that you *see* what's happened.

I emailed Dr. Jemsek's office right away, around noon on Friday and, for the first time, did not hear back from them before the week was out. So, I hit the internet and dove in. There are many names for what this could be, but it all comes back to central pain, an issue coming from the cortex of my brain. It keeps coming back to Lyme in the brain and spinal cord.

I really do not know much about this yet, but I am now certain it is something I will learn more about and most likely medicate sooner than later. I feel it is of concern, especially since the sunburn sensation seems to be spreading. I have it on my face and hands now. Does this mean I will lose sensation in those places too? I have no idea.

I'm also itchy. Not in the way one might imagine. There are these deep itches, that only require a couple of good scratches, especially on my face, hands, arms, bottom of my skull, and soles of my feet. I continue to feel like I have been hit by a truck. I am *so tired* all of the time, but I have Lyme and a three-year old, so exhaustion is just plain on the menu and I am still learning to deal with that. I am getting lurking headaches again in my left frontal lobe.

The *tops* of my feet continue to be excruciating and if I have any trouble walking, this is why. I do need to have this dealt with. It is just torture and I cannot stop thinking about it because every step reminds me they are there and screaming. They also feel *very* hot to me, while my body temperature is so cold I am buried under my comforter half the day, yet I feel like I have a sunburn. I just feel like a freak of nature, honestly.

And yes, as I mentioned on Day 5 of my helliday, just like last month, my ACA started to come back. Now it's back and my fingers are like hard swollen sausages on the inside again, that look like they might pop. They haven't split…yet.

My schedule has begun to overwhelm me. Between my IV meds and my appointments, I really am starting to feel tied down. During antibiotic weeks, I tend not to have any appetite at all until the second evening IV of Zithro. Then I am ravenous, even if I have eaten dinner. It is so weird. So, on those days, I have stopped eating dinner, knowing I will be starving in two hours again anyway.

I have people all around me. I am getting an immense amount of help. I have people inviting me to lunch, etc. I never feel up to it, as much as I crave social *anything*. But I still feel so alone. I feel cluttered in my body, like my insides are just an episode of "Hoarders." I want them out. So yes, I am crying again and very depressed, but it is, after all, a "holiday" and we know this is the hardest time for me. Right now is Day 8 and I am not seeing my promised blue skies, though I am desperately looking everywhere for them. It's hard to explain an emotional and physical pain wrapped all in one. I often wonder if it's a chicken or egg thing. I frequently tell myself to buck up and pull myself out of this funk, but it's not happening. I am just waiting for it, honestly wondering if it will ever come.

Sometimes I wish I had a partner in all of this. Someone who I wouldn't feel badly asking for help with my daughter. Someone who would just sit with me and hang out. You know, just someone with that special connection. At the same time, I think it might be even harder for a loving partner to watch me go through this than it is for me. Because what is "real" to someone who is not in my body? I mean, something is wrong with everything, so I suppose that would get tiresome. But the longing is there. Maybe I just need someone to bring me an iced green tea and a hug right now. Hmm, maybe what I need is a cabana boy.

Sunburn From the Dark

October 8, 2012

I sit here with a red burning face. A face that has not been in the sun since I was on a cruise in March. After letting Dr. Jemsek's clinic know that I was experiencing sunburn-like feeling without a rash or redness, I was prescribed the third and only other neurotrophic possible. I have now added Trileptal to my Lymeopolitan cocktail. At this point, I see how much these multiple diseases have turned my brain into a Not So Fun House. My mind jumps up and down and my eyes are blurry. I feel like I am walking on unstable ground. But I am used to it now and barely notice it.

Trileptal greatly reduces sodium levels, so I also have to take salt tablets with it. Because of my adrenal insufficiency, I have low sodium issues anyway. I remember for years and years the taste of my tears having no salt at all. And then I started cortisol treatment (Cortef) and my tears tasted as they should again. And that made me cry too, because it meant something was going right. And so now to take a medication that reduces sodium disturbs me a little.

I am on the first of two antibiotic drips now. The sunburn on my face happened before I started the drip. But now on this Clindamycin drip, I kind of feel like my head is rocking back and forth horizontally, as it is propped up on a pillow. I feel tired and the thought of having to go down and put the dogs to bed, take care of what needs to be done before bed, and check on my poor three-year-old who is sick with a wicked upper respiratory viral infection seems impossible. How am I going to get this done?

Today we returned from three nights in a cabin in Maine. As you know, I have been *dying* to get out of my house and it was great to be there. The loons called at night. My parents and I played Scrabble as my daughter slept. My dad played super grandpa and made hand puppets from bags, taught Mini to play Go Fish and Chutes and Ladders, took her fishing, and held her open s'more while she licked it, as she wouldn't hold that sticky thing. Mom was her usual nurturing self and tickled and loved on her a lot. And I sat like a lump. My mood was quite good, but things were going on in my body.

I did the two antibiotic drips on Friday while playing Scrabble with my mother. The first one went fine, unlike it's going now, but the second one, the Zithro, had an almost instant visible effect on my body. I could feel it running through my body and then burning my stomach like someone threw a fireball down there. My face changed. I slumped back into the sofa into a disengaged pile of nothingness. It was the first time my mother watched this happen. It was not the first time Zithro has had that effect on me.

My legs cramped up. They still haven't let go. My right elbow joint began to throb again. I had some needle pain in my legs. And I was tired. But I have to say, I was able to think clearly and care for my sick little one while taking it very easy.

My next appointment with Dr. Jemsek is next week. It's crazy how fast these six weeks went. I am curious about what is next, as always. We need to have a real discussion about this sunburn sensation. It started on the plane on the way to see him last time and now it is very bothersome. Even my ears are burning.

I am going to Mexico in January. It's there that I hope to have this kind of sensation in a good, healthy way. I cannot wait to lay in the sun, have a virgin margarita and enjoy. To be honest, I think *that* is my light at the end of the tunnel. But we shall see. It will all depend on if my line is out by then. If it's not, should I go? I wouldn't be able to swim, and that would be torture for me. I love to swim underwater where it is silent and peaceful. I long to dunk my head under the water in my deep tub. I want to dive into the freezing lake that I gazed at last night. A shower. A real shower. I guess this sunburn has awakened my inner mermaid. I need water.

But in a few minutes, I will remove the line from the Clindamycin, flush the line with sodium chloride, and then dig into the evil Zithro, making the rest of the evening an arduous process. If only I could put my head underwater to escape the chaos in my head.

Faceoff
October 8, 2012

—◦◦◦—

I can tell you, for the last two nights, I have literally felt as if my face would melt off. The sunburn feeling, ears burning, face bright red. It felt as if it would need to be picked up off the floor. Gruesome, I know, but it's exactly how it felt. My best friend is here to help me, helping out while my parents continue their vacation. She couldn't believe the bright redness of my face. I have emailed the office to see what it could be.

I was exhausted yesterday, on my "off" day. It seems that those days and the holidays are the very worst for me. These are the days that the spirochetes float around dead, spreading their neurotoxicity until they are expelled from my body. This Babesia co-infection is a wicked one. The symptoms are endless and every time a new one arises, I write it down here, in my journal to prepare for my next "presentation" at my next appointment.

My eyes are blurry pretty much all the time. I am exhausted *all* of the time, but I will say, I sometimes feel some cognitive clarity, reminiscent of how I felt before therapy, when I could actually work coherently and have a conversation that made sense. I did really well with work during my first months of treatment, but now, I'm struggling. I'm not keeping up. I'm not understanding everything. I'm just not the force I used to be. I should accept that and commit to my naps, but something inside me *just can't.*

My seizures seem to have subsided with the increase of my epilepsy meds to the highest dose (yikes). My speech is clearer and I don't stutter as much, although I will stop completely mid-sentence and awkwardly try to find my way back to what I was talking about. This happened today on a National Conference Call and, while many may have noticed the brief silence, for me it felt like an eternity and I know that my inner overachiever is beating myself up about it.

I am tired. So tired. But it's hard to fall asleep at night. Once asleep, I stay asleep, but getting there is an issue again. An unwelcome issue: the addition of the Trileptal has helped with my sunburn on the rest of my body and my itching, but is it the cause of my face burning off? I am not sure. It's cause for further investigation. For sure, the question of the day is, "Why is my face melting off?"

Flagyl – The Five-Hour Energy Drink
October 12, 2012

Well, kids, we've found the culprit. You may remember two weeks ago or so when I mentioned my insomnia. It's 1:00 a.m. and here I am. Despite having taken (as directed) two Seroquel, two Ativan, two Klonopin *and* a Benadryl, I have that wretched Katy Perry song, "I'm Wide Awake," playing in my head again and again. But tonight I figured out why. It's the Flagyl.

The friggin' Flagyl. Now, I know it's doing its job, attacking the cystic form of the spirochete, but this shit has my eyes wide open and all I know is that I have a three-year-old who will be bright-eyed and bushy-tailed in less than six hours. So much for my prescribed sixteen hours of sleep, but we knew I wasn't getting even half of that. I swear this stuff for me is like No Doze.

Several things have occurred to me this week and I've been able to make many new connections between my condition and my treatment. One thing I have noticed in great detail is the mind/body connection that I'm now experiencing. I firmly believe that we store emotions in our body cells.

I have noticed that, as I change treatments or get further into a phase, that memories come up of unresolved issues in my life. Often painful memories, ones that I thought I had moved on from but clearly are filed away in my Lyme Library. And now these meds are shaking things up and, one by one, I am again faced with working my way through things that happened five to twenty years ago. It's so weird. Believe me though, after five years of getting my head shrunk by the world's most wonderful therapist, I know how to work through this and if I get stuck, I will call her.

I am currently working out a phase of my DC life, whereas for the past two months it's been working through the dreaded later years of Sweden. I am happy to have moved on from that. It kind of feels much like when an alcoholic "comes out" and there's this blanket spillage of information that comes out too, with no boundaries. That's what's happening in my mind. It's like some kind of PTSD projectile vomit. All of a sudden, there it is again for me to clean up. But you know, my daughter was once a baby and my French Bulldog has a severe gastrointestinal disease. I am used to cleaning up puke, so I will be fine.

Random thought: I want very much to bake an apple pie. I used to do this every year. And when I bake, I mean I yank out the Martha Stewart magazines and create those perfect Stepford Wives-type pies with meticulously cut out leaves and such on them. I really have made a great wife to myself. That said, every time I pull out the ingredients, I take one look at them all and go lie down on the couch. Maybe I should have planned to do it at midnight when I am taking Flagyl. Friggin' Flagyl.

I am getting headaches again. They start in my upper cervical area and spread to my temporalis and now they're also yanking on my jaw muscles. Tonight I had to dig up the Tiger Balm, the big guns, to penetrate the locked jaw muscles and pieces of granite on top of my shoulders.

Last night, as I did my second drip of the evening, third of the day (it was Zithro), I experienced that feeling of knowing exactly where it was in my bloodstream, feeling it burning every inch of the way. Again, my face burned up and got bright red. It then led me into a full-fledged panic attack, which I now think was actually a limbic seizure, though I'm never really sure.

I broke down today and bugged my nurse at Dr. Jemsek's again for the, a'hem, fourth time in four days this week…and asked her what this was about. After a while, she emailed me back and said they had all met and agreed that it's a Herx reaction to the Zithro, not to the new neuro-trophic I just started, and that I should take a Benadryl and an Ativan before starting that drip. This is in addition to the two anti-nausea meds I have to take before this drip. Let me tell you, this is *some drip*.

My visiting nurse came today as scheduled to change my dress-ing, take my vitals, and do a draw – three tubes of blood through my PowerLine. For the last month or so, we have not been able to easily get a draw. Last week, the nurse had me cough, which worked. Today I realized that very deep breathing allowed the blood to release into the tube. I took this as a message that I need to be taking deeper breaths.

My temperature was 96.4°, pretty low, even for me, so we need to watch that. But today was too crazy for me to harp on anything. My best friend had to leave earlier than usual for a work thing that came up. My wonderful cleaning lady came at 8:15 a.m., the same time the guys from Lowe's arrived with my new freezer for the basement, and the same time my dad came to take Mini to school. Then at 10:00 a.m., my plumber came to do a burner service so it wouldn't blow like it does every year when I forget I'm supposed to get that done. I *won* this year!

It's gotten very cold now, which means my wars with the mice in the basement have begun. It may sound cruel to you, but I live in the woods. Mice carry ticks. Therefore, if mice come into my house, they enter a sea of land mines. I don't know why I find this amusing. I am an animal lover. But I admit, I look forward to seeing my progress every morning. I am even tempted to go downstairs now and check, but nah… that would make me the crazy mouse stalker lady. I will let that one sit until the morning.

Tomorrow I get my hair washed. Believe me, it will make the world a better place. Or at least this town.

Zithro Strikes Again
October 13, 2012

————◆————

It's amazing how the effect of the same drug enhances as you continue treatment. At first, I had little to no reaction to the Zithro IV. As I previously mentioned, this second two-week round has posed an entirely different set of challenges for me. My strong reactions on Monday and Wednesday, slumping over into a pile, bright red burning face and sensation of sunburn all over, and complete panic attack on Wednesday that took eighteen hours to subside, were enough to actually really freak me out for the first time.

When Dr. Jemsek's office suggested I add a Benadryl and Ativan to the Zithro drip, I figured that it would be a good idea to have my dad here for that evening (I only do the Zithro drip at night). I'm glad I made that decision.

He came up to keep me company. During my first Clindamycin drip, which is harmless enough, we played a game of Scrabble. Just as we finished, I took the Benadryl, Ativan, two anti-nausea prescriptions, and hooked up the Zithro. The office had asked me to slow the drip down to half the rate, so it took an hour rather than thirty minutes. My father later told me that I expressed a sensation of it moving through my blood system, that I knew exactly where it was. Again, it burned. After a time, I began to slur my words, said I couldn't see, faded out and then passed out sitting up. Dad finally woke me once the drip was done, which is good, so I didn't end up with blood in the line. I really don't remember that drip. That is scary.

If my observations of this treatment serve me correctly, I believe this next phase, Phase 4 which starts after my next DC visit this week, will involve me dropping the Clindamycin, and doing the Zithro twice a day and adding a new IV drip. Lord help me. I expect this next month to be a challenge.

I am now on my next helliday. I had to put on my happy face today and attend my daughter's Fall Festival at school. I try so hard to make sure she doesn't miss out on anything, but I admit, it does happen and the guilt is rough. But we went today and had a good time. Granted, we left more than an hour early, but I did what I could do and we came home and she took a nap as I did an IV drip. After that, Mom played with her for a while and I took a one-hour nap.

Now that I am on my twice-daily Lactated Ringers, I have a lot of chaos going on. *My legs.* Oh, my legs. I feel the sunburn, but also small needles pricking me around my calves. They are also kind of numb. I find myself moving them around a lot. I have that same large needle feeling in my left thigh, a symptom I have had for years.

My left knee and right elbow have been periodically popping up with some joint pain, and my jaw muscle is completely stuck. I have several muscles in spasm that won't release: my hamstring, my calf, my right bicep, and my jaw.

When I start the Ringer, I always start coughing and I get very mucousy throughout, with post-nasal drip, deep coughs, and general discomfort. Yes, it all sucks, but the thing is, I just know in my gut that we have hit something. We've pissed some infection off, be it Lyme, Babesia, Bartonella, or Ehrlichia. These bastards are pissed. There's a war going on here.

Almost this whole month my vision has posed a real issue. I can see, but everything is so blurry. On the Zithro, I can barely see at all. I can make out shapes and shades of light, but that's it. I know when to ask for help, when not to drive, when to call in the troops. Once again, I can only say how lucky I am to have a support system.

I leave this Wednesday to meet with Dr. Jemsek on Thursday to discuss Phase 4. I am not sure if this next phase will be a four- or six-week session. I am not sure what the cocktail will be. I am not sure how life will be. But I know I will fight on. I know I will do my best. I am a hard worker. I will work to maintain my business so it continues to thrive and grow. And more importantly, I will work to be the best mom I can be, even if it means cutting some corners. There may not be a mountain of homemade Christmas cookies this year, but dammit, Santa will get a couple.

An Increase in Slumber Parties

October 17, 2012

I seem to finally be coming out of it, just in time to fly down to DC today for my appointment tomorrow. From what I understand Phases 4 and 5 are supposed to really be hell and if the past two days are any indication of what's to come, I know what I'm in for.

During this past phase I was also told to do two liters of Lactated Ringers, rather than one, to flush out the toxins faster. I have done this diligently and have still feel like complete crap the entire time. But these last two days were something to talk about – if only I could talk.

I have spent the past forty-eight hours mostly in the fetal position, sicker than I have ever been. Flu-like symptoms, fever, trouble breathing, the deepest cough you can imagine, and non-stop tears. This, my friends, has been *the* helliday of all antibiotic hellidays.

What I am afraid of is that the next phase might up that Zithro dose to twice daily plus add another nasty bastard of a bag, my fear being Cipro, although I am not sure if I am at that point yet.

We had an earthquake in the northeast last night, which proved to me that my legs still work. I scooped up my daughter and ran like the wind to get to my mom and dogs. Mom has spent the past two nights here because I've been so sick. Dad spent last Friday night here. If you notice the number of slumber parties increasing, you're right, and it's not a good sign.

And so, I leave for DC today feeling a 4 out 10, trying to muster every bit of energy I have to get down there alone. Dad's already down there on business and will meet me at the hotel tonight.

As you may suspect, it might take me a day or two to digest all I learn tomorrow, but I will share in its entirety upon my return. Until then…

Freakish Health Issues, Starring — ME!

October 20, 2012

———◦◦———

It's as if I am watching the Discovery Health Channel about someone else's life. Except it's not. This is about me, and that makes it scary. Don't get me wrong – this was a good appointment. I learned a lot. I have a groove with Dr. Jemsek now. We get each other's sense of humor and the appointments flow very nicely. I know how the appointment is going to unfold, step by step. I have an idea what the treatment will look like.

At this point, I am kind of used to the misery. With each appointment, it strikes my dad and me more and more that even though we are seeing the top specialist in the world for Lyme, I am, in fact, one of his worst cases. It really is a miracle that I function as well as I do. At each appointment, Dr. Jemsek makes it pretty clear that my case is unusually difficult and severe. He is often amazed that I can walk and talk at all, that I am as functional as I am despite my condition. However, it seems as if all of that is about to change. I am used to asking for help, although have never gotten over the guilt of asking for it.

The good news is that there should be some kind of turnaround, a blue sky or two – in December. I have been at this since July, so six more weeks of hell seems doable. There will be more hell after that – the line will likely not come out until February – but there is an end to this tunnel (at least the IV portion). This next phase, Phase 4, it seems as my father put it, "Entering the Jaws of Death."

We are deep in the trenches of this battle now. Apparently, what we have been doing so far has been working up to these next two phases of blasting everything wide open, to kill the Lyme and get them out.

———o———

My appointment started right on time, as usual, with Monet, who weighed me (I didn't look this time), took my vitals, and asked me a few questions. I always seem to get asked the same questions by all three people who see me, though they get a little more in depth each time. Monet is really just the sweetest thing. She is very steady, understanding, and professional. You can tell she listens and she cares.

The RN came in and asked her questions and I spouted off the three pages of explicit notes I had taken about what happened during each week of the six-week cycle I had just finished. Ashley was new to me and I liked her too. I asked her to look at my sterile dressing and requested a redress, because when I was sleeping in a sweat, the sterile field had opened, as it sometimes does.

From Ashley, I learned that the IV flavors of the month would be Zithro, which has given me such a problem, and Cipro. I showed her that gross picture from a previous post of my green tongue and she mentioned that she had seen it, as had everyone, because they had never seen anything quite like it. Dr. Jemsek later confirmed that the infamous wall-to-wall carpeted tongue thing was due to the mountain of toxins being released. When I think about it, I cringe. It's so gross. I cannot wait to be done with this and just drink kale juice. Blech.

I told the RN that I was concerned about having trouble getting a draw from the line for blood testing each week. Ashley, and the others I asked about it, confirmed that it is likely due to the fact that the line is pressed up against a vessel and I should do as I have been doing: take very deep breaths and cough in order to get the draws done.

Erica, the infusion nurse came in to change the dressing while I was on the test Cipro dose. She sterilized the whole room, we all put our masks on and she took *forever* to clean the area. It was kind of a mess, but that's okay. Erica was a bit suspicious of the entry site and of a potential infection, so she asked not to use the Bio-Dot, a circular pad that covers the entryway for protection (and then is sealed by the patch itself), but she wanted me to watch it to see if the swelling and redness spread. Well, I would keep track of that if only I weren't bleeding through the entire dressing. *Anyway...*

I was told that the Cipro IV might cause previous joint pain to reappear with a vengeance. The Cipro really goes into the joints to attack Lyme and Bartonella.

Dr. Jemsek came in next and we went through it all again. My dad later mentioned how much he liked this appointment because first Dr. Jemsek listened to me, then he asked some questions, did a brief physical check up, and then told us in a few sentences what was happening and why, and what the next steps will be and how I will likely react.

After I went through all of my symptoms, he mentioned that my limbic system is cycling and triggering. He said that we needed to increase the Ativan and switch the Neurontin to Lyrica, which will hopefully help me get into a true deep sleep, something I haven't experienced for years. Lyrica will likely impair my vision even more than it has been, so there's some question about driving. That can all be worked out between my parents and my assistant.

Dr. Jemsek said that I "have a few more areas popping up than most." He mentioned that there are many compartments in the brain element of all of this and that I "pretty much have them *all*. The good news is, you are doing it."

I have now been prescribed Marinol to take away the sensation of the sunburn I have been experiencing. While this is a medical marijuana pill, most tend not to get high from it. I will be taking it in a very small dose, and only when my non-existent sunburn is problematic. It can also be used for nausea from the heavy IV meds, especially Zithro.

The bulk of my problematic symptoms are neurotrophic. It's strange to think that pain in my foot is actually based in my brain. I have major neurotrophic issues and central pain. My flu symptoms are normal for my treatment, as is my deep unproductive cough. This is another way my body is ridding itself of the toxins.

I explained to Dr. Jemsek about my strange sneezing episodes of fifteen to twenty enormous sneezes, and he agreed that it is some kind of seizure activity. I also described the headaches that I have had my whole life that begin in my upper cervical area and then spread around my skull to my temporalis and then to the plate right at the top of my skull. "You have more than most people," he said.

If I could only tell you how many doctors have told me I am their most complicated patient. It's hard to hear because I feel like I will never get out of this, yet I know I will. I have recognized that once the physical treatment is over, I will need to do some energy work to clear myself of this self-image of myself, the girl whose life was destroyed by Lyme. I will need to let that go. But first things first.

Dr. Jemsek promised me again the blue skies that I did not see this time around. They are coming, he said. He expects me to have some good moments, hours, even days, by the time I return to DC. The next cycle consists of two weeks on antibiotics and one week off, repeated for another six-week cycle. If my final helliday is too much for me, I can tell him and we will shorten it. What he is looking for is any kind of trend, the start to something positive. If all hell breaks loose, we will shorten the cycle and regroup. The IV Cipro, which I will take in the morning may exhaust me and may cause more bone pain.

I was asked *not* to do deep tissue massage anymore because it seems to be causing more inflammation in my body. I will be switching to lymphatic, Bowen, and cranial-sacral massages instead.

We discussed my gnarly green tongue again, which had made its way around the office. He said that the discoloration comes from the lower brain stem from my thalamus, which sits under my hypothalamus. So we add more fun to the equation…

Diamox has been added. It drains potassium, so I have to take an extreme dose of potassium pills with it, along with vitamin C to counteract the alkalizing. I was told that if I experience more dystonia (basal ganglions letting go) that means something is firing in my brain and I need to calm it with the Marinol and Ativan. This will also help with my "stiff man syndrome," where my muscles are tight like a rock, sometimes so much that it's painful to walk and move.

I will also finally be switching off the B12 injections because they are still causing inflammation and irritation, which is counterproductive. Instead, I will be taking 10,000mcg B12 sublingually every day.

I left the meeting feeling positive and scared at the same time. I know there are bright skies and a turnaround ahead. I also know that these six weeks promise to be some of the most challenging of the entire IV process. I can expect to be mostly bedridden, although I will do my best to schedule my meds around times when Mini is awake and wants to play and have my attention. If I can find a groove for that, I think we will all be okay.

The truth is, everything has changed now. Many of my neurotrophic meds have changed, so I don't know how I will react. I know that I am always more sensitive than most, so it could be a wild or very calm (passed out in a state of hypersomnia) type of cycle. We shall see.

Empty
October 21, 2012

———◦———

Do you see me? Because I have nothing left. My gas tank is running on fumes. I am maxed out. I feel scared and while I have a lot of support, I feel ferociously alone. I am so sick of being around myself, lying in bed, watching the same shows over and over again. Sometimes I just feel like I don't exist.

When I see people, it's mostly for a transfer of Mini or to help clean up or help with my business or the dogs. But while everyone else is being taken care of to help me out, I am left in a deafening silence with an empty heart, alone in this hell that is so physically and emotionally painful. I feel invisible. It's the right thing to do to make Mini the priority, to keep her as entertained and secure as possible. I get it.

But for a moment, I am going to allow myself to be selfish. Very selfish. All of the support I get aside, I need a body next to me, whether it's in bed or on the couch, watching TV with me, reminding me that I once had a social life, reminding me that someone knows that I am desperately alone. Someone who makes me feel like they *see me*.

At my last appointment, when I went to the bathroom, I overheard my dad talking to Monet. When I came back and asked what they talked about, he told me honestly that sometimes he and my mom wonder if I am exaggerating the details and explanations of what I am going through because they just cannot understand what is happening. They cannot understand why I seem okay sometimes and that, while I say I am having trouble seeing, I was able to read my list of symptoms. I will admit, this sent me off the deep end.

Exaggerating? I have such a vast list of tangible things going on that I couldn't even *begin* to exaggerate anything. He was trying to express that they are still struggling to wrap their minds around my experience. He told me not to think more of it than it was because he and my mom had long ago decided to just take everything "at face value" and know and trust that it's all real.

But I can't let go of it. That kind of mentality is exactly what I have heard through all of these years. It reminds me of the doctors I saw pre-diagnosis: "You are depressed," or "You should have a baby so you won't be so selfish," or "It's all in your head." I realize that I am a great burden on many people right now, but guess what? *I don't want to be. I don't want help. I* need *help*.

I really wasn't going to write about that part of the appointment, because I have no intention of presenting my parental help as anything but above and beyond the call of duty. They have been incredible. But that moment, I just cannot get it out of my head. Hearing those words from my dad made me realize how profoundly lonely I feel. How much I just want to run away and start my life all over again. I long for my old independence. I long for my life in Sweden, where my life was my own. I long to be *myself* again, that girl who could pull anything off.

I hope this will validate the thoughts of many of you who may struggle to understand their loved ones with Lyme. You may be as supportive as my parents are to me and still have your doubts. Or perhaps this chapter will open your eyes to the fact that everyone doubts various aspects of Lyme at a certain point, even the patient. This was a story worth telling, for my sake and for yours.

Impaired
October 22, 2012

———◦◦———

I can honestly say after all of these years of exhaustion, I have never known a day like this. This will have to be very short because I have nothing in me.

I woke up this morning, took my stomach protector pill, and then took Mini to school. As soon as I got home, I started my IV Cipro and took my handful of supplements, neurotrophics and antibiotics, which I will only take Monday Wednesday, and Friday. Afterwards, I took a quick "up to the belly button" bubble bath, used a cloth to get at my arms, carefully, to avoid the water contacting my sterile dressing.

I tried to watch a little TV in bed, but by 9:30 a.m. I was *out* like a light and didn't wake until 2:30 p.m. I thought and hoped that perhaps I would be able to come out of the state I was in: blurred vision, poor balance, slurring of words, etc. I called my mom to say that I would try to get Mini. Then I had to call back to say I couldn't do it. I passed out again and slept until 4:45 p.m. I swear I could go to bed now and sleep through the night.

I now understand what Dr. Jemsek meant when he said, "Driving will be a problem this month." In the morning before I take meds it seems to be fine so far, but I will need help with school pick up for sure. I have never felt so out of it in my life.

I continue to be completely overwhelmed by my schedule. Tomorrow I will have no time to sleep, as I have school drop off, straight to hair wash, then to lymphatic drainage, then twenty minutes away (feels like a thousand miles) to get my prescriptions and grocery shopping done. By then, I am afraid that if I fall asleep, I may not wake up when Mini gets home from pre-school.

This part of treatment makes me panic with exhaustion and I haven't even done the first Zithro bag; which we know puts me in a slump over the edge. I do not look forward to the six weeks ahead. In fact, I am terrified of them. How will my life move forward? How will I manage all that needs to happen?

> "I know God will never give me more than
> I can handle, but sometimes
> I wish he didn't trust me so much."
> —Mother Theresa

Hello? Is It Me You're Looking For?
October 30, 2012

———◦———

Good Lord, I just titled this entry after a Lionel Richie song, but it seems so apropos. I haven't written in a week, mostly because I can't. It seems every word I type must be rewritten. Writing is a very daunting task for me at the moment.

My vision, motor skills and speech are all affected this month, as I beat at the Bartonella and Lyme with a side order of Babesia. My biggest worry has been my walking. I have fallen many times and am very unsteady on my feet. It's as if the room starts spinning as soon as I stand. As such, I taught Mini how to call 911 today and how to call my parents' house phone and her grandpa's cell phone. She gets it. She is very smart.

Thank goodness my assistant is back from her various vacations and weddings for good now, because I absolutely cannot drive. I figured that out on Day 1 of the new meds and pulled over halfway on my way to pick up Mini. I called my mother. "Mom, you need to pick us up at dance class." I haven't driven since.

It became quickly apparent that the Cipro IV makes me very loopy and completely exhausted. Once I get off that drip, I sleep for *hours*. The really problematic one for me has been the IV Azithromycin, which I know I need to do supervised. So, on my antibiotics nights, Dad sleeps over and hangs with me until I am done.

I have a fear about what it will take and how it will be to start my life over, anew. Many say, *how wonderful* you will feel. But how do you relearn to live the life you have lived since you were eleven years old, full of pain, exhaustion, dismissal from every "expert MD," and the cognitive behaviors that go with it.

How will I get used to not taking four-hour naps every day? Pretending that I feel well, when really, I'm a mess. What does it feel like to truly feel – good? Mentally, emotionally, physically, and spiritually? I have *no idea*, because my *best* day could be your day from hell. I just have no idea what it feels like to feel good.

So this is where I am. Thinking about some big things, very tired, people around me. I'm just trying to survive this brutal Phase 4 of Treatment.

Anything a Fortune Cookie Says...in Bed

November 2, 2012

—◦—

Remember that dumb thing in the '90s that when you pulled out a message from a fortune cookie you added the words "in bed" at the end of the fortune? It was usually funny and usually worked out. Well, that's how my life has been this week, "in bed."

I did some work… in bed.

I snuggled with my baby girl…in bed.

I read some books to her (with gigantic words that I could barely read)…in bed.

I ate once in a while, in bed.

So now that I am on my last day of this first of two two-week antibiotic routines, I can say that the IV Zithro does not like me at all. I guess my worst two symptoms have been exhaustion at a level I never knew existed – among other disagnoses, I have adrenal insufficiency which, by definition, creates complete exhaustion – and my vision; I have to move this computer close to my face, then far away, close then far away all over again…in bed. My vision is so blurry now that it is really unnerving. It's likely due to my switch from Neurontin to Lyrica, but who knows. I just want to be able to read a book…in bed.

On the bright side, my burning is gone. No headaches. My muscles are looser. I think I am just in a state of hypersomnia where the whole point is to heal while you sleep and sleep and sleep. It's hard for me to reconcile wasting so many months sleeping. I mean I have been sleeping since April 2011. That just feels shitty. Thankfully, I have a lifetime of memories to feed off of and many, many more to look forward to in the future. I cannot wait to take Mini on a safari in South Africa. How fun will it be to take her to Disney's resort in Hawaii? It will be important to take her back to the country where she was born, too.

I have been unable to drive now for an extended period. This means I am stuck at home and it's making me *crazy*. I was actually the one who realized it's just unsafe for me to drive now, so my parents have valiantly taken over the driving duties of getting Mini to and from places. She seems to be getting used to it, but it makes my heart cry when a weekend roles around and she asks about school, and I reply with, "No school today!" and she jumps and claps yelling, "*Yay!* It's a Mommy Day! Is tomorrow a Mommy Day too?" Breaks my heart every time.

Dr. Jemsek said a while back that we should plan a family vacation for when this hardcore part of treatment is over. So, last night I started looking at trips to Disney World. My girl has been through so much and has been such a good sport about it all. I just cannot wait to see her have a magical week that's all about her. Am I trying to vacation her troubles away? Um, *yeah, I am*. And while I think she would be just fine, she deserves this. I really look forward to being a mommy again. One that's *not*… in bed.

Desperate
November 8, 2012

It's been days and I really should write something, so here I am, with my Mac screen zoomed in as much as possible, trying my best to articulate what has happened during the last few days.

I am on day five of my helliday and I can do nothing but sleep. And when I say sleep, I mean sleeping eighteen hours a day of a sleep so hard that I don't hear a thing until my daughter is poking me to wake me up after she gets home from school.

It's hard for me to put it all out there. It feels very emotional. I feel naked; exposed. But I think it's so important for others out there to know that they are not alone. And so I will share some very personal details.

I have been hallucinating a lot lately. Not scary hallucinations, and I am able to distinguish them immediately as such, but they happen and it affects me. The most common one that I have experienced is when I sit downstairs in the corner of my sectional and, out of the corner of my eye, I see someone sitting next to me. It can be someone I know or not. Mostly, it seems to be someone I don't know, with long, dirty blond hair.

Today my French Bulldog kicked his tennis ball and I thought it was a rat. That wasn't awesome. And sometimes I see worm-like things making their way across my eyes.

My vision is deplorable. I cannot see a thing. I mean it. I have had to allow Mini to play an educational game on her iPad because I cannot read to her. I'm completely freezing at all times. Mom just bought me an electric blanket that I am waiting for and now I want a new comforter. I am freezing. All the time.

My newest issue is that I am very short of breath. It's hard for me talk without any kind of slur, stammer, loss of words, or loss of breath. So, I am still awaiting the turnaround I was promised. I see no evidence of it yet, but he did say December. I would really just like to feel okay on Thanksgiving.

Mom and I went to some shopping outlets yesterday to get me out of the house. Bad idea. Everyone was looking at me like I was on drugs and… I was, just not what they thought. I was completely shattered after that experience and will not leave this house again anytime soon.

I feel I have been a really good sport so far, but now I want to yank this thing out of me. I am so tired. I am tired of being tired. I am tired of multiple IVs every day. I am done. *Done.* I want a week at Canyon Ranch. I want to go swimming with my head under water. Take a *real* shower. Jump in the lake. I just need to be done with this. I feel desperate. That is the word.

Desperate.

Antibiotic Cycle 2 of Phase 4
November 17, 2012

I have been pretty much house-bound for the past eight days. I should have been sleeping, but haven't been able to pull much of that off. I am working on a huge marketing distribution that has required all my time, as well as my assistant's. But now she is on vacation, and I am in a mad race to get it done.

I've had a couple of days where I've managed to experience the kind of sleep that I've been prescribed – eight hours at night and eight hours through the day. This is no easy feat. It may sound like heaven (or hell) to some of you, but staying in bed for that long, giving in to your body's need to just pass out, is not a simple task. For me, it means removing all methods of distraction from my bedrooms (computer, cell phone, real phone, TV remotes, magazines, and even books.)

It's been an excruciating week, having been put on new neurotrophics, which absolutely shattered me into a rag doll. I started waking up at three or four in the morning for the day, which was not conducive to this treatment protocol. I basically need my parents to be here every waking moment to help me with Mini. I am very lucky that they have been so great.

I gave it several days, assuming that taking a neurotrophic would require a few days to settle, but it never did. And so, I thought through the whole thing and came up with a treatment plan that I deemed appropriate and necessary, and then called Dr. Jemsek's Physician's Assistant for an appointment to discuss my plan.

I spoke with the PA for a half hour as we laid out my plan. I told her I was already going off the Lyrica and refused to go back on it, and that I wanted to go back to 1200mg of Neurontin three times a day. I then suggested that I try Seroquel with time release to help me sleep.

The PA agreed that this was the right treatment, only that she would *add* the Seroquel with time release to the regular Seroquel I am already taking. So, those adjustments were made, and I am already beginning to get my sight back and am feeling more myself. I was really proud of myself after this call. I have always known that I am unusually aware of my body and what is happening with it and that I can name almost everything right away.

I am now in a better state, although I am reluctant to say that I have had hallucinations during this entire time. They aren't scary ones, but rather people that are peacefully sitting next to me. None of them make me feel uneasy and, when I turn my head, they are not there. I have had a couple of scary moments thinking I see people looking in the windows, but I quickly realize those are hallucinations too. This is quite common when treating the co-infection Bartonella, which is what we are primarily attacking at the moment, along with the Lyme. So these hallucinations qualify as Herx reactions to treatment. All good. It will go away.

I am trying to stay positive, but I still cry a lot and sometimes in front of my dad. It's a helpless feeling. Where are those blue skies? Those weeks, when you are off antibiotics, are supposed to give relief, but for me they cause nothing but havoc. I will say that my hands did *not* peel wide open during the last holiday. They usually do on day five.

I've had *no* appetite during this phase of treatment. Sometimes if Dad brings me something, I will eat a bit of it. Mostly I drink half lemonade, half water, with a splash of ginger ale. That's refreshing.

Besides that, my upper cervical headaches are still bothering me, but my muscles are feeling better from the Marinol I take at night. It's been a long phase so far. I have a couple of weeks to go until I head back to DC. I wonder what he has in store for me then, and I wonder how he will work this next phase around my trip to Mexico, which he said he could. I won't be able to swim, but I will be able to feel the warmth, sleep as I should, and eat as I should.

On a positive note, we have now planned our trip for Mini to go to Disney after treatment. She has been *such* a good girl, and I want to pull out all of the stops for this angel. I know she will remember everything. It's just who she is. But first on the agenda – Santa's Village!!!

Alert! Alert! Blood Work Train Wreck!
November 23, 2012

Phase 4 has been rough. It only took my writing that one sentence to make me cry. It's 1:00 p.m. on the day after Thanksgiving and while I've taken a bath, I'm still in jammies. The bottoms of my feet are killing me.

Today is the last day of my Phase 4 antibiotics. I want to sleep all day. I did have the opportunity to do that one day and it was amazing how much it helped. I insisted on going off the Lyrica and they agreed, so now I am back on Neurontin and more stable, hoping to drive after this weekend. We'll see.

Falling asleep is no problem, but I am waking up unbearably early, at 4:30 or 5:00 a.m. I am so tired I could easily fall on my face, but my three-year-old keeps me running. It's a rough combination.

Dr. Jemsek just ordered some blood work, which was, for the first time, a complete and utter train wreck. My primary called me and flipped out, then my naturopath called me and told me I had to call Dr. Jemsek right away, though for some reason Dr. Jemsek's office, the ordering physician, got the blood work a full two days later. They emailed me and made a plethora of changes and now it's completely impossible for me to remember anything so I have to use a chart to prepare my gigantic week's worth of four daily doses of handfuls of pills plus IV bags.

Now, look, I know there are people who have it much worse than me, but this is my experience and I have decided to own it, experience it, and learn from it. And I am miserable. I've never been so miserable in my life. Here I lie, while my little one naps. My feet hurt so much that I can't sleep, so I write and wipe my tears, wishing someone would do that for me.

This afternoon I have to go to the grocery store. It feels like such a production. My mother will drive me, Mini will have to have the cart with the car (yuck, germs), and I will have to buy absolutely everything because I have not been shopping in four weeks.

I know I am to learn from this, that it is a lesson, but I am too exhausted to learn anything. I am too exhausted to even feed the dogs. But I do it. Then I collapse. I hate walking funny, having to hold onto things. I hate that I can't pick up my little girl who today just started crying and said, "I just want my mommy to be happy." What do I say to that, besides "It's not your fault"? I will not lie to her. I am not happy because I am very, very sick. And it really isn't her fault. And I love her to the moon. It's all I can do.

Yesterday in the bath I noticed that I had black freckles all over my chest and left arm. No idea what that was about, but now they're gone. It was like a freak show. I also had bruises in a straight line down my inner forearms. They were purple/black. They too are now gone.

My hallucinations continue, mostly out of the corner of my eye. I am never scared and know they are just my mind playing tricks on me. After all, I am pretty much taking every brain drug one can take at the same time.

All the while I am trying my best to keep my business together. It's going okay. My business is fine, but my team management has suffered and therefore my organization will suffer. It's a tough challenge and probably one I should lighten up on. I can't want something for someone more than they want it for themselves. I just wish there was some effort that my middle management team could offer to fill in the blanks that I can't cover right now. Sometimes I just want to say "*Come on!!!!!*" But I can't. I have to take a deep breath, and be a leader, and so I trudge on. But I have no energy for that.

I go to see Dr. Jemsek on December 6. I am hoping for "the okay" to go to Mexico in January. I think some warmth, quiet, and peace

would do me some good, but we will see how he deals with that. Phase 5 is supposed to be a rough one. My travels will take place during what was supposed to be an antibiotic holiday week, which I find a relief – I hate the holiday weeks. They're miserable for me. I guess I am a freak of nature because most people feel much better when on that break. Not me. No way.

In any case, that's my update. I know you're waiting for the upbeat turnaround. Believe me, I am too. I am still waiting for those blue skies I have been promised.

What a Loooooong Strange Trip It's Been

December 3, 2012

I can't get that Grateful Dead song out of my head. If you had told me when I was a teenager that I would be a thirty-seven-year old single mother nearly debilitated by a misunderstood and even unrecognized deadly illness which would take almost three decades to diagnose, I would have laughed in your face. I also would have laughed if you had told me that my body would reject the usual tried and true International Lyme and Associated Diseases Society (ILADS) treatment, not being surprised that my body defied something. If you had told me that I would have to fly monthly to see a world specialist and feel inconceivably helpless, I would have broken down and cried.

I don't think I would have made different choices in life, because I am someone who believes you create your own reality. While still I believe that to a certain degree, I have been proven wrong and now know that the universe has its own plan for me. It may be somewhat affected by my decisions, but my expectations are moderately useless in this sense. All I can do is be a good person, be a loving person, defined by me and me alone.

What I am saying is, I didn't ask for this. I am not one to ask, "Why me?" very often, but right now I do feel helpless. I am exhausted. I am frustrated that a minor activity can knock the hell out of me for three days. Mom wanted to try to get me out of my pajamas and take me somewhere so we went to buy some decorations so that Christmas would vomit all over my house to bring a little Christmas cheer. It took me days to recover from a three-hour excursion. It's so frustrating I cannot even tell you.

I have driven once in the past six weeks, so my poor parents have basically been Mini's taxi. I am so grateful, but it is so devastating to me. I have felt judged several times and that is, of course, saddening – and irritating. Mostly people have been supportive, but it's been very interesting to notice the loud silence from friends I thought would be there for me. It's not unlike any other situation; you learn who your friends are in difficult circumstances.

My grandparents were here for Thanksgiving and it was the first time they have been able to really see the toll this illness and treatment have taken on me. There are days, such as Thanksgiving, that I have to hold on to things to walk, that I fall down or up the stairs. Sometimes my legs just collapse and I sit there helpless.

I am also extremely emotional and cry out of nowhere. I try to hide it from my girl, but she knows. The bottoms of my feet are swollen and painful. My right eye has started to move more slowly than my left, making it hard to read anything at all, unless I enlarge it. No more handheld books or magazines. No more simple emailing. Now it's all about the grandma-font and closing one eye to read.

This has been Phase 4 of treatment, the second of my two six-week treatments. I have had two weeks on antibiotics and then one week off. It's also been the first time I have had to schedule an emergency phone appointment to make changes to my protocol in order to dig me out of my rag doll state. I am now on day 9 of my holiday and my tongue is once again *hulk green*, a color I think should be a crayon color. It is seriously so nasty I can barely look at myself.

The worst part is that I have this nasty sour taste in my mouth which trumps all other flavors, including cinnamon toothpaste, peppermint mouthwash, you name it. It's so gross. I have had several episodes of the sensation of complete body itches. Torture. The only thing that seems to help with that is the Marinol, which I also use for nausea and that sunburn sensation.

Mini and I had our Christmas portraits taken. I was so proud of myself. I got our matching jammies ordered with our names embroidered and a beautiful dress for her to wear in other pictures and for once in a very long time, I was very excited about something. That is, until I saw the shots of me. I didn't even recognize myself. Mini was, of course, perfectly adorable in every picture. She is astonishingly photogenic. We do these every year and usually there are three or four acceptable pictures of me. But this time, I could actually see in my eyes and in the puffiness in my face that I am drugged into oblivion, battling the nasties. It was devastating to see myself like that. I truly did not recognize myself.

I'm incredibly depressed. There you have it. I said it. I'm so depressed I don't quite know what to do. I'm a prisoner in my own home. I can't take off and just find some solace somewhere or do some retail therapy. I'm stuck here. And when my mom or someone else tries to get me out of here, I pay for it in spades. It's just not worth it.

I'm thankful that finally, after all these years, all of my family understands. They know I'm not being lazy. They know I'm genuinely in pain in varying places every day. And they now know that my tears, that seemingly come from nowhere, are actually limbic seizures (which are now pretty much controlled since I now know what they are and how to treat them).

I was hoping for some kind of turnaround by now. I'm still waiting. For the first time, I have no real idea about what Phase 5 will have in store for me. I hope I'm done with the Zithro, since we are not friends, but suspect I will remain on Cipro. I am curious about what will be in the other IV bag.

I am also curious to see if it will be at all possible for me to go to Mexico for a business trip. To be honest, I cannot imagine not going. On the other hand, I cannot imagine going. I need to get the "okay" from Dr. Jemsek first and then see the antibiotics schedule and see if I think I can pull this off. One thing is for sure – I have worked too hard to get to this phase in treatment to postpone it for a week that might make a difference or a dent in my treatment. If it comes to that, I will not go.

Phase 5: I Need a Medical GPS

December 8, 2012

⸺·⧫·⸺

This, in a nutshell, is kind of how I find myself weaving through this plethora of new information and news, both good and bad.

This Phase 5 that I am entering is supposed to be the last of the phases, but not for me. I am clearly too neurotoxic to follow the typical schedule. And so, my program has been lengthened and my PowerLine will remain intact until at least April 2013 (not February, as we originally expected). I will stay in treatment for an unspecified amount of time, when we can begin to taper off the meds and work down to a lifelong antibiotic schedule of an expected three days a month of antibiotics for the rest of my life to remain in remission.

This time I won't bother you with the regular stuff. We saw everyone we needed to see and I IV-tested Tigecycline, which was referred to as "kind of the big guns," meaning a few days into treatment, the nausea is brutal. I was advised to take all four nausea medications I have, *plus* the Marinol. Sounds like a barf-fest for me.

The Tigecycline drip takes thirty minutes. I will do that nightly *before* I do the one-hour Invanz drip. Invanz is similar to Meropenem, which I took for two months at the beginning of the protocol, but is now on a national backorder. So Invanz it is.

Dr. Jemsek had gotten hung up with some guy in a suit (I saw him when I wheeled myself to the bathroom). I am assuming he was some pharmaceutical rep who, ahem, greatly values Dr. Jemsek and his patients who write $6,000-$7,000 checks each visit for IV meds alone. And none of it has to go through insurance as it will currently be denied. Anyway, Dr. Jemsek is one hour and twenty minutes late to my appointment. The first time always hurts the most. We miss our first flight.

When he comes in, I explain that I have given my dad notes to speak for me because I am not sure I can make it through a sentence. And for the first time ever, he seemed to purposely position himself in a place where he was looking straight at me, not my dad, as if to suggest it was safe for me to talk. I wonder if Dad caught onto that. He asked my dad many fewer questions this time. I think that was because he wanted to know from me what was going on, but also to suggest to me, "You can do this." That's how I interpreted it anyway.

So we started talking symptoms and meds. Clearly, as I write this at 4:30 a.m., I have a sleeping issue. Dr. Jemsek quickly picked up on that and my Hulk-colored tongue after detoxing for thirteen days, and mentioned that my lack of sleep and toxicity are working against my recovery and that sleep has to become my #1 priority.

I explained that I am now experiencing tingling in all digits and in my upper back, sometimes mistaken for MS, but often a symptom of Lyme. I have not had this problem before, until the last month or so.

I asked him why I am sleeping later while on holiday and he replied that, when on holiday, it's like the brain is rebooting. "We don't usually have this much of a hard time with sleep… We're tweaking involuntary parts of the brain."

At this point, he told me that because I am clearly quite toxic, even after thirteen days of double detoxing (I do two-liter drips rather than one), he is inclined to have me do yet a third detox week before starting this upcoming mine field (Phase 5). He explained that his job is to find a balance for me, and I am obviously uncomfortable and upset.

I explained that the Marinol at very low doses took care of my sunburn feeling, but that the sunburn feeling has been replaced by itching. Itching, itching everywhere. He reminded me that itching is a form of pain and that I took the right pill to deal with the problem. Amen, I did something right!

So I am about to get personal again, but I have vowed to share it all in support of my Lyme sisters and brothers out there. *My God*, the smells that come out of me are atrocious. It can be in the bathroom (either way), it can be if I forget deodorant and so on. Dr. Jemsek explained that this is all very normal and will subside. When in oxidized stress, sulfites come out in urine, stool, tears, body odor, etc.

So mission #1 is to get me sleeping – sleeping long and hard. After I get up for Mini, I need to sleep long and hard again during the day. Dr. Jemsek will tweak the sleep meds I already take because I do well on them and because it's tough to switch sleep meds. Plus, we really only have one "big gun" left and none of us wants to go there. We'd rather play with dosages of what I am taking now, because for a time, it worked well.

As for detoxing, they are doubling that in every form for me too. We have already doubled the Lactated Ringers and now we are doubling the sublingual B12 that I used to take as a shot but which used to cause inflammation and itching for weeks. So now I am doubling my detoxing B12 pills (this is not your run of the mill B12…)

Because I have been hallucinating so much, the doctor now wants me to back off of the Lamictal by one half. I've been taking Lamictal for pain and epileptic episodes. He believes the Marinol will take care of any pain issues I deal with and that we can start weaning me off some of the neurotrophics.

I explained that my instinct never liked the Trileptal. Amazingly, he respected this and said, "Then let's just take it out of the equation. You know what's right for you." I expressed that I would be happy to slowly lower the others, but that I want to stay steady on Neurontin so we're not messing with all of it at the same time. He agreed.

Dad explained my body temperature, how the latest reading was 95.8°F, always after a Lactated Ringer. Usually I end up around 96.4°F, but it's getting colder. Basically, my thalamus, hypothalamus and amygdala nerve, which is a bit lower than the thalamus, are all in flight-or-flight mode. Basically, the entire lower portion of my brain is pissed off and fighting back. *Hard.*

Dad told Dr. Jemsek about the day I took a bath (you know – the PowerLine dry, sitting in a hot puddle bath) and when I looked down I noticed all of my freckles and small moles I had had turned *black*. And I mean *black*. I started to think it was skin cancer or who knows what, but within an hour they were all back to their normal color. I have also noted a great increase in skin tags, most of which have now fallen off. Dr. Jemsek asked me all about this. There are no studies to prove the correlation, but they are seeing that many patients with strong Bartonella disease (which is my strongest co-infection on paper) are developing more moles and skin tags. Oh, how interesting! *Gag!*

So, that's my version of Phase 5. If you are seeing Dr. Jemsek, this will not necessarily be your schedule and you should be prepared for any of your stages to look different than mine. We are lucky to have a doctor who treats the *individual*.

The good news is that he is giving me a two-week holiday in the middle of the phase to go to Mexico. I worry a bit about getting down there and will very likely use a wheelchair service, etc., but I am going to do it. I just know the heat and the option to sleep and eat good food (I have barely been eating) will be so good for me, and from past experience, I come home from these trips a better mother.

There will be no removal of the PowerLine until I can prove to him that I have had several good weeks of blue skies. I am searching for them, looking hard. I am working hard at getting healthy, and now I have to sleep hard at getting healthy.

One thing Dr. Jemsek said that seemed to relieve my dad, but that I heard very differently was, "This is not what I like to see, but I think we can still get you there." It was very different than what we have heard in the past: "The goal is for long-term remission." Knowing doctors as I do and knowing what marvels they are at tiptoeing around exactly what a patient does not want to hear, I realized that I might very well be different. I may not get that long-term remission we were hoping for.

You have heard a great deal of griping from me, but in actuality, I am a glass half-full kind of person, at least when I am not Lymie. I kind of consider having Lyme as having a child. You keep an eye on it; if it starts to get sick, you medicate either naturopathically or with western meds; if it gets out of line you go to military school in DC and have it slapped around a little. But mostly, you allow it to become a part of your life, because in some sense, be it physical, spiritual, mental, or emotional, it will always be a part of your life. It is better to embrace then to struggle, hide or run. Once this battle is over, I plan on giving my Lyme a big hug and asking it to cooperate with me and to free me, to allow me to have a life for the first time in twenty-eight years.

Phase 5 Starts with a Bang
December 18, 2012

—————— ◉ ——————

I was warned that the IV Tigecycline was considered "the big guns" and that, "there is a possibility that you may experience some nausea. *Um…*

I spent three hours last night praying that the next thing I would vomit would not be a major organ. The strangest part of it was that it took me a minute in the morning to figure out if it had really happened, because I am on so many sleep drugs that I wasn't quite sure. Well, I figured out it had. It happened.

So, this should be a long seven weeks. I wonder if my tongue will look like a lava lamp on the off weeks this time. This past week was the extra week Dr. Jemsek had given me to detox. Three full weeks. The first two were hell, the third was just unfortunate, not hell. I have still needed help with everything, virtually everything, but in that third week, my mind started to clear up a bit. That said, my sleep issues returned with a vengeance, my digits tingled uncontrollably, I still had trouble finding and using words, and I certainly wasn't driving. So, a glimmer of clarity was nice. That, and my Hulk tongue subsided.

I have spent a lot of time trying to sleep as instructed. I have had such a hard time with that. I know the treatment has helped, but I don't think this infection is gone yet, by any means. My clock is still turned upside down, I still have pain issues, headaches, etc., though they have lessened. The problem is, these are bacteria and the like, and can grow back. And they do. At lightning speed. So I want to be sure everything is as "in remission" as possible before I get this PowerLine out.

And then there's that. He didn't mention the word "remission" at the last appointment, as he has at all other appointments. Last time, it was more like: "While this is not at all what I like to see, I do *think* we can still get this." I'm not going to lie, his words have been echoing in my head since he said them. I know how doctors leave hope in uncertain situations, but I wonder, will I ever really get into long-term remission? I know I am in the right hands. I know I am doing everything right, but the uncertainty is just crushing.

The Thing Is, I'm Ready Now
December 29, 2012

———◦———

The thing is, I am ready now. That's the truth. That's what has been tearing me to shreds. I am ready for the blue skies, for remission. I have done the work. I have lived in near isolation for two months; I have dug deep and scrounged every bit of strength I have and when I have no more I dig deeper. It's who I am. It's how I have survived almost thirty years with this undiagnosed illness.

I have been on this aggressive IV and oral antibiotic protocol since July of 2012 and have followed nearly every single minute detail to a tee. And yet here I lay, on a scavenger hunt to find some kind of positive development. There have been some. I am definitely more mentally clear than I was during Phase 4 (when I was a virtual rag doll), and I can read again for the most part.

My pain continues, although it has morphed its way from a feeling of sunburn to horrible itching. As I mentioned earlier, most people don't know that itching is a form of neurological pain, and I have it in full force. And let me tell you, it will drive a girl crazy.

Two days ago, I broke down. I haven't *really* left my house or driven in two months, I can't sleep because I'm so itchy, and I'm so sick of sorting medications, hooking up to IVs, and trying to keep my happy face on, mostly for my daughter, but also for myself.

During the past couple of weeks, everything came to a head. I am now on a specially designed plan of one week on treatment, nine days off. We needed to cut back a bit, but I do fear that my infection may be returning a bit and I want to make sure that doesn't happen.

Mostly, I sleep all night and for a good part of the day. When Mini is home, we watch movies or do puzzles and crafts, but it's challenging for me. I am not going to lie, being a mother with Lyme can be hellacious some days. I suppose the season has a lot to do with it too. We had a nice Christmas with lots of family and fun, but it is energy-draining for anyone and I am no exception. I wish the tree fairy would come and put away Christmas.

I'm in a place where I need to pull it back together and get back into fight mode. Currently, I am in flight, which is not like me. I do feel that this latest cocktail of around sixty pills a day has brought out a weakness in me with which I am unfamiliar, and quite certainly uncomfortable.

What I have needed to express today is the emotional toll of it all. Today, this is where my therapeutic writing has led me. The physical stuff has been brutal: raging GI issues, adverse reactions to IV meds causing violent vomiting, *no* appetite for two or three weeks, tingling fingers and feet, and of course the itching. *Everywhere*, but especially on my legs. But what no one really seems to write about is the emotional pain of it all. Lyme *sucks*, and I just have no idea how long this treatment will take. Because then and only then, will I be able to get back to having a normal life. It feels like it will be an eternity. Actually, to be totally honest, while I know it *will* turn around, it feels like this will never end. So there you have it. The raging silence has broken. As a result, I feel broken.

Amuse Bouche

January 7, 2013

Here I sit, fearful. Fearful of what my future will look like. Fearful that I may never reach true remission. Fearful of what I may look like in the future. Fearful of how I will feel. Fearful of actually feeling good.

You see, I've had some blue skies now, an *amuse bouche* (a one or two-bite teaser preselected by the chef and offered free of charge to all present at the table) of sorts. I can hear the cheers from all of you and, believe me, I am thankful and excited to have these short moments, sometimes hours of clarity, having energy to put the dishes away, or just getting out of bed. When you are in my shoes, "blue skies" does not mean I'm out walking the dogs and going out to dinner. It means that, for a moment, some longer than others, I feel a bit better.

And yes, I still feel like shit. But now I have some hope. It scares me though, because hope is a powerful feeling that does not always actualize. I am still stuck in my house all day and, at this point, I feel like that is a good thing, considering this horrendous flu that is going around. But I am tired of looking at the pink pashmina that has been draped over the door knob of my closet for who knows how long – some may call that laziness, but I call it impossible right now. But it's there, glaring at me. Maybe that will be the last thing I move when I am finally declared "in remission."

I'm on a much lighter antibiotics schedule now, which I think has helped a lot, at least with my brain. Who knows what it does to the little PacMen eating at me. The truth is, I have no idea what is next and, after twenty-eight years of Lyme, I have *no idea* what is "good," which is a rather overwhelming concept. I mean, how do you identify a feeling you cannot remember ever experiencing? It's daunting, to say the least.

I don't mean to be negative. I mean to be real. I don't remember what a day without pain feels like. I don't remember what a day without exhaustion feels like. I don't remember what a day (outside of treatment) without an excruciating headache or migraine feels like. And I don't remember what it will be like to be able to control my emotions.

I still feel as if I am watching myself unfold. I am not used to watching. I would like to be controlling it. But I am happy for the total of maybe seven hours of blue skies that I've had in the past month. I have been fighting so hard for this. My whole family has. But I threw off the gloves in 2011 and went to war with this a full year before the doctor got involved. It has been a long road for us all.

And now, while I am thankful to have a taste of what may come, I am also terrified because I do not know how to manage the new me who may be approaching. I fear I won't even know who I am.

Where to Begin?
January 29, 2013

———◆———

Phase 5 has had some better and worse moments. It's been another winding road, but a less aggressive one. Since I am, as they say, "so reactive" to the treatments, they have slowed it all down.

Week 1 on antibiotics was rough. It affected my vision, sometimes my speech, my balance, and certainly my energy level. I have also had *no* appetite. *None.* These antibiotic weeks have also brought out the chills in me. I've always said how I suffer from low body temperature, but on the antibiotics and up to three days afterward, I can and do experience hypothermic-like temperatures of plus or minus 95°F. Dr. Jemsek wanted me to go to the Emergency Room during the last one and I was like *no way* am I fighting the Lyme fight there, so I snuggled up in my current sleeping arrangement – an electric blanket on high, covered by two down comforters and a faux fur blanket to weigh it all down on me. That seems to do the trick.

My first week off of the antibiotic schedule was sticky to say the least. I remember forcing myself to eat, freezing to death, experiencing great pain in my feet and legs, and feeling general muscle weakness. Not to mention the exhaustion.

The best part of this phase was during the second week of my holiday. I took off to Playa del Carmen – pure relaxation: no kids, no phone, no bills or dogs. Just a chance to soak in the heat and eat and sleep well. I actually *had* an appetite down there, drank fresh cactus and hibiscus juices, ate sushi, and just enjoyed the good company. It was a wonderful week of pampering. It was sheer medicine for my bruised soul.

It's amazing what heat does for me. At this point, I have to seriously consider moving south. My time in Mexico took away most of my pain and, with the exception of a few tumbles, I did relatively well. I had a distinct strategy. Once I got to know the group (colleagues from around the country), I began having breakfast in my swim-up suite room and started my day slowly. I then took it easy, but stayed with the group for the day, retiring after dinner while the others went dancing. I knew that I needed to have a steady, conservative schedule and it suited me well.

There were outdoor beds, under thatch-roofed palapas, and we just made ourselves comfortable. I put my IV pole up in a discrete place behind the palapa bed, which allowed for an inconspicuous drip by the pool. It really was an incredibly healing time for my soul. The cabana boy always looked a little puzzled, but who cares? We needed ceviche and mojitos, STAT!

And then I came home… Back to reality and back to round two of antibiotics. This round had me again feeling a bit like a rag doll, but also set me into complete panic attacks. I really hate these panic attacks because I cannot find anything, reason with myself, or do anything other than cry, shake and panic.

My meds are kicking in for sleep now, so I should go before I face plant. Since I took Marinol last night to help me with my neurological pain and then proceeded to have uncontrollable munchies for an hour, I will be skipping that routine tonight and hope to sleep through the sunburn and itching sensations without it.

I head back to DC tomorrow. Another month of IV meds was con-firmed today. I hope this is the last. I want this *out*.

Phase 6 _ Hunt 'Em Down and Smoke 'Em Out

February 2, 2013

———◦◦◦———

During the several weeks I haven't written, I have suffered from hypothermia several times. While it seems to be somewhat normal to the doctor now, it really freaked me out, as well as my nurse. I was advised by the doctor to go to the ER, but you bet I was not going to fight the Lyme battle there. By the time I received the email, I actually had a fever of over 100° from burying myself under my two comforters, electric blanket on high, and faux fur throw.

I went for my next visit to DC. Dr. Jemsek came in after the usual hoopla about blood pressure and body temp, and meeting with the infusion nurse about my symptoms in the last phase. She said I wouldn't have to try any new infusions today, as I've experienced all of the antibiotics before. This month is quite a cocktail. Make that a double.

I immediately asked him if I should be treated any differently than other patients since we now know that I carry both North American and European strains of Lyme (as it turns out, I got bitten at least twice by those little bastards). He was very honest and said, "We just don't know." Lyme research is an ever-evolving process. While relatively little is known about such details, it was a straightforward answer I could accept.

I explained how well I felt in Mexico and that, while I was somewhat symptomatic, I felt good enough to consider a move to the south. I went on to summarize my struggles on the Phase 5 antibiotics. I had to take multiple anti-nausea meds before infusing. Invanz was used to replace the national sell-out of Meropenem (which had given me no side effects), and the dreaded Tigecycline, which immediately makes me nauseous and then literally turns me into a slumped-over rag doll to the point where my Dad either had to be around during infusions, spend the night, or just talk me through the whole thing. That drug causes a battle for sure. I explained that, at the end of the Tigecycline infusion, my left chest area hurts a lot and then my left arm feels very sore and heavy, but that seemed okay with him. I'm all "*Ahhhhh!* Heart attack?" He was fine. Okay, then.

This past phase, I was only on antibiotics for one week, then two weeks off, then. I also explained that my holidays have been very predictable. Day one brings on the peeling of my palms (ACA), day three creates unbearable, 36-hour panic attacks, and day six results in the dreaded green Hulk tongue.

I explained that I am now able to sleep, that I've found the right combination of seven pills that make me sleep the way normal people do. So that's a positive. Another positive is that during the last phase, I regained my mental clarity. With a few exceptions, especially in Mexico where I pushed my energy levels a bit, I've been able to speak at a normal speed without slurring – another plus. I've gained more control of my legs, though I have "tripped" a few times and once in Mexico my left leg completely gave out. Nothing a mojito can't fix.

I explained what had been different this past month was that when I have to go, I have to go – and I mean pronto. TMI, I know, but this is my reality.

I did tell the doctor that I have crying seizures still. I am, in general, a very emotional person, but this is a whole new level. These limbic seizures occur and I just start crying for no apparent reason. It goes on and on. My coughs are still metallic.

I admitted to skipping some Lactated Ringers (which I am to do twice daily) out of sheer exhaustion. I was just plain afraid that I would fall asleep on the drip. He told me to do them anyway. Okie dokie.

At one point he said, "We are looking for glimpses of green pasture where you don't feel quite so toxic… I don't think I ever said it would be easy." Well, true that, dude. I told him that we will be taking Mini to Disney in May as a reward for being such a trooper through it all and he said, "You will be in the pool in May. Your PowerLine removal won't even be close." *Hooray!!!*

I explained that the Marinol pills just aren't working for me beyond giving me the munchies. It was supposed to help with pain management, but instead just makes me eat the house, completely stoned. I am glad that he said I shouldn't take them if I don't want to. They don't feel right for my body or good for me.

My DHEA levels were so low on the last test, they were off the charts. They had originally told me by phone to go on 50mg of DHEA, but I didn't. I waited to see Dr. Jemsek and told him, "I have no desire to grow hair on my chest. When I was on twenty-five milligrams my DHEA was way too high, so I'd like to suggest ten to fifteen milligrams, if you agree." He did, and so I will start that as soon as I get some.

He said it would be okay to try using my sauna for about twenty minutes if I secure my patch with press and seal wrap (like I have done twice in the shower). I look forward to this and will do it first thing when Mini goes to school on Monday.

I have a couple of tiny new moles, grey to brown in color, that I showed him and he immediately said, "Bartonella. Don't even think twice about them." He also said this about my age spots. "We're starting to round the corner," he said. "You've been pretty darn sick."

He asked for labs toward the end of week one and on my illegible sheet that he always gives me regarding my current schedule of drugs for the month, I could read with great certainty, "The next round will be the last." I keep staring at the sentence. I live for that sentence.

So after Phase 7, I will have surgery to remove my PowerLine and then I will be on multiple oral antibiotics for one to two years. Then I will be on three days of orals for the rest of my life. If symptoms reappear, we regroup and make a new plan.

Dr. Jemsek said, "Show me you can do a week in New Hampshire like you did in Mexico. Then you will be done with IVs."

So, this month promises to be my roughest yet, though knowing that there are only eight to ten weeks of this left is a dream. I can do eight to ten weeks. Much more and I would have ripped this thing out myself. So, here's to hoping for an easier than expected month and a quick run toward Phase 7.

In this phase, we will, pardon the quote from one of my least favorite people on Earth, George W. Bush, "hunt 'em down and smoke 'em out." We will be focusing more on the Bartonella infection. This one should be a doozy. But I'm ready. Let's be done with this already.

Phase 6 – First Night of Antibiotics
Snap, Snap, Snap
February 6, 2013

———◦◦◦———

Do me a favor. Sit in silence for a moment and start snapping your fingers to a steady beat, then sing, "When you're a Jet, you're a Jet all the way…" from *West Side Story*. Get ready to rumble, my friends, because if this first day of antibiotics is any indication of how this month will be, it will be the battle of all battles.

Each day, I take sixty to seventy pills, and each day it feels like I take sixty to seventy pills, which stand firmly center stage. Enter the IV protocol from stage right, quietly holding the antibiotic bags. I can hear them snapping their fingers, getting ready to rumble, and continuing their song, "from your first cigarette till your last dying day." And there I stand, front and center, staring out at the audience, the spotlight on me. The star of a show, a show I never auditioned for, but there I am, the star.

My first night on the IV meds was a nightmare. It seriously was one of the Top 5 worst nights ever. I began the Meropenem drip, which is now back in stock, but I have to break the tube and swish the medication in the liquid bag myself, which I did not have to do before. I have never had a hard time with Meropenem in the past, but this time it made me instantly start wailing uncontrollably and for no reason. It didn't hurt and I wasn't sad, I was just wailing. So, my dad came over to sit through the drip with me. Poor guy, he has so much work to do and he's in his car constantly, only to hear me bawling and begging him to come over here at 8:30 p.m. on his way home from a long day. I started the Tigecycline drip, which feels like a hot worm going through my bloodstream. I always feel nauseous on this one, so I take multiple anti-nausea pills before starting the IV.

My poor dad was so tired and just kept yawning. So as I neared the end of the Tig drip, I just told him to go home and get some sleep. I thought I would sleep well given all of my sleep drugs, etc., but at 12:30 a.m. I woke up and immediately knew I had to *run* to the bathroom. I ended up spending six hours in there. There was no use going back to bed because the second I got in bed, I had to puke again. It was a full-on nightmare. I don't know where it all came from because I haven't had much of an appetite these days.

About fifteen minutes after my six hours in the bathroom, Mini woke up and was ready to start her morning routine. I soldiered through it and off she went with one of her grandparent personal drivers or her Royal Advisors, as she sometimes calls them. So off to school she went, and I could not *imagine* how I would get the seventeen pills down my throat after vomiting so violently for so long. So I waited and took a nap. After some tea, I decided I needed to get back on the wagon and that's what I did.

Tuesday was a day off from all antibiotics. Tonight I have the pleasure of taking those IVs again. I am already on an anti-nausea schedule, so I hope it works. Dad will be sleeping over just in case. I mean there is not much he can do if my face is in a toilet, but he can be useful if Mini wakes up. My ACA (peeling of skin on palms) is getting better with the antibiotics, but my vision is severely impaired and my speech is slow and slurry again.

I have a 1:00 p.m. call with work, and then I plan on a solid nap. A much needed nap. Oh, I need a nap. But let's not play now. Next week will be *waaaay* worse and, while many of you see just eight to ten more weeks of this, you cannot even imagine how far away that feels and how much hell I will have to experience to get there.

I Love a Man Who Keeps His Promises

February 15, 2013

———◦———

Dr. Jemsek has told me again and again that there would be blue skies. He promised me. He told me I had to prove to him that I had several in a row before he would consider taking out the PowerLine to my jugular.

After the hell I've been through, I started to doubt him. Being told by a world specialist again and again that you are one of the most re-active cases he has had makes you wonder if you will ever *really* be in long-term remission. I still wonder, but he promised me, and I love a man who keeps his promises.

Blue skies came from the four IV bags of Cipro I had this week. After the first bag, I noticed that *all* of my psoriasis disappeared, including the inside of my ears and my knees, which I have never been able to get rid of, even with the steroid Clobetasol ointment.

And then, on the third day, just like that, I could breathe for the first time through my nose. I didn't know people could actually take such deep breaths through their noses. I have never been afforded that luxury in the past. I knew I had a chronic sinus infection, as seen on an x-ray and from experience, but I had no idea how significant it was. Sometimes a Z-pack would make a difference, but nothing like this. It's amazing. So just like I never knew people had sensation in their shins, I never knew – or had completely forgotten – that people could actually breathe "for real" through their noses! I have even contemplated a nose job for a deviated septum. But praise Cipro, I have a newfound appreciation for yet another basic quality of life that I never knew existed.

I've had energy this week for four days in a row. I have been able to get some work done, actually eat something, make my doctor appointments, etc. The one thing I am still not doing is driving. I took a short drive to the hospital for some blood work and promptly decided I'd wait a bit longer. Dr. Jemsek had said to just take it slow, and that's what I am doing. Not ready to drive yet. Okay.

I've been through a lot and now that I am nearing the end of IV treatment, it's starting to hit me just how much I *have* gone through. The pain, the emotions, the inability to drive, to have a social life, to be the mother I want to be. The sleepless nights, the meds adjustments, the trips to DC. Being a burden on my parents. It's all been a nightmare.

Next week, I will only be taking one antibiotic which blasts the Babesia co-infection and then I return to DC on March 4. At that point, I anticipate that Dr. Jemsek will assign me one last round of IVs, and the next trip will be a two-night trip including the removal of my PowerLine in April. I cannot even imagine the freedom I will feel when they take this thing out. It's just overwhelming.

I may just get my shot at living a normal adult life, a life I never knew existed. I am excited to do things with Mini. I cannot *wait* to take my first shower since July of 2012; to take a swim in my sister's pool and in the lake; to cook for my friends again; to participate in friendships again; to not have to be hooked up to a pole that stares at me in my bedroom and follows me wherever I go; to be done with sodium chloride and Heparin flushes.

Once my PowerLine is removed, treatment won't be complete. I'm in this for life. Let's just all hope that remission is the final chapter of this journey; that I get my shot at a normal life.

I Want Him Back...

February 17, 2013

———◉———

Well there goes the honeymoon, before we even got married. I mean, we were fixed up by a worthy source and just getting to know each other. That week, I felt better than I ever have. It was love. I want him back. So much so that I wrote an email to my infusion nurse asking her to please ask Dr. Jemsek to do what he can to help me win him back, my Cipro that is. This coming week I am still on antibiotics, but an oral one, Coartem, which cannot be taken with other antibiotics. And so as I yearn for my love, my sinuses begin fill back up, there is a hint of my psoriasis coming back, and I miss him. *(Aaaaaand scene – taking a bow.)*

IV Cipro had an amazing effect on me both times during its role in my protocol. I plan on asking if the oral Cipro will be as good. I know it will tear my stomach to shreds, but will it do the same amazing job it did this past week? I would even consider keeping that PowerLine in and prolonging treatment for a month if it meant I could have Cipro again. Now *that's* love.

So, eye on the ball – two weeks left until Phase 7. It feels like it's been an eternity in a living hell and at the same time, holy crap, March will mark my first anniversary with Dr. Jemsek. One year. That's the longest relationship I have had since I was in Sweden.

As Depths of My Mind Surface
February 21, 2013

You know how when people are in dangerous, near death experiences, that they often see their whole life flashing through their mind? Well, that's where I have been for the past few days, experiencing emotions of all kinds, reliving various parts of my past. I have found myself here, in my bed, and thinking about all of the "what ifs." What could have been? What have I completely missed because of my unknown almost three-decade-long battle with Lyme.

It's a completely unconstructive, almost torturous direction for my mind to go, but as you know by now, there is little I can do about where my mind wanders off to these days. In a way, I feel it's important to just let it happen. Clearly my brain has been through a lot, between the Lyme, the encephalitis and the cerebral vasculitis, and the handfuls, literally, of medication four times a day. I feel it's important to allow my poor brain to just let it flow wherever it needs to go.

Allowing this, however, interferes with my life. It involves some tears, some deep longing to seek closure with various experiences. But in many cases, the closure I seek would seem inappropriate and impracticable.

This kind of purging creates desire in me as well. Desire to live a normal life, whatever that is. I am now watching many of my friends enter their second marriages and, while I am more than happy to have waited, to have missed that first wave of divorces, I do hope to find someone special when the time is right. There are so many things I hope for that, at the moment, seem out of reach.

I want *big* things for my career. I don't want to slow down and, amazingly, I haven't. I am fortunate enough to telecommute, so I am able to do 95% of my work from home. That's a blessing that I don't believe was any kind of mistake. I believe the universe delivered this job at the right time, so that, by the time I just *had* to leave my office job, my home-based business was bringing in enough money for me to support my family.

As my brain travels in time, I try hard to be thankful for all I *have* accomplished. According to Dr. Jemsek in one of my first appointments, he was shocked by the severity of my infections and was surprised that I came in walking and talking. I've been lucky in that regard and, as such, have been able to accomplish many of the years abroad, career successes, and relationships with friends around the world. I have loved, and loved deeply. I have experienced debilitating loss, which has left me terrified of that ever happening again. But mostly, I have lived an incredible life against the odds.

As I continue the battle, I feel that however painful the memory or "what if," no matter how awkward, angering, saddening, invigorating, or motivating, I feel myself entering a form of mental detox. While I may be very fragile right now, I am and always will be stronger than most of the people I know. I consider myself an awfully busy full-time mom, a dedicated spokesperson for my career, and at the moment, the lookout at the top of the tower, ready for the next attack (Phase 7) that will begin in two weeks, after my next visit with Dr. Jemsek. I am a warrior for my own health, as I am the only one who truly knows what it feels like to be me. And I am trusting that my next step will be the right one.

And so, as the depths of my mind begin to surface, I stare Lyme straight in the face ready for battle. As a former peace educator, it feels strange to say this, but it's true; I stare in the face of my enemy, prepared to torture and kill every single one of its soldiers, no matter where they hide. They've taken over my body for long enough. Now it's my turn.

Do Badgers Have Growing Pains?
February 22, 2013

I'm willing to bet some solid cash that no one has ever asked you if badgers have growing pains. Well, I think it's a valid question.

I felt okay today. Mini gave me a real run for my money and was *very* fresh all day, but besides that and not getting a long enough nap, I felt okay. But now, I find myself buried in my deep sea of comforters, electric blanket, faux fur blanket, warm jammies with fuzzy robe on top, and yet, I still lay here with a baby washcloth between my teeth so as not to damage my teeth from the chattering. I'm cold.

It has been ten years since I left Sweden, but tonight one memory lingers in my mind. I remember Gustaf thinking it was hilarious that I buried myself in my comforters. I'd say I was wrapped like a burrito and he'd echo in Swedish, "No, like a cabbage roll." I still giggle at that.

When he awoke to me like this, he'd dig through the layers to give me a good morning kiss, and then he'd chuckle under his breath and whisper that I was just like a badger. They have a lot of badgers in Sweden, and they're not known for being particularly gentle, sweet animals. Most often you see them by the side of the road as road kill. *Nice thing to call your girlfriend.* But what he was referring to was how badgers bury themselves for warmth.

And so, I lay here, perhaps the best-looking badger you have ever seen. But I wonder, do badgers have growing pains? Because according to my parents, the pain that I now have at this moment in my thighs were always growing pains, even when I was thirty. Since I am now pushing forty, I am pretty sure I am not growing. Regardless, I associate the pain I am experiencing with growing pains.

I'm not sure how to describe it. It's not like restless legs, but a deep ache that makes me want to get out of bed and stretch my quads. But that's not going to happen because this badger plans on hibernating until tomorrow when Mini decides it's time to climb into bed with me around seven and ask me to get her kefir and juice, as she climbs into my warm Utopia. *Total buzz kill.* That little badger.

Drop It Like It's Hot
March 3, 2013

If you don't know this Snoop Dogg song, don't worry about it. If you do I am not talking about dropping "it" like it's hot. Actually what I am talking about is everything I have dropped today. I have been back on antibiotic holiday for nine days now and sure enough, on Day 5 all hell broke loose.

It started with impaired vision and exhaustion, lack of appetite, white tongue (at least it's not green this time), and some slurred words, but Day 6 would prove to be much worse. I could barely see, was putting together incoherent sentences and that night needed an extra Ativan to calm me, which works.

On Day 7, I got my floating headaches back. The kind I described before with the headache floating outside your brain. I believe this to still be pressure on my left limbic system. My lower thalamus is still screwed up because sometimes I am not hungry, but most day I eat mangos and watermelon.

And today, I'm dropping *everything* like it's hot, hence the Snoop Dogg reference. I wonder if' Snoop Dogg' and 'hence' have ever been in the same sentence before. Anyway, everything I have touched today has hit the floor. Yesterday I was off balance. The day before, my parents had to come put Mini to bed. But today, I am just dropping things. Mini's lunch, spoons, my tea, a carton of blackberries, the dog, pillows, etc.

All of this is coming to a head, I have unfolded through my mental, emotional and physical layers, as if they were an onion. But in that onion, there is a core. And that is what I believe this final IV chapter will unveil for me on Tuesday when I head back to DC. I also believe this is what the next one to two years of aggressive oral antibiotic treatment will finally unveil: a chance at long-term remission, the core of the onion.

I'm not going to lie. I have a secret fantasy that Dr. Jemsek will come in with a big lab coat, open up one side and allow me to buy a bag of IV Cipro. That is a true fantasy. Yes, it is time for remission and for me to get the hell out of this house!

IV Phase 7 — Hand in Hand
March 6, 2013

———◦◈◦———

It's what we have all been waiting for. Tears of joy. My treatment is nowhere near over; as I have over a year still to go, but yesterday's appointment with Dr. Jemsek was a breakthrough and all the tears that ran down my face were those of joy. This is what we have been waiting for.

By now, Dr. Jemsek is well aware that I use humor to get through the hell that I have been through. I explained to him that the first IV dose of Meropenem several months ago had no side effects at all. I was spoiled. Then the national sell out of Meropenem later led to the use of Invanz instead, which went marginally well to really sucky. Well, turns out the pharmaceutical industry caught up and last month I was able to have the Meropenem again. I explained to Dr. Jemsek that, this time, the Meropenem produced limbic seizures in the form of uncontrollable wailing, so much so that my dad came to spend the night.

I explained to him about my extreme nausea and the evening I was up all night with that. I then told him that I decided to go on a regimen of anti-nausea pills every day, as there were many times I felt extreme nausea. His response was, as usual, clear and calm, that the Meropenem must have killed a bloom of spirochetes (Lyme) in my spinal fluid. He explained that it had been a long time since I had taken anything that killed spirochetes on contact, hence the purging.

We agree that my increased base temperature to the low 96°F range was a positive change, thanks to Clonodine. He described that as a "big deal," a positive one.

We then left my father for a full physical in the exam room. Dr. Jemsek then tested the strength of my fingers, hands, feet, legs, neck, etc. My right leg was a problem. Then he dug up in under my right ribcage. Remember now he knows I cope as a jokester and a minor pain in the ass. While he was poking under my right rib cage I whispered, "You know I had that taken out," referring to my gall bladder. He burst out in a chuckle, shook his head "*I know*," and did the same thing on the other side.

My reflexes took a while to cooperate, but they eventually did. "Okay, they work." Then I was asked to stand up and extend my arms while watching his finger. I could feel my left eye moving more slowly than the right. Then he asked that I put my arms straight out and, one hand at a time, touch my nose with my pointer finger. Oops.

Then he asked me to close my eyes and walk in a straight line. Epic fail. Epic.

Back in the room with Dad, we went through the physical assessment. He determined that my grip was normal. *Yay! Something is normal!!!!* My strength is better, but I have moderate cerebellar issues. I mean, really, I almost slammed my head on the counter walking like a close-eyed drunkard, but minor cerebellar issues it is, then. And then he said I had some carotid neck issues around the area of my degenerative disc disease, not a huge issue, but something to address.

Dr. Jemsek explained that the main issues now are neurologic, and suggested that I continue the Lamictal and Neurontin, which was a wise choice on his part because, let me tell you something, I am not letting those go anytime soon!

I told him that my pain is mostly relieved, that the sunburn and itching are gone, and that I don't have any consistent, pronounced pain in one area. That is a *major* feat. Then I had to break it to him (or rather be honest with myself) that some days my speech is slower than others, I sometimes slur words, I lose my balance a lot, drop things and other fine motor issues. I am also photo- and sound-sensitive and in any given situation one of these things can still set me off into a Lyme Rage or a seizure.

Dr. Jemsek determined that this is not unusual and that these issues would slowly continue to improve with the oral antibiotic treatment to come. No, kids, I am not done yet. The issues above are traced back to the thalamus in the mid to lower back of your brain. This lower part of my brain also controls my desire, or lack thereof, to eat. I know I have to eat, but I get to the fridge and I want *nothing*. This is a lower thalamus issue.

I came home with four new prescriptions, three of which I asked for, one new, and a much lighter bag of IV meds and tubing. Yes, my friends, assuming my holiday is a series of good days, I will have my PowerLine removed at George Washington University Hospital on April 8, 2013. Writing this brings me tears of relief, joys, shattered dreams pulling themselves back together to realize possibilities that may await me, and pride in all I have accomplished. It has been hell and I still have seven months to go, but this is a major corner to have turned – kind of like when you land on the ladder that goes three levels up on Chutes and Ladders.

After my line is out, I will be prescribed physical therapy on a very gentle level in order to increase my core strength and balance, which will help loosen my trapezoid muscles and carotid artery.

At my appointment, we discussed detoxing and he explained that detoxing does not only occur in the liver, but in fat cells and other organs. "As sick as you are," said Dr. Jemsek, "it usually takes six cycles. We are now on cycle seven." He made it very clear that I am not to overdo *anything*. You know what that means? I need to completely change everything about my personality, but I will do it. It's worked so far!

So how do I *feel* about all of this medical mumbo jumbo? I remember being a three- or four-year-old girl and listening to an album by Nicolette Larson with my flower-child mother, and her song lyrics, "One step forward, two steps back, you start to say you love me, then you take it back." That's how I have felt all during treatment. Many times, I've wondered if this was really working, if I would *ever* really get better. I'd feel better one day, and get hit by a train the next.

And now, here I sit on my bed, clear-minded at 7:30 p.m., when I used to go to bed, preparing for an 8 p.m. conference call that I'm going to run. I call it progress. I still have a hard time with my vision, but I can see the screen at night, though not in the morning. I have very few seizures now that aren't medication-induced. I kept my business thriving. I put my daughter to bed almost every night and dress her for school virtually every day with only a few exceptions. I am still mostly exhausted, but I can function. And to be honest, I feel like a bad ass. I have made some major progress and congratulate myself because I have worked endlessly to be compliant with treatment, and have learned on a whole new level how to listen to my own body, and listen to others.

I know myself on a new level. I understand myself on a new level. I accept myself and my flaws on a new level. And I know how blessed I am to have my family. They have never flinched, at any time, when I needed them.

As my daughter listens to Nicolette Larson's lullaby album, we begin this next seven-month chapter as a team. Rather than a scattered group, unaware of pretty much anything, we stand hand and hand and walking fearlessly toward the next stage. Ready to kick some serious butt.

The Beginning of the End of an Era
March 10, 2013

Merriam Webster's online dictionary defines an era as: "a memorable or important date or event; especially : one that begins a new period in the history of a person or thing."

Tomorrow marks the beginning of the end of an important era in my life, as I begin my last phase of IV treatment before the PowerLine is removed. I admit, in some circumstances, I am self-conscious of my bandage and BioDot, especially in situations where strangers are looking at my chest (ahem) and discover that I have some major health issue that is none of their business.

On the other hand, I've become accustomed to this apparatus as if it is some new part of my body. Yes, it itches sometimes, but in all, I barely notice it's there anymore. It's been a royal pain in the ass for everyone in my family to have to go through the IV process, as I have put a self-imposed and wise halt to my driving for almost six months now. That got old on day three. So, I've been dependent on others to drive my daughter to and from school, go grocery shopping for or with me, take me to appointments, etc. I have had virtually no social life since July 2012 when the PowerLine was inserted.

There are no new surprises this month. I do IV Meropenem and IV Tig again, but, during week two, I get to add five days of Cipro (*yeah, baby*), which made me feel *amazing* last time. Please let that be the case this time!

I will remain on oral antibiotics for the next one to two years until we start to wean me off of the antibiotics first and then the neurotrophics, which I think will be more difficult, as I still have some pain in the form of itching.

In the meantime, I look forward to even a glimpse of a real life again. To be able to drive to my work events again, to take Mini to school again, to go out to dinner again and to generally feel good, however it is that feels. I look forward to a social life beyond my family, although they have been wonderful.

And so the beginning of the end of an era is here. It's a time to prepare for celebration, though I can't celebrate just yet. Patience and diligence is the name of this game and I plan on continuing to be fully compliant, so that I can actually go to West Palm Beach in April with one less body part.

Cry Me a River
March 13, 2013

———◦◉◦———

For better or for worse, my life is driven by emotions. I have always been profoundly emotional in all situations throughout my life. I am not only the hot or cold girl, I am the one who *weeps* at every emotion. When I get really angry, I cry. When I am happy, I cry. When I am sad, I cry. Overwhelmed, proud... and so on.

Right now I can feel that I am on the brink, but I don't know why. I can't put my finger on the emotion. As always, I have some unrelated-Lyme stuff going on in my life, but that's all good. My family is coping well with it all, so what is it?

The Lyme rages are long gone (thank goodness for all of us). I know my emotions are not Lyme-related, but are authentic pieces of me. And I love that about me – and I hate that about me. Sometimes it makes life really hard.

I really cannot figure out why I'm crying, beyond the fact that this chapter is nearing its end and I am so relieved, overwhelmed, happy, kind of sad, nervous, you name it.

I'm now staring at my IV pole, "Pol-ine", and my triage table next to the bed, full of boxes of supplies, syringes, alcohol swabs, tubing, IV antibiotics, massive amounts of prescription drugs and supplements, and so on. I'm re-alizing that, in two weeks, all of this clutter can be removed from my room.

And it makes me cry.

I will have my space back, but what does it feel like to have space back? I will declutter my room but, you know what? I don't know what uncluttered feels like. Okay, I'm crying. At this time two weeks from now, all I will need are two boxes for my prescription meds and my sodium chloride and heparin flushes for the line. And even that box can go on April 8.

As I look at the one box that will remain, I feel sorry for it. It's like sitting in detention. For the next six months. And what will I do with all of this space? *Nothing!* That feels good, so of course I want to cry about that too.

I know how positive these weeks have been and will be, but I am completely overwhelmed. As I dig out of this minefield of medical supplies to be thrown out, I feel uneasy about what's to come. This ending means another new beginning. Another uncertainty. Another reason to take a deep breath, dig deep down and find the strength to accept change. Again.

Rise and Shine

March 15, 2013

I really thought that, since I had been on the IV Meropenem and IV Tigecycline, this week would be a cakewalk. And the beginning of the week was okay. I had *no* appetite and, much to my own chagrin, did not eat *anything* at all for a few days, though I was careful to keep my fluids way up there.

I took my assistant to get manicures and that was fun. I always feel better when I spend time with that ray of sunshine. But today, even as her light shone on me, I felt completely drugged. I could barely see. I couldn't remember anything. I couldn't put two words together, much less a sentence. I wasn't understanding or remembering what people were saying. My balance was off. It felt like a setback.

I was unable to take Mini to dance class; she was wailing when my assistant got to school to help her get ready. I felt like the worst mom in the world. But my dad was waiting there after school with a phone and I spoke to her to calm her, and yes, to bribe her with something special tomorrow morning if she was a good listener and a good dancer.

It was neat for Hoovie to get to see Mini dance her recital dance. He's never really been in the dance studio before, except to pick her up and then the waiting room outside the studio is so crazy so he usually chooses to wait outside.

I stayed in bed until it was time to put Mini to bed. Dad read two books, as my vision is impaired at the moment. Before he left, I laid there with her for the usual three songs and then I went and got back into bed. Once again, my parents saved the day.

I'm really struggling with dry mouth, which I just cannot seem to get rid of. I broke down and started drinking the healthiest kind of rehydration drinks I could find. Not an easy task. And no, water does not do it. I drank a liter of water before going into my doctor today and could barely pee.

I went to my OBGYN, told him what was wrong and he too wanted me to pee. *Rise and shine!* I got away without a yeast infection for a year but now *poof!* Like magic! A miserable state to deal with. *Blah.* I warned the doctor that I will be on oral antibiotics by the gazillion for the next year or more, so he should consider himself on call because I am not coming in to get probed every time I know what's wrong. He laughed and said that was fine.

I realize that this is a lot to share, but it's a reality of Lyme. I'm one of the lucky ones. Many people have these issues right away. So, excuse the nature of the end of this post, but I have been real all along, exactly my intention.

Magical Old Soul
March 17, 2013

I sit here, trying to type quickly, but all I can do is look at the ceiling right now. My child is magnificent. She is spectacular. She is special and insightful on a level I have never seen.

Every night, we read two books and, as I mentioned before, listen to the same lullabies she has listened to every night since she was a baby. Some nights, such as tonight, I cannot read because my vision is so impaired by the Lyme drugs I'm taking. So tonight I allowed her to play a game on her iPad. Then we laid in bed for her usual lullabies album and during the first song she said, "Mommy, can I tell you something? I wish you had someone to love you and take care of you."

Suddenly a stream of silent tears ran down my cheeks as I laid on my back trying not to let her notice that I was crying. But she knew. I managed to keep it under control besides the tears and then I felt this little hand reaching down my leg, searching for my hand.

And so for three songs tears poured down my face and my four-year-old, my magical old soul of a child, silently comforted me. It was one of the most profound moments of my life and made me realize that she is ready for me to get back in the game. She wants me to be loved. And so now, as my little rock holds me up just as I am about to fall. I will open myself to love again, almost ten years after I watched Gustaf walk out of the airport in Stockholm. I will put the pieces of my heart back together again and find the right man.

If she is ready, then I am too. What a profound, confident, old soul she has. The beauty of her heart astonishes me. And here I sit in a sea of tears, floating away from my past and nearing my future with my little girl happily taking on the role of first mate.

Exhale, With a Side of Nausea
March 23, 2013

Last night marked my final IV antibiotic treatment. I actually forgot about it until my dad texted me a congratulatory text this morning. We are so modern. Or sucked into an age of sad technology, you choose. I am so used to this thing that it hadn't even occurred to me that it was – it *is* – over. I still have to do the daily Lactated Ringers and I still have to have the surgery and antibiotics, but that aside, I am done, more or less.

I spent most of yesterday wondering if I had gotten a stomach bug or something because I was so incredibly nauseous. That was when I remembered I had forgotten the previous evening to take the five anti-nausea pills I usually take with the IV Tig. I also neglected to take the Benadryl. I am lucky I didn't spend all of yesterday sprawled out on the bathroom floor like last time. Instead I loaded up on anti-nausea pills all day. I got through it.

This morning I find myself in a sea of IV flashbacks. I think back to the very first time I administered my own IV treatment and how half the IV line was filled with blood by the end. I think back to the nights that the Meropenem made me weep uncontrollably. I shudder to recall the many seizures I have had on the line and after an IV treatment, the sleeping for two to four days except in the morning and evening when Mini was home, the inability to read for several months, and the not being able to drive for what will soon be six months or more. And now I find myself here. And you know what? I'm okay. I feel okay.

I'm in a place now where I need to keep things very mellow, even though I feel all right. I cannot overdo it, which I am very good at doing. There is still aggressive treatment to be had, and it will take its own toll on me. For now, for the next couple of weeks, I will allow myself to exhale and pat myself on the back for a job well done.

Free Falling
March 28, 2013

Yesterday I received a call from Dr. Jemsek's office confirming that my surgery to remove my PowerLine is on April 8 at George Washington University Hospital in DC, where I had it put in. I cannot even express to you how relieved I will be to have this thing removed.

I have been feeling lucid, even "normal" for me, most of the time, even during this past week when I had oral antibiotic treatment. I did give driving a shot, which was a little iffy and had my friend take over, so I am not totally there yet, but in all, I am well. People notice that I feel well.

I went to pick up Mini at school today, and within five minutes, I was told multiple times how much color I had back in my face, that I was glowing and I looked happy. It's so strange to hear these things after a full year of tearful hugs and arms around me asking how I am holding up. It's almost startling to experience the opposite.

I think today I finally realized that people beyond my family and close friends, genuinely care about this whole process. I have been unable to hide my PowerLine, so it's always been very obvious that something serious has been going on. Sometimes it's been a relief to have it there, because then I can just skip the smiles and niceties and just get things done. And now, I realize that I have not had the capacity to be grateful enough to those who really do care.

I sit here, alone in the corner of my couch – dogs snoring away, Mini asleep – staring around my living room and kitchen. On the kitchen island, I see a gorgeous bouquet of roses brought by one of my closest friends. I see the drapes which another loving friend helped me design and have delivered. I stare at the kitchen I haven't touched for over a year, until the past few days, and I realize how far I have come.

There are so many parts of my experience that I wish I could forget or even hide from future friends and lovers, but this is what has made me who I am today. I have been through a lot these last twenty-eight years and I pray that I will now be granted the serenity to live a life without physical and emotional pain, without trying to hide symptoms, without defining myself as my diseases.

I realize that the best hope is for long-term remission. I know I will be on three days a month of antibiotics for the rest of my life. I wonder if there is someone out there who will love me the way I am, for who I am, for what I have accomplished. I've tried my best to be a warrior, yet sometimes I find myself in the fetal position wondering what is yet to come.

Why me? It's a question I've avoided for some time now because we all face our own demons in life, and I've refused to pity myself for the hand I've been dealt. But we all want to be loved and, now that I am nearing the end of this nightmare, I think I am just about ready for that to happen.

I feel surrounded by friendly love, yet so alone. But sometimes, like this afternoon, I cherish my quiet space where I can just think my way through life's challenges, desires, and realities. Today I realized it's not enough to want something, that the universe has its intended plan for us all and we are to surrender to whatever it is that is intended for us.

It's time for me to set my ego aside and just be open to what I have been granted. I simply cannot be all things for all people. Women in this country, in this age, are expected to be superwomen: great moms, successful in the workplace, sexy lovers, fierce defenders of our families, homemakers, good cooks, etc. It's a lot of pressure, pressure that I have always strived under to be perfect. But tonight, all I wish for is a bit of luck. I wish to be granted the ability to take the pressure off of myself and be who I am. I just want to be me and be loved for me. I have spent a lot of time figuring out who I am and I finally accept and appreciate who I am. Tonight, my wish is much like the Tom Petty song: Tonight I would like to free myself of all of this and peacefully fall into my future.

Easier said than done.

Perfection in Imperfection
April 2, 2013

I have been blessed in my life. And I have endured great suffering. I think this is true of everyone in his or her own way. I often see life like a canvas and various pieces of life's puzzle are added to that canvas. From afar, the picture of one's life may be a very beautiful image, but as you get closer, there are sure to be varying degrees of darkness. Or, like many, such phases of my life, it might just be a plain old hot mess.

We all go through it. It's the what, when, why, and how that makes us unique.

This past year for me has been one of the darkest of my life. I've been largely confined within the four walls of my home, unable to drive for the past six months, and with far fewer visitors than I had expected, mostly because I have not been in a place to handle visitors until recently. I have gained friends and some have disappeared, perhaps to return when they emerge from their own struggles, but I feel fulfilled for the first time in many years, knowing that all is unfolding as it is meant to. There's nothing I can do to control it other than to choose how I react to what life hands me. I have tried endlessly during treatment to be brave, strong and vulnerable, all at the same time.

I have dug deep, often in my writing, to work through various stages of partially painted components of my own life's canvas, many times, unable to complete the picture, as much as I would like to. What I am realizing is that there is great perfection in imperfection and it is with that sentiment that I allow myself to move on.

I have experienced and witnessed what may have felt like perfection, only to discover that behind the appearance of perfection often stands dysfunction, unhappiness, or denial. What I now know is that the beauty in life lies in the flaws. And it is from here that I decide to move forward with my approach to my self-worth regarding the past twenty-eight years. I am no longer in pursuit of being perfect, for that pursuit is what has broken me on multiple occasions. Instead, I now choose to acknowledge that my life has been a series of great highs and lows, and yet somehow, I find myself in perhaps my most stable mental state in many years.

I am getting better and better. It is amazing to see that in words. There was a time when I thought my canvas would shift from the most beautiful colors to the darkest of gloom and stay there. I felt that way as recently as six or eight weeks ago. And here I am, prepared, not scared, to have my PowerLine removed, to drive safely behind the wheel again, and to start dabbling in some resemblance of a social life.

And yes, I am lucky for so many reasons, but I know deep down that true growth comes from what is learned by our struggles. And so, if I were to describe how I see my current life canvas image, it would be a ticking clock, ticking away from the darkness toward an array of stunningly beautiful colors, just in time for spring. And those colors grow more and more vivid with each step I take toward my own truth, which is and will always be flawed.

I have a way to go in terms of treatment, but it is so much nicer to look at that future with colorful glasses and a smile, than with dark night goggles fogged with tears. And that is where I find myself at this moment, at a place on the clock where time still moves at a steady pace, but that with each second, a lighter moment arises.

Removal of PowerLine
April 10, 2013

———◦◉◦———

It's been a bit of a whirlwind and, to be honest, between my exhaustion and the sun in my eyes, I can barely see the screen. Dad and I arrived in DC on Sunday night, this time staying at the Westin Georgetown.

The day had been worrisome for us all. After about three good hours, I found myself in a deep Lyme ditch, unable to walk straight, bumping into things, and angry. My mother who is staying with Mini while I am away, asked a few questions about how to feed the dogs and I snapped at her, "I can't talk about that now." I vaguely remember going to the bathroom, putting my head against the wall, and almost falling asleep. I was exhausted and in a serious crash.

I'm not sure what set me off after almost three weeks of being my old happy self, but it was rough. Perhaps it was the anticipation. Maybe I just haven't gotten enough sleep or nutrition. Whatever it was, it got me badly.

Dad drove the two hours to the airport, and I was slumped over nearly the entire way like that old rag doll. And I mean straight slumped over, head in my own lap, unconscious. It was awful. I ate something, drank my first real Coke in years, and while it helped a little, I passed out again on the flight.

Since we were at a different hotel, just a block from Dr. Jemsek, we tried out the Latin restaurant there. It was fantastic and, by the time we got there, I was feeling fine. And I ate because I wanted to, not because I had to. That too was a nice feeling, one I have not experienced in a long time.

We went to our rooms around 8:00 p.m. and I did some work. (After this DC trip, I am on my way to a national conference in West Palm Beach. I do not know how I will have the energy to survive this but I've given myself a day and a half when I get there; I think I'll spend much of the day napping.)

The next morning, we got to GWU Hospital, and I was told that the procedure would take an hour to an hour and a half. I waited in the same place with the same nurse on the same gurney as last time. The wait was long, and the department, very cold. I asked for a warm blanket and promptly received one.

Over the loud speaker, it was announced several times, just like on Grey's Anatomy, the hospital was proud to welcome the Joint Committee. Well if you could have seen the nurses start scurrying around, reading their manuals, testing each other, giving the already clean floors a good mopping... I was pretty sure I would have a smooth operation. Last thing you want to do when the Joint Committee is in the house is have a patient croak on the table. I found the whole thing hilarious, but I felt extra safe.

Now, despite my "glamour years" in and after college, I'm not a big drinker, nor do I do any drugs, but I was giddy with excitement about the happy gas they were going to give me. I'd been looking forward to it for days. During the first operation, it took me to such happy places: to my hot rock in the sun in Sweden, to the beach at my parents' house, to a place of love and euphoric peace.

They wiped what looked like Betadine on my skin after they removed the patch and the surgeon explained that it would sting, tug and burn a little. Fine with me because the happy gas comes next. "Okay, now this will tug a bit. Now a bit of a burn. Tug. *You're done!*" It was like pulling a shoelace out of a shoe. *With no happy gas – downer.*

So that said, the operation took five minutes and I felt *fine*. I went and washed up. Dad and I went to drop off my huge suitcase at Dr. Jemsek's, and then we went out to lunch like nothing had happened. We had lunch and got back to the doctor's office nineteen minutes early. Such pros now.

I skipped to the scale, knowing I had lost more weight but, the ding dong that I am, forgot that I had just eaten. I also had heavy jeans on and two bottles of water in me. So according to chart I lost two pounds. *Ha!* Whatever. I'm killing it here. We went through the usual three phases of saying the exact same things to three different people, Dr. Jemsek being the third.

I explained how amazing I'd felt on this last holiday, even on the antibiotic Coartem week, and Dad said I'd been back to my normal self. I told him I'm driving again, except for the mornings when my nighttime drugs make it still a bit iffy. But by the time those have worn off, I'm good to go.

We discussed some continued neurological issues: lack of balance, minor memory issues (nothing like before), confusion regarding numbers and sequence, etc. He just said that I'll stay on my neurotrophics for a good while and then we'll start to slowly taper off. We discussed my current nights of incredible pain in my legs (also a neurological issue). He basically told me to stop playing doctor and just stick with the protocol. And I will. It's just been hard, now that I am finally out and about, to stick to a medication schedule. I mean, I take four doses a day of at least ten pills each, and now it will increase with my oral antibiotic treatment. I will be doing two weeks on antibiotics, and then three weeks off to see how I do. There will be two of these cycles before I return in June.

Lately, I've been having frequent issues related to aggressive antibiotic treatment. Dr. Clark at home had done an alternative test by Doctor's Data, which indicated that Diflucan is bothering my girly issues, so now we will be using Grapefruit Seed Extract. Throughout my treatment, Dr. Jemsek has paid more and more attention to the testing I bring him. I greatly respect him for being such a highly regarded Lyme expert who is still open to integrative methods of treatment.

I hope people with Lyme will now understand that, even when in the darkest pit of treatment, there is light. I would not say it's at the end of the tunnel – I would say it's more like a guiding light through a pit you must climb up out of with every ounce of strength you have. I am still nearing the light. I am not there yet. I still have at least over a year of treatment to go and then we will see what happens. So please, if you are like me and have Lyme along with all of the co-infections, climb. Keep climbing, no matter how slowly you must go. Rest, then climb, then rest some more. Climb.

Weak_Willed

April 18, 2013

————◦◉◦————

The day after my surgery, I flew to West Palm Beach to my company's annual conference. I flew down early to give myself a day and a half to rest and get acclimated, but I really just worked on my presentations the whole time.

The conference was pretty grueling on my body, especially with the air conditioning worsening my 95.2°F body temperature. On breaks, while my colleagues caught up with one another, I raced to my room and threw myself into a scalding bath to try to get my temperature up. I changed my clothes several times, but nothing really seemed to help.

I spent a wonderful day aboard a yacht, an incentive I had won for my sales achievements, and the next two days were nitty-gritty conference days, which included a cocktail party one night and a dinner and awards ceremony the next. Now don't get me wrong, I loved every second of it. Having been imprisoned in my house for six months, the social aspect was amazingly good for my soul, but physically, I would pay.

I flew home and, the very next morning, I began my new oral antibiotic treatment. *So many pills.* If I thought I was taking a lot before, man was I wrong. I now take over seventy pills a day. It feels like a full-time job to get them all down. And these new antibiotics, well, they do what high doses of antibiotics do: they attack your digestive track. And so, I am finishing my first week completely miserable. To be honest, it makes me miss my PowerLine. Who knew?

I am pretty miserable right now. I'm back to no driving and imprisoned by new issues that are driving me mad. Right now, I am so frustrated I'm weeping. In the past, treatment weeks have been better weeks for me, while the holidays were worse. But now, I'm among the normal Lymies, feeling completely horrendous on the treatment weeks.

The good news is that I have two weeks on and three weeks off, so I am hoping for some sort of normalcy during my off weeks. Thankfully, I will be on an off week when we take Mini to Disney World for being such a hero and a sport throughout treatment, never complaining when someone else had to step in and take over Mommy's duties. My little four-year-old just gets it. It's amazing.

And so I fight on, but my will feels weaker. My optimism is taking a break. My body is beat up. I so want to be done.

Merry-Go-Round
April 19, 2013

It's as if I am sitting on the biggest horse on a merry-go-round, the one that goes up the highest and then quickly dips down the furthest. It's amazing how fast this merry-go-round is. I am holding on for dear life and have my seatbelt on.

Yesterday was an emotional pit, the horse moving as far down as it could. My physical symptoms began to manifest into a one-night emotional breakdown. I couldn't articulate how I was feeling and so my night became somewhat of a train wreck, which I took out on a very patient and special friend. I was so difficult and I knew I was being difficult. I knew that the conversation should happen at another time, but Lyme ripped through my filter and I just let into him. It was the first time this has happened in over a year. And it saddens me. It's so hard for me to apologize when these moments occur, when it's as if I am outside my own body watching the scenario unfold. Like it's not even me. I was just so frustrated by how I felt physically that I let it get the best of me.

In some ways it feels like a setback, but I just remind myself that I am in a new phase of treatment, attacking areas that have not yet been treated, and so it is normal for some of my old symptoms to reappear as a Herx reaction. I just wish it didn't always have to include people I care about. I wish I could get out my nasties in some other way.

Today the horse flew up again. I feel like I was pretty busy all day, but I can't remember what I did. I should ask my assistant who knows what I did, because I certainly cannot remember. Whatever I did, it did not include a nap. I am back to having trouble getting the prescribed amount of sleep. I can't blame it on Mini, since she sleeps twelve hours at night and naps. In fact, I can't blame it on anyone but myself. As a result, my eyes are burning and the horse goes down again. I'm exhausted, but I can't seem to sleep. Last night, I fell asleep around 11:30 p.m. and woke up every other hour for the whole night.

But today, my horse was up! My digestive issues can reoccur at any moment, but they were under control today, which helped my emotional state and well-being. A mom at dance class made a point of coming across the room and telling me how great I look and that she had noticed a huge difference in me. That brought me up too.

My biggest issue right now is getting all the pills down. It's really so hard to do it and I often find myself gagging. I dose ten to twenty pills, four times a day. Some are supplements, some are chemo drugs, and some are for malaria. It's bananas. They all wipe me out. Some mess with my eyesight, others with my mind, fatigue, balance, and pain.

So what I've realized is that this merry-go-round, on which I will stay for one more week, then three weeks off, then climb back on for two weeks, then three weeks off – seems more like a roller coaster.

My Blue Sky
May 5, 2013

———◦◉◦———

He has no idea what he has done for me. He has no idea about the darkness that he's turned to light. No idea how much he's reminded me of my life's dreams. He just doesn't know.

For many years now, things have been blurry for me. Many times, I have found myself in a fog of depression, my deepest being during various stages of this treatment.

When nearing the end of my IV treatment, a childhood and most trusted friend, Leah, contacted me and told me she wanted me to meet someone with whom she worked, someone with whom she knew I would share a mutual attraction. I was not open to letting anyone in at the time and falling in love was certainly the last thing on my mind, and she knew it, so when she was so insistent, I was listening, but my heart was still closed in my pit of Lyme.

The timing was all wrong, I thought, but Leah was sure and insisted we meet immediately, that we would be the remedy to one another's deepest, darkest pain. If only she knew the depths of my pain. I was completely opposed to the idea, but she yacked my ear off and told me to look at the pictures she had sent to my email.

When I saw his smile in the pictures she showed me, and in that picture of him in the bright yellow shirt, something convinced me that he was special. I had no idea that he would change my life. He would be the one to finally open my eyes, if even the slightest crack, to let in the light of life beyond illness.

There is so much he doesn't know. So much he was lucky enough not to witness. They say timing is everything and I believe that to be true. Had I met him ten years ago, he would have known a different person. Had we met five years ago, I would not have Mini. Had we met a year ago, he would have known a woman broken in pieces, writhing in pain, drowning in tears, paranoid because of hallucinations. He would have known a lost woman with little hope, struggling to live each day for the sake of her three-year-old daughter. He would have known a woman who was so lonely in her illness that she was nearly paralyzed within the walls of her own home. A woman who had a paid assistant who was more like a paid friend. Someone to keep her company in her misery, something that her parents feared with every second would be what could kill her.

Self-administered injections in the abdomen, several IVs a day in the chest, sixty to seventy pills: her treatment had become her life. She could barely care for her own daughter, whom she had fought for and "given birth" to on a 48-hour airplane ride across the world to a place that looked like the moon. That baby was her life's dream and, for a time, she could not be the mother she had promised to be. And it tortured her inside. That is who he would have met. But that was then.

I met him. And while my eyes were still closed, I experienced an internal gasp. My stomach flipped. My heart pounded. Every inch of me melted into a puddle. We had spoken on Facetime for seven weeks, to get to know one another. He was beautiful. He was masculine and smart. He was a good father to his children. He was a reason to yank myself out of my deep depression to explore something that could be real.

Real. For the first time in ten years, I was open in an instant to something so real it shocked me. He finally came to visit me, driving over to spend the weekend. By then we knew we liked one another. By then, we had decided beforehand that he would approach me with a kiss to take away the awkward suspense of his arrival. And for the first time in my life, I wasn't nervous. I felt secure. I felt at peace. I felt happy. My eyes were open.

It takes time to learn to know someone deep down, but sometimes just an instant to recognize a connection, and that we had. I knew it was real from the moment he got out of the car. From the moment he kissed me. From the moment he held me in his arms and all my fears went away. I felt it. I knew there was a mutual connection. And for the first time in my life, I was not afraid of how he felt about me.

Our first weekend together was so natural. With every kiss, with every touch, I walked away from my past with an open heart, without looking back. I allowed him to touch my soul on a level I had buried for so long. I let him in. I feel truly happy. And while I have completely opened my heart and eyes to him and decided to allow myself to speak my truth without reserve, he still has no idea the freedom he affords me just by the way he looks at me.

It has taken me several months to decide if I wanted to share this chapter, but at the time, I still had my PowerLine. I was self-conscious about my PowerLine and my patch and as he pulled me closer, I covered it with my buttoned down shirt, trying to hide what he had already seen. It's hard to miss. And this man, this amazingly sensitive man, put an end to that pain, that feeling of unworthiness, by gently moving my hand away, opening the top of my shirt, looking at me, kissing my patch and then me. It was one of the sweetest and most meaningful moments of my life. He clearly wanted more than my body. He wanted me. And I knew it. And finally with one big exhale, I was able to let go of my fear and allow him to see all of me, my flawed body, my PowerLine, my patch, and my open eyes, not looking down, but straight at him, allowing him straight into my soul and, more importantly, allowing myself reentry into my own soul.

And it was so real. And natural. And at I wanted to let him in. At that moment, I knew I could love again.

He spent two nights with me and, when he left, I knew we would meet again. But how was it possible to feel such an emptiness, when someone you have just met pulls out of your driveway to go back to his life. In a way, it scares me, yet I know this could very well be the relationship I have waited for my whole life. I knew I was in love. Just like that. Truly falling deeply in love with this man who appeared out of nowhere when I least expected it, in a condition when I was least open to it.

We are the same age and at thirty-eight, there are always obstacles to overcome. I don't like to think of it as baggage, because baggage you can just leave behind, lose, or trash. Obstacles involve patience, work, and a desire to overcome. And we both have our own obstacles. And that is okay. Because within imperfection lies the most beautiful sort of perfection: honest and true reality.

When he left, he texted me before he was even off my street. Then he called me from the gas station a few miles away, telling me later that he almost turned around and came back. However, he continued home to his life and responsibilities, as did I, but we never stopped contacting one another for even an hour. We missed each another and communicated that freely with sweet affection. He helped me relearn how to reopen my heart and keep my eyes open to the world even while away.

Much to my surprise and delight, he returned the following weekend. We strengthened our bond, and he grew an even larger place in my heart, and I in his, I believe. Our passion, undeniable. Our understanding of one another – emotionally, physically and mentally – grew with each look, smile, and kiss.

He guards his heart just as I have, only he is a few steps behind me in letting me in, but I slowly feel him letting me get closer to him. And that's okay with me, which is shocking. Earlier in my life, it would have bothered me to not be on the same level, but now, I trust that, as he slowly lets me in, it will be real, authentic and long-lasting.

And now, several months have passed and with each day and every second, I love him more. I love him as I have never loved another. With him and away from him I feel a secure sense of serenity that has been foreign to me in my thirty-eight years. He has not only been the catalyst for me to dig myself out of an endless pit of darkness and let the light in, but he has also revealed a light that shows me the way to my future.

I feel a warmth about him that I have never experienced. I feel no sense of uncomfortable desperation to know where things are headed. The only desperation I feel is to be with him when we are apart. I am not an easy woman, this I know; yet he handles me in a way that is so loving and understanding, it makes me strive to be the woman I have always known I could be, but that I could never quite become. In finding him, I have found the missing pieces of myself.

With him, I feel safe form the world, from all harm, from being judged by my illness, and from another broken heart. He holds my heart in his hands with such care.

For me, he is the best medicine I have been granted by the universe at this very moment, a moment to focus on health and love, on what could be in the future, rather than pills, illness, and the depressing present. He has made me feel alive again.

I believe that people walk in and out of our lives at given times for a reason. This is no exception. This man, who has no idea that he has helped me find my way back to myself, is the best medicine I could ever have asked for. An answer wrapped in a gift. And no matter what the outcome, I will forever be grateful for what he has done for me. For showing me that there is light in my future. And I love him; something I never thought I would ever do again. I love him.

Afterword

My treatment is nowhere near its finish. In fact, I still have a long way to go before I hope to be in remission. It is expected that I will take three days of antibiotics per month for the rest of my life, but who knows? As research evolves, so will treatment.

I still take about fifty pills a day and I still have one to two weeks a month where I am floored and cannot move, as every little breath causes great physical distress. I still see Dr. Jemsek on the same schedule and will continue to do so for at a year, until Summer 2014. By then, we all hope for long-term remission and an end to my nearly thirty years of suffering from Lyme and Multiple Chronic Infectious Disease Syndrome (MCIDS).

I decided to end this book with a beautiful experience in my life, a period of time I will never forget. One never knows where a relationship may lead, but its relevance to the book is that all cures do not necessarily lie solely in a bottle, a machine, or a vegetable. There are matters of the heart that can change energy to help one realize that there is a chance at a normal life. Perhaps your light will not lie in a romantic relationship, but a deep friendship, a support group, or any kind of human or pet interaction. That light is extremely helpful in finding the energy and will for compliance with medications, physical therapy, and other treatments.

In a way, I dissected myself in this book. A portion of it felt very much like writing a novel, recounting my past, but then, as I'm not into the nitty-gritty of treatment itself, I wanted to bring the book back to the positive: that you *can* get better, that attitude matters, and that support matters.

If you are a partner of someone with Lyme use your words of love from the heart, as you did when you first met. Find the spark that brought you together, for it might be the light that ignites a desire to climb out of the pit of Lyme darkness. It's easy to get caught in the web of these little monsters. Sweet gestures go a long way. If you are a loved one who wants to support someone with Lyme, please be patient through the rages, the depressions, and know that the patient is not at fault.

And if you are alone, my advice is to make the choice not to go through this journey alone. Don't be afraid to ask for help. Embrace support.

Thank you for following my journey. It has been incredibly therapeutic for me to write my deepest experiences through this process. I will continue to write on my blog on my website TwistofLymeBook.com and who knows? Perhaps there will be a sequel. But for now, I will continue to take things day by day and be grateful for all of the gifts I have been granted.

Helpful Resources

TwistofLymeBook.com

International Lyme & Associated Disease Society – ILADS.org

Tick testing, UMASS – ag.umass.edu/services/tick-borne-disease-diagnostics

Tick and human Lyme testing, IGeneX – igenex.com

Jemsek Specialty Clinic – jemsekspecialty.com

Steve Clark, ND (Lyme-literate naturopath in New Hampshire) – steveclarknd.com

High alkaline detox mail-order juices – BluePrintCleanse.com

Non-toxic personal and home products – AvaAndersonNonToxic.com/andreacaesar

Index

About the Author

Andrea Caesar grew up in Barrington, RI, and holds a BA in International Relations from American University in Washington, DC, and an MA in Teaching from The School for International Training, a division of the NGO, World Learning, in Vermont. She speaks fluent Swedish and Spanish and is proficient in Russian.

It is believed that Andrea has suffered from Lyme disease for the past twenty-seven years, since she was eleven years old. She now lives in the Lakes Region of New Hampshire with her four-year-old daughter, where she continues her battle with Lyme, under the guidance of Dr. Jemsek

Made in the USA
San Bernardino, CA
15 March 2017